Essentials of Child Welfare

Essentials

of Child Welfare

Rodney A. Ellis
Catherine N. Dulmus
John S. Wodarski

 John Wiley & Sons, Inc.

Library of Congress Cataloging-in-Publication Data

Ellis, Rodney A.
    Essentials of child welfare/Rodney A. Ellis, Catherine N. Dulmus, John Wodarski.
        p. cm.
    Includes bibliographical references and index.
    ISBN 0-471-23423-0 (pbk.)
        1. Child welfare—United States. 2. Social work with children—United States. 3. Family social work—United States. 4. Social case work—United States. I. Dulmus, Catherine N. II. Wodarski, John S. III. Title.

HV741.E39 2003
362.7'0973—dc21

                                                                          2003045096

Printed in the United States of America.

10 9 8 7 6 5 4 3 2 1

To the children in the care of the state.
May this book help make your days better,
your lives safer, and your futures brighter.

CONTENTS

SERIES PREFACE

I n the *Essentials of Social Work Practice* series, our goal is to provide readers with books that will deliver key practical information in an efficient, accessible style. The series features books on a variety of topics of interest to clinical social workers, such as child welfare, case management, social work policy and practice, to name just a few. For the experienced professional, books in the series offer a concise yet thorough overview of a specific area of expertise, including numerous tips for best practices. Students will find here a prioritized assembly of all the information and techniques that must be at one's fingertips to practice knowledgeably, efficiently, and ethically in the social work field.

Wherever feasible, visual cues highlighting key points are utilized alongside systematic, step-by-step guidelines. Chapters are focused and succinct. Topics are organized for an easy understanding of the essential material related to a particular practice area. Theory and research are continually woven into the fabric of each book, but always to enhance the practical application of the material, rather than sidetrack or overwhelm readers. With this series, we aim to challenge and assist readers engaged in providing social work services to aspire to the highest level of proficiency by arming them with the tools they need for effective practice.

Essentials of Child Welfare provides important foundational information about the child welfare system. The first chapter describes (a) the agencies and individuals that are involved in the investigation of allegations of child abuse, neglect, or abandonment; (b) the legal processes that decide the fate of children and families; and (c) the processes used by child welfare agencies in making permanent living arrangements for children. Chapters 2 through 8 describe the essential information and skills required to understand and function within each component of the child welfare system. Chapter 9 then describes the process of preparing children in foster care to enter independent living, whereas Chapter 10 describes the importance of cultural sensitivity as an early step in the development of cultural competence as a practitioner. The book's goal is to acquaint the reader—whether student, child welfare worker in training, or practitioner—with the core issues and components of the overall processes in the child welfare system.

One

INTRODUCTION

Laws governing child welfare exist at virtually every level. Federal law requires states to have a continuum of services and provides funding to them as long as specific requirements are met. Based on the federal statutes, states develop their own policies that define exactly how services will be provided. In jurisdictions where all or part of the services are contracted to local government, the governing body of that jurisdiction has its own ordinances. In each case the law of the higher level of government is regarded as superior, and each jurisdiction drafts its policies in accordance with what has been enacted at higher levels. One example can be found in laws regarding the investigation of allegations of abuse and neglect. Federal law requires that a system be in place for conducting investigations and provides general guidelines for what should happen in the course of those investigations. State law tailors these requirements to its own jurisdictions by mandating the operation of hotlines and abuse registries, as well as creating the agencies that are responsible for facilitating the process. In some cases local governments have assumed responsibility for some portion of the investigation; for example, medical examinations of children who have allegedly been sexually abused are sometimes conducted by employees of local governments. When this is the case, local policy must create and direct that agency.

It is important to recognize that the structure of child welfare systems across states and even across counties and cities is often varied. Although the legislation that mandates protection for abused and neglected children is federal, that policy offers little specific direction as to how services are to be delivered. The vast majority of the policy that directs child welfare is at the state level, and it differs somewhat from state to state. This short volume does not allow for a full investigation of the specific policies of each state. Rather, it focuses on the policies and procedures that are most common across states.

Putting It Into Practice

The Sexual Abuse Response Team (SART) of Broward County, Florida, is an example of a local government using state dollars in combination with its own to provide a specific service in the child welfare system. State child welfare investigators transport children who are believed to have been sexually abused to SART for medical examination, medical treatment, and the initiation of intervention to help children deal with their abusive experiences. The centralized location permits resources and expertise to be focused in a single office, optimizing quality and speed of services as well as promoting the efficient use of supportive funding.

Readers should consult the policy and procedure manuals of the agency in charge of child welfare in their own states.

It is also important to understand the way in which the child welfare system works. It is a vast system, with its own language, procedures, funding sources, and problems. Without knowing the terminologies that are used and processes that must be navigated, the child welfare practitioner cannot function effectively, resulting in personal ineffectiveness and inadequate services for children and families who are desperately in need of help and support. Foundational to such knowledge is an understanding of the agencies and individuals that comprise the system, the legal processes that drive it, and the process in which child welfare agencies engage.

THE AGENCIES AND ORGANIZATIONS

One of the most important pieces of information involves the agencies and organizations that comprise the system. Without understanding them and the roles they play, it can be difficult or even impossible to function successfully within the system. When participants in the system cannot function effectively, the system breaks down, and children suffer as a result. Rapid Reference 1.1 highlights the agencies and individuals that make up the child welfare system.

The Court

The juvenile court operates under a different set of philosophies and rules than do the courts that try adults. The difference is in large part due to a pair of legal concepts that underlie and direct the court's decisions: *parens patriae* and the rights of parents (Ellis & Sowers, 2001). The rights of parents are sometimes seen as working in concert with *parens patriae*, sometimes as opposing it. For example, *parens patriae* supports the right of the state to remove children from their biological homes. When parents recognize their inability to deal with a child's needs and seek the assistance of the state, *parens patriae* allows the court to provide relief. However, when parents do not wish court intervention and find it forced upon them, the rights of parents are in opposition to the doctrine of *parens patriae*. Whatever the dominant philosophy, the

> ≋*Rapid Reference 1.1*
>
> ## The Agencies and Individuals in Child Welfare
>
> - The juvenile court
> - Child welfare agencies
> - Ancillary service agencies
> - Volunteers
> - Foster parents

> # DON'T FORGET
>
> *Parens patriae* refers to the responsibility of the court to act as parent to a child if parents are unable or unwilling to do so appropriately. Parental rights refer to the right of a parent to make primary decisions regarding a child's future and welfare.

courts were originally designed to ensure that children are protected and that they have a reasonable opportunity to develop successfully either in their biological homes or in some alternative setting.

Although the original intent of the juvenile court was that the best interests of children could be considered in a nonadversarial environment (Mather & Lager, 2000), there is, in fact, a great deal of controversy surrounding many child welfare cases. Parents often feel that child welfare agencies and the court are unjustified in their interference. Court personnel and agency workers may disagree as to what intervention would be appropriate for a child. Agencies that provide ancillary services may accuse a child welfare agency of insufficient activity on behalf of a child or vice versa. Volunteer advocates who speak on behalf of children may charge that an agency is acting to protect itself rather than to help a child and his or her family. All too often the needs of the child and family are lost in the controversy between interested parties.

CAUTION

Both a judge's spoken and written orders must be completely understood. Failure to comply may result in a finding of contempt of court or even charges of criminal neglect.

It is also important to understand that the juvenile court exists in various configurations and functions under different names in different jurisdictions. In some areas the judges hear all cases related to delinquency and child welfare in the same courtroom. In other areas some judges hear only delinquency cases and others hear only dependency cases. Some jurisdictions have family courts that oversee all issues related to families such as dependency and divorce. Other specialized courts are sometimes involved. For example, jurisdictions may have mental health courts, teen courts, substance abuse courts, and others that play some role in decision making (Ballou et al., 2001).

Regardless of their structures, courts are composed of persons in various positions. These include judges, referees, court administrators, employees of court-operated programs, and court staff. Practitioners must understand the role of each, as well as the way in which they interact, in order to interact successfully with this component of the child welfare system.

Rapid Reference 1.2

1. *Case plan:* Strategies are designated that are intended to facilitate the reunion of the child with its parent or parents.
2. *Termination of custody decisions:* Children are released from state custody and returned to their biological parents.
3. *Petitions for the termination of parental rights:* Custodians such as state agencies apply to have the rights of the parents to custody and control of a child permanently revoked.
4. *Adoption petitions:* Individuals or agencies ask the court to allow a child whose parents' rights have been terminated to be adopted by another responsible person.
5. *Emancipation petitions:* Custodians ask the court to release children who have attained the age of the majority in that jurisdiction from their custody and control.

Judges hear cases and make many decisions regarding the fate of children who enter the system. Although children are most often taken into custody by an employee of an investigative agency, judges usually make the final decision about whether that child will remain in custody or will be returned to its family. They usually also have the power to approve or disapprove plans developed regarding the child's future. Cases that are scheduled to come before the judge are placed on his or her *docket*. Judges are provided a daily or weekly listing of cases to be heard. Such cases include case plans, termination of custody, termination of parental rights, adoption petitions, and emancipation petitions, which are described in Rapid Reference 1.2.

Judges appoint referees to perform specific actions in their stead. Typically, referees supervise hearings that are not expected to require judicial decisions. This provides a means of observation and communication for judges whose overloaded dockets do not permit their personal involvement. Referees may be authorized to make specific kinds of decisions but may be required to refer cases to judges for other decisions. One example of a type of hearing a referee might supervise is a regularly scheduled report on the condition of a child in custody. If, however, the time had come to consider the termination of parental rights, a hearing would be scheduled with the judge.

The daily operation of juvenile courts may be supervised by a judge when in smaller settings. In larger jurisdictions there is often an employee of the court known as a court administrator who performs these functions. The court administrators supervise other employees to ensure that such tasks as docket development, paperwork processing, collaboration with external agencies, and operation of internal programs are adequately and efficiently performed. Although judges are the persons who are in charge of the courts,

Putting It Into Practice

Imagine that a caseworker had spent months working with a mother on issues related to substance abuse, parenting skills, and responsible behavior. Should this mother consistently fail urine tests, miss scheduled visits with her child, and display poor interactions with the child, the worker might eventually decide that she would make no improvement and that this represented a danger to the child. The worker might then arrange a hearing to discuss the possibility of the termination of parental rights.

they are often very dependent on the administrators for daily decision making and in their interactions with the community.

Some courts operate their own programs for the children they serve. These programs may include counseling services for children and their families, sexual abuse diagnosis and treatment teams, review board supervisors, intensive home-based service programs, and others. The programs are typically funded by outside sources that can create a degree of accountability outside the court, which is often a desirable commodity.

Juvenile courts frequently include various staff members such as administrative assistants, secretaries, and security personnel. Each of these persons typically provides very specialized services within a fairly limited range of activity. For example, judges often have assistants whose responsibilities include developing dockets, scheduling appointments, interacting with the offices of other judges, initiating and receiving correspondences, and handling the office telephone. This assistant often shares an office with a law enforcement officer whose duties include controlling access to the courtroom and maintaining order within the court. Although these two work in close proximity, neither would be likely to attempt to perform any of the duties of the other. Also important to remember is that each may wield a significant amount of power related to the access of judges, program directors, and others. The reason is that they may have the judge's trust and can cause access to the judge to be granted or denied with a comment or brief note to the judge.

Given the sometimes extensive and always variable construction of the court in different jurisdictions, it is very important to understand whom the court employs, what their roles are, and how the functions they perform relate to one another. One useful way of developing such an understanding is by creating an *organizational table,* which is a graphic representation of an organization that identifies positions in boxes or circles and the direction of authority with lines or arrows. An example of a hypothetical organizational table can be found in Rapid Reference 1.3.

CHILD WELFARE AGENCIES

For the purposes of this discussion, child welfare agencies are considered those agencies that fund, monitor, or facilitate the investigations of abuse, neglect, and abandonment of children; arrange alternative placements and case plans

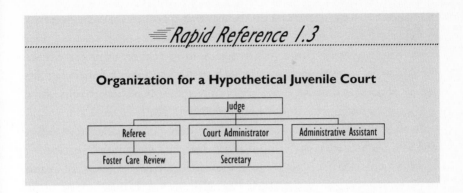

Rapid Reference 1.3

Organization for a Hypothetical Juvenile Court

for those removed from their homes; and are responsible for developing long-term arrangements for the care of children who will not return to their biological parents or be adopted. Traditionally, these services have been provided by state agencies, but in recent years states have begun to contract with local governments and private agencies to provide many of these services.

In jurisdictions where the state provides direct child welfare services, there is often one large agency that provides the bulk of those services. Divisions of those agencies with names like "protective investigations" or "child protective services" conduct investigations of abuse, neglect, or abandonment. Other divisions locate alternative housing, provide supervision for children in care, facilitate the adoption process, and help older children prepare for independent living as adults. These agencies typically receive money from the federal government to conduct their operations. Federal money is sometimes supplemented with state, local, and private dollars.

In other jurisdictions child welfare services are provided by some combination of public and private agencies. The private parts of the system are often funded with dollars distributed by the state agency responsible for child welfare. In such cases the state agency also typically performs monitoring functions designed to ensure that services are being adequately provided by the agencies that receive their funds. Some jurisdictions have privatized the entire service system so that someone other than the state government provides all direct services.

An additional and critical service offered by child welfare agencies is early intervention. In some cases the investigatory unit may visit a family and determine that although conditions in the home are not sufficient to warrant the removal of a child, sufficient risk exists that specific services are necessary to reduce the risk of future harm to the child. In these cases specialized units of child welfare agencies or ancillary agencies may offer to provide services to the family on a voluntary basis. The agency's activities might include a wide variety of services from accessing financial resources or painting bedrooms to providing counseling or other mental health services.

As with the juvenile court system, it is critical to understand the structure and role of the direct service agencies in the child welfare system. Specific divisions and agencies often provide specialized services and may be unable to perform any of the tasks assigned to other groups. It may be helpful for each practitioner to develop an organizational table of the agency or agencies that provide these services in his or her community.

Ancillary Service Agencies

In addition to the agencies that provide direct child welfare services, a variety of agencies provide ancillary services to both the children in custody and their families. These include mental health providers, substance abuse treatment providers, home service agencies, medical providers, educational systems, and intensive case management providers. Services may be provided in the agency's offices, in the family's home, at the child's school, or in a variety of other settings.

Mental health agencies provide a variety of services to children and families. Services may include individual and family counseling, group therapy, assessment and diagnosis, and more intensive treatment of mental illness. Treatment settings may include in-home, in-community, outpatient, day treatment, or residential programs. Often, mental health needs are recognized or suspected by an employee of the child welfare agency and may be mandated by the court as a part of the plan to reunify a child with its parents. In these cases the court usually requires a satisfactory report of progress before children are returned to their parents. Before services are mandated, a judge typically requires a mental health evaluation. The evaluation usually begins with a psychosocial assessment, in which the identified client and sometimes significant others are asked a series of questions about several dimensions of the client's life. Certain kinds of answers to these questions can alert the evaluator to the need for deeper investigation. If deeper investigation is required, the client may be asked to complete a series of interviews or pen-and-pencil question-naires that are designed to reveal the presence of specific mental disorders.

A second type of ancillary provider is the substance abuse treatment agency. As with mental health agencies, substance abuse providers most often become involved because of a referral from a child welfare agency, and often at the order of a judge. Services may be provided to the child or children taken into custody, to siblings, or to parents, depending on what the need is believed to be. Substance abuse providers also typically initiate their services with a psychosocial evaluation that may differ from that of the mental health provider in that it may include more specific questions about a history of substance abuse. Substance abuse professionals may also conduct chemical testing such as urinalysis to determine what drugs are present in the person's system. Following the presentation of the findings to the court, the judge may elect to mandate treatment, or the client may elect to undergo treatment voluntarily.

The term *home service agency* is used here to designate agencies that provide a broad range of physical services in the homes of families whose children have been taken into custody. Some children are removed in large part because the dilapidated condition of their homes constitutes a signifi-cant risk of harm. Home service agencies help to alleviate those dangerous conditions. Although their role varies from family to family, these agencies engage in such activities as housekeeping assistance and training, nutritional advising, and home maintenance. The activities are often initially very inten-sive and then diminish as work is accomplished and competencies are gained.

Other agencies offer medical and dental services. Children who are taken into custody have often had their physical needs neglected. Some may be malnourished or suffer from a long-term untreated illness. Others may have undiagnosed problems with vision, hearing, or their teeth. Other children in the home or even the parents may have similar difficulties. Child welfare agencies often refer children or family members to such providers for diag-nosis and treatment.

Children who are taken into state custody frequently experience educa-tional needs. They may benefit from testing, tutoring, or educational guid-ance. Children generally are either part of or associated with local school systems. Child welfare workers suspecting these needs may refer children to these agencies (often associated with the school system) for assistance.

In some jurisdictions there are agencies that provide intensive case management services. These services are often selected for specialized situations, such as when child welfare workers think that the removal of a child may be avoided. Teams of workers from the agency provide a very broad range of services, often helping with housework, engaging in minor home repair, assessment, counseling, psychoeducation, and referral to additional services.

Volunteers

A fourth group that plays an important role in child welfare is the volunteers. Volunteers may be professionals, paraprofessionals, or persons without a professional background. Volunteers are trained to engage in specific activities to help children and families in the system. Volunteers may include attorneys ad litem, guardians ad litem, court-appointed special advocates (CASAs), human service boards, and service review boards.

Attorneys ad litem are attorneys who represent children on a pro bono (free of charge) basis. In a system where families and agencies may become so embroiled in controversy that the interests of the children are forgotten, attorneys ad litem are responsible for keeping the interests of the child paramount. Although other attorneys are often involved, including lawyers representing parents, child welfare agencies, or other providers, the attorney ad litem exists to provide a voice for a child who might otherwise be forgotten.

Some jurisdictions have volunteers and paraprofessionals who receive specialized training to speak on behalf of children even though they do not have formal legal training. These volunteers, often known as *guardians ad litem,* cannot act as attorneys but are respected by the court and participate actively in advocacy and decision-making processes. The use of terminology regarding guardians between jurisdictions can be confusing. In some areas the term *guardian ad litem* may refer to attorneys. In others it may refer to citizen volunteers. To further complicate matters, either attorneys or citizen volunteers may be referred to as CASAs, depending on the jurisdiction in which they are located. In either case their functions are similar, except that citizen volunteers cannot perform the legal functions performed by attorneys.

Human service boards are composed of local agency heads and other community members. Their function is to provide support, advice, and guidance to child welfare administrators. In some jurisdictions these boards have a tremendous amount of influence. In others they do little more than offer their insights and opinions. In still other areas these boards do not exist at all.

Some jurisdictions also have service review boards. These boards are responsible for monitoring specific activities of child welfare agencies and the children in their care. One example used in several jurisdictions is the foster care review board. Foster care review boards consist of concerned citizens from diverse backgrounds who receive specialized training and become members of panels that conduct periodic reviews of the condition of children in state custody. They are typically unpaid and serve a term with a specific limit, such as three years. Although these boards have no real power, they do have the authority to make recommendations to direct care workers. Should the direct care workers not comply, the board can bring the situation to the judge's attention.

Foster Parents

Foster parents are persons who agree to house, clothe, and care for children in state custody. They have some, but not all, of the authority of biological parents. Typically, they receive a small monthly stipend to help support the children they care for and have some assistance from a direct care worker. Children with special needs are often assigned to specialized homes. For example, a child with an emotional disorder may be placed in a *therapeutic foster home* with *wraparound services,* as described in Rapid Reference 1.4.

Another example of a specialized home is the *medical foster home,* in which children with severe medical problems are supervised by foster parents who are trained to deal with those conditions. Other specialized homes exist in some jurisdictions. These homes may be operated either by the child welfare agency or by an ancillary agency. Yet another specialized form of care

═Rapid Reference 1.4

Therapeutic foster homes have parents with specialized training to deal with the child's problems (e.g., medical or behavioral). Wraparound services are provided by ancillary agencies to support the family and include services such as counseling and skills training at no cost to the foster family.

is commonly known as kinship care or relative care. In these situations biological relatives agree to assume responsibility for the child. They may be identified as foster parents or relative caregivers or may adopt the child.

LEGAL PROCESSES

Children who are taken into state custody are subjected to a series of legal processes by the court system. These processes begin shortly after the children are removed from their homes. State guidelines vary for the permitted delay, but many require that a child come before the judge within 48 hours of being taken into custody. The processes include shelter hearings, adjudicatory hearings, dispositional hearings, supervisory hearings, permanency hearings, hearings regarding the termination of parental rights (TPR), adoption hearings, and hearings to approve the release of the child from state custody. Other hearings may be held to deal with specific situations. The names of all of these types of hearings vary between jurisdictions. Hearings may be initiated by the agency that is supervising the child, by an ancillary agency, by the attorney for the child, by the attorney for the child's parents, or by the court itself.

The first phase of the legal process is the shelter hearing. At this hearing the judge determines whether sufficient evidence exists that the child has been harmed or is endangered to warrant remaining in temporary custody while the cases for all parties are being prepared. If sufficient evidence is

DON'T FORGET

Court Processes

- Shelter hearings
- Adjudicatory hearings
- Dispositional hearings
- Supervisory hearings
- Permanency hearings
- Hearings regarding the termination of parental rights
- Adoption hearings
- Hearings to approve the release of the child from state custody

found, the child is placed in temporary shelter with the child welfare agency. Alternatively, the judge may place the child with relatives, return the child to the parents with recommendations that specific services be received, or reverse the action of the child welfare agency, releasing the child from custody.

The next major step in the legal process is the adjudicatory hearing. At this point a decision is made as to whether abuse, neglect, or abandonment has actually occurred. All parties present their cases, and the

> **CAUTION**
>
> The names of types of hearings vary across jurisdictions.

> ≡ *Rapid Reference 1.5*
>
> Case plans (discussed in greater detail in Chapter 4) are essentially written strategies designed to facilitate one of three outcomes for a child: reunification, long-term foster care, or adoption.

judges rule based on the evidence that they provide. Although the adjudicatory hearing determines whether abuse has occurred, it does not determine where the child will reside. The judge may choose to return the child to his or her parents with no stipulations, to return the child to its parents with specific provisions to be overseen by child welfare workers, or to adjudicate the child dependent and place the child in the custody of the child welfare agency.

A dispositional hearing follows the adjudicatory hearing. Here, a more long-term decision is made about the fate of the child. Namely, a decision is made as to where the child will reside, and a *case plan* (described in Rapid Reference 1.5) is approved by the court.

The case plan includes a series of activities in which the children and their families must engage in order to achieve reunification. If the parents do not wish to regain custody of the child, a plan may be developed to arrange an alternative placement and terminate parental rights.

Often, a series of supervisory hearings follows the adjudicatory hearing. These hearings are intended to ensure that the child is receiving adequate care and that the case plan is being followed. In some jurisdictions these may be overseen by referees or service review boards rather than by judges. When this is the case, reviewers have the right to schedule a hearing with the judge when necessary.

The successful completion of a case plan leads to a hearing to review the possibility of release from state custody. If the parents have been diligent in their efforts and have, as a result, demonstrated sufficient willingness or capacity to provide safe and adequate care for their child, the judge may order that the supervisory activities of the state be terminated and the child be reunited with the parents. Such hearings also occur when a child who has reached the age of majority (generally age 18) is officially released.

When parents make little or no progress toward case plan completion, a hearing may take place in which TPR is considered. At these hearings, those petitioning the court to end the rights of parents present their case, and those who oppose it argue theirs. Many TPR hearings occur with little or no opposition from the parent. Many others are vehemently contested. The foundational philosophies of the court may come into conflict here, as was mentioned earlier in this chapter.

When parental rights have been terminated, an attempt may be made to arrange that the child be adopted. When a prospective parent has been identified and prepared, the child welfare agency may petition the court to allow this to occur. The hearings in which the petitions are presented are often called *adoption hearings.*

The court system is replete with specialized documents, motions, and orders. One of the essentials of child welfare is a basic understanding of the most common of these. Petitions are documents presented or prepared by an attorney that ask the court to consider making a decision that changes something about the status of a case. Participants then argue in support of or in opposition to the petition in order to inform the court's decision. Court orders are legally binding statements or documents that compel persons named within to respond in certain ways. For example, a judge might issue an order requiring that the child welfare agency seek psychiatric care of a juvenile in its custody. A specific type of order is the *rule to show cause* when a participant in a case is required to explain why specific essential actions, often part of a previous order, have not been taken. Participants who do not respond appropriately to the requirements may be found to be in contempt of court. Those who do not discharge their duties in a responsible manner may find themselves charged with criminal neglect. Each carries its own specific and undesirable (for the errant participant) consequences.

DON'T FORGET

- The structure of the child welfare system may vary significantly across jurisdictions. Some are operated primarily by the state, whereas others are principally in the hands of private agencies.
- Despite the intention that the juvenile court be nonadversarial, it is in fact often very adversarial.
- Two of the central philosophies of the juvenile court that often conflict are *parens patriae* and parental rights.
- The right of judges to make specific decisions varies across jurisdictions.
- Child welfare agencies are required to ensure that allegations of abuse, neglect, or abandonment are thoroughly investigated.
- Permanency plans must be developed within 18 months of the time children enter care.
- Ultimately, children may be adopted or placed in long-term foster care.

The authority of the court varies somewhat across jurisdictions. In some areas, for example, a judge may order that a child be placed in a specific home or treatment facility. In other jurisdictions the judge may decide on the level of care a child will receive but be restricted from identifying a specific facility.

CHILD WELFARE AGENCY PROCESSES

The previous section provided an overview of processes that occur in the juvenile court. Child welfare agencies have their own set of processes (summarized in Rapid Reference 1.6) that typically initiate or respond to court activity.

Child welfare activities are typically initiated when an *allegation* of abuse or neglect is received. Many states operate telephone hot lines that receive these allegations. Trained operators collect essential information and screen the calls for those that can be identified as errant or fraudulent. Reports that are screened out are logged and filed. Those that appear to have merit are forwarded to investigatory workers at the child welfare agency.

≡ *Rapid Reference 1.6*

Child Welfare Agency Processes

- Allegation
- Investigation
- Supportive services
- Placement
- Reunification
- Termination of parental rights
- Adoption
- Long-term foster care
- Independent living

The investigators who receive the report also review it for credibility before proceeding. If an allegation is believed to be credible, an *investigation* is initiated. Investigators may visit the child's home, neighbors, school, church, or other locations to determine whether abuse appears to have occurred and what its nature and severity has been. If it appears that abuse has occurred, the investigator may take the child into custody or take other steps to ensure that the child experiences no further harm.

Often, investigators determine that conditions in the child's environment are bad but not sufficient to warrant removal. In such cases the worker may recommend that the family receive *supportive services* from an agency that provides early intervention. The goal of the services would be to reduce the risk that abusive conditions might occur or reoccur. Families might choose to accept or reject these services. Support services could include child care, homemaker services, transportation, and parenting classes, among others.

Children who are taken into custody are provided living arrangements in what are commonly called *placements*. The initial placement is the *shelter*, a temporary arrangement (which may actually be a foster home) in which the child resides until the court determines whether the child will remain in custody on a longer term basis. If the child is adjudicated dependent, he or she is moved into foster care, kinship care, or some form of more specialized care.

The case plan for each child should state the ultimate goal for the child. Historically, federal and state legislation have required an emphasis on *reunification*, which is a return to the biological parents. As the number of children in foster care has grown and it has become clear that some parents will be unable or unwilling ever to resume caring for their children, legislators have

CAUTION

Generally, a permanent plan should be made within 18 months of a child's entering care.

moved to compel child welfare agencies to make speedier decisions about long-term goals for children. If it appears that the child cannot be returned to the parents by that time, plans must be made either to attempt to find adoptive parents or to place the child in long-term foster care.

If reunification cannot be accomplished, the child welfare agency must petition the court for the *termination of parental rights*. When parents' rights are terminated, they lose all legal authority and responsibility for the child. Rights may then be transferred to the agency or to some other person through the adoption process.

Adoption occurs when an adult or pair of adults assume the legal responsibilities as parent of a child. The rights of the state as parent are terminated, and the new parents assume full responsibility for the child. Historically, *adoption* has been seen as the ideal situation for children who cannot be returned to the parents because it most closely approximates a natural family environment.

When a child whose parents have had their rights terminated cannot or will not be placed in an adoptive home, the child is given a goal of *long-term foster care*. An attempt is normally made to place the child in a home where it can stay indefinitely, that is, until it reaches the age of the majority in that jurisdiction. Some children may become eligible as older teens to participate in a program known as *independent living*. These children are placed in an environment in which they live semi-independently, for example, in their own apartments in a cluster of other apartments inhabited by other children in the program.

When a child who has remained in foster care reaches the age of majority, the child welfare agency's responsibility to provide for the child ends. In some states certain conditions may allow a child to remain in care for a longer period of time. For example, some jurisdictions allow custody to continue until a child has graduated from high school or has received a university education. Typically, a child's exit from custody is acknowledged for the records of both the court and the child welfare agency in a final hearing.

CHAPTER SUMMARY

This chapter described the essential players and processes in the child welfare system. If these persons and processes are not understood, the professionals attempting to function within the system are likely to be frustrated and ineffectual. The next chapters discuss the essentials of each of the phases of the child welfare process.

 TEST YOURSELF

1. **The structure of child welfare systems is consistent across cities, counties, and states.** True or False?

2. **Some jurisdictions have privatized the entire child welfare system.** True or False?

3. *Parens patriae* **refers to the responsibility of the court to act as parent to a child if parents are unable or unwilling to do so appropriately.** True or False?

4. **Ancillary service providers include all but which of the following?**

   (a) Mental health counselors

   (b) Foster home placements

   (c) Medical doctors

   (d) Intensive case managers

5. **Investigations into allegations of abuse and neglect are typically reported to**

   (a) Police departments

   (b) Mental health providers

   (c) Telephone hot lines

   (d) Foster care workers

6. **The term *placements* may refer to**

   (a) Foster care, kinship care, or residential care

   (b) Protective investigations or child protective services

   (c) Alternative arrangements of the juvenile court: dependency, delinquency, and family

   (d) Shelter, adjudicator, and dispositional hearings

7. Termination of parental rights typically occurs

(a) When parents have successfully completed their case plan

(b) When parents have shown themselves to be unable or unwilling to complete their case plan

(c) When foster care workers develop a case plan

(d) When allegations of abuse and neglect are found to be substantive

8. Adoption is a legal act in which

(a) The rights of biological parents are terminated

(b) A child is placed in the care of a foster family

(c) An adult or adults agree to become the legal parents of a child, assuming full responsibility for the child's future and well-being

(d) A judge concurs with the findings of a protective investigator and orders that a child be placed in the custody of the state

9. Independent living refers to

(a) The process by which a child is declared dependent on the state

(b) The process by which a child is emancipated from state supervision

(c) The process of preparing a child to live on its own as an adult

(d) The process of arranging a long-term placement for a child

10. Permanency plans must be developed within what period of the day a child enters care?

(a) 18 months

(b) 6 months

(c) 2 years

(d) 12 months

Answers. 1. False; 2. True; 3. True; 4. b; 5. c; 6. a; 7. b; 8. c; 9. c; 10. a.

Two

ESSENTIALS OF PROTECTIVE INVESTIGATIONS

Activity within the child welfare system is initiated by an allegation of abuse, neglect, or abandonment. If the allegation is regarded as sufficiently credible, it is given to an investigator who will actually visit the child's residence to assess the situation more closely. State statutes provide general guidelines regarding what conditions may warrant action by the investigatory agency beyond the investigation. Agency procedure manuals offer additional guidelines that help investigators recognize when one of these conditions has been met. When one or more of the conditions exist, investigators may chose to (a) facilitate the provision of services to the family or (b) remove the child from the home and assume custody as a representative of the state.

This initial stage of child welfare activity is known by different names in different states. For the purposes of this book we use the term protective investigations. The policies and procedures for investigations also vary between states and often between jurisdictions (in practice they may also vary even between investigative units). This chapter summarizes the essentials that are reasonably consistent between jurisdictions, including (a) the investigatory agency, (b) the types of child maltreatment, (c) the nature of the reporting system and structure of investigations, (d) evidence that maltreatment has occurred, (e) means of assessing risk to the child, (f) alternatives to removal from the home, and (g) the process of assuming custody of the child.

THE INVESTIGATORY AGENCY

The agency in charge of investigating allegations may be either public or private. Traditionally, the agency responsible for these activities has been a state department or division of child welfare. In recent years some states have contracted these responsibilities to local government, private social service

> ### DON'T FORGET
>
> This initial stage of child welfare activity is known by different names in different states.

agencies, and law enforcement agencies. The responsibility for the initial receiving and screening of allegations may lie with the same agency or may be placed with some other organization.

Investigations follow protocols described in agency manuals that are used for training new hires. Such manuals and related training include an introduction to the statutory definitions of abuse, a discussion of the indicators that may be a clue to the presence of abuse, and a review of the procedures that investigators are expected to follow when they conduct their investigations. In some cases, trainees may get an opportunity to shadow or observe more experienced investigators in action for the first few days on the job.

TYPES OF CHILD MALTREATMENT

Children may be mistreated in a number of different ways. Whether any of these forms of mistreatment constitutes a reason for intervention by the child welfare agency depends on definitions in state statutes. These definitions vary to some degree between states, making a thorough discussion that is comprehensive for all jurisdictions somewhat challenging. Several authors have developed typologies of maltreatment that can help facilitate that discussion (Christoffel et al., 1992; Rycus & Hughes, 1998). We use the term *maltreatment* to depict all forms of inappropriate, harmful behavior directed toward a child. Rapid Reference 2.1 lists seven categories of child maltreatment. Maltreatment may be active or passive. Active maltreatment involves deliberate, willful behavior that brings harm to a child. Passive maltreatment includes neglect by those who are unable to care adequately for their children as well as *failure to protect,* in which a parent is aware of abuse by another adult but fails to intervene to stop it.

Physical abuse refers to actions that cause or permit significant physical injury to the body of a child (Christmas, Wodarski, & Smokowski, 1996). Physical abuse may be in the form of beating, cutting, burning, slapping, or other injurious behavior. It is important to note that in most jurisdictions corporal punishment does not constitute abuse unless it is exercised with sufficient force to cause injury. Most types of physical abuse result in some injury that can be observed either externally or through medical examination. Harm caused by abusive behavior can often be distinguished from accidental harm by looking for the indicators of abuse. The indicators are discussed later in this chapter.

Another form of maltreatment is *sexual abuse.* Sexual abuse occurs

when a person or persons of a more advanced developmental stage take advantage of a person at a less advanced developmental stage for their own gratification. This may occur between adults and children or between children of different ages. Sexual abuse may include vaginal intercourse, anal intercourse, oral stimulation, manual stimulation, touching, penetration with objects, exposure, voyeurism, and sexual comments or conversation (Faller, 1991; Mather & Lager, 2000). Depending on the nature of the act, the jurisdiction, the age(s) of the perpetrator(s), and the discretion of judges or prosecutors, sexual abuse may result in either a civil charge of child abuse or a criminal charge.

Neglect involves the failure to provide adequate resources to protect a child from harm, to provide a reasonable assurance of health, to receive an adequate education, or to promote adequate emotional development (Child Welfare League of America, 1991). Neglect is often difficult to detect, and

≡ Rapid Reference 2.1

Types of Child Maltreatment

- Physical abuse
- Sexual abuse
- Neglect
- Abandonment
- Inadequate supervision
- Heightened risk
- Emotional abuse

investigators who are responding to allegations of other forms of maltreatment may easily overlook it. Comprehensive assessment that considers every aspect of a family's life can help to guard against such oversight.

Abandonment occurs when parents forsake their children altogether. This may occur when a child is simply left somewhere, perhaps as a baby on a doorstep or a child dropped off at a mall and never picked up. It may also occur if parents leave children with relatives or friends and never, or very rarely, return.

At times supervision of a child may be so lax as to constitute maltreatment. *Inadequate supervision* refers to a gross failure on the part of a person responsible for supervising a child that results in death or physical harm or sufficiently threatens to allow that harm to occur. Situations such as leaving a baby alone in a bathtub or allowing a child to play with a handgun may constitute inadequate supervision.

Some jurisdictions consider *risk* to be a sufficient criterion for intervention by the child welfare agency. Risk usually refers to the presence of sufficient accumulated conditions so as to place the child in danger of experiencing injury. Risk can sometimes be difficult to identify, and it is frequently difficult to justify. Issues include determining the degree to which a child is at risk. One example would be a dirty and untidy home. A kitchen floor in serious need of mopping might indicate a fairly normal degree of risk. A floor that includes an overflowing garbage can and mounds of dirty dishes in the sink might constitute another. A kitchen including rotten garbage, a dirty sink, and piles of cat feces would clearly constitute a higher level of risk. Despite the clear levels of risk in this example, it might still be difficult for an investigator to determine at what point in-home services might be offered and when removal of the child would be necessary. Some jurisdictions have adopted risk assessment instruments, questionnaires that can be completed to help determine the severity of the risk. Risk assessment instruments are discussed in greater detail later in this chapter.

Emotional abuse probably occurs in many homes, but it is difficult to identify and measure and must be extraordinary to allow intervention in most jurisdictions. Emotional abuse may occur when a child is harshly and repeatedly criticized, blamed, or made to feel guilty. Emotional abuse has severe consequences for those who experience it, but it usually does not constitute a reason for intervention.

THE REPORTING SYSTEM

Many states receive allegations through a telephone hotline. Operators are trained to take calls and ask appropriate questions to determine which allegations have merit. Those that are believed to have merit are often assigned a level of urgency based on the degree to which assessors believe that there is "imminent risk" to the child's welfare. For example, a situation in which a child has been seen being beaten severely might warrant a "critical" status. This would mean that an investigator would need to respond immediately. An instance in which a child was not being required to attend school, however, might require a response within 48 hours.

In order to determine the credibility of the allegations, operators are trained to ask questions, summarized in Rapid Reference 2.2, that address several issues. These issues include the following:

1. *Is the witness credible?* The operator needs to ascertain whether the person making the allegation can reasonably be believed. Even though filing a fraudulent allegation is a crime in most jurisdictions, people sometimes allege that maltreatment has occurred when they are aware that it has not. The motives for such allegations may vary but are often intended as an act of revenge on the accused. False allegations are also made by persons under the influence of alcohol or other substances or by persons experiencing episodes of mental illness. Additionally, not all false allegations are fraudulent. Callers sometimes believe that they are reporting maltreatment when, in fact, it has not occurred. Anonymous calls are generally regarded with skepticism. Professionals such as social workers, psychologists, psychiatrists, teachers, and physicians are generally required to report maltreatment. The credibility of any call is enhanced when the caller begins by stating his or her name and professional position.

2. *Does the act described constitute a legislatively defined abusive act?* Some acts may be harmful or perceived as harmful but are not defined in state statutes as maltreatment. Many people, for example, are opposed to spanking. However, spanking is not considered abuse in most jurisdictions unless it is sufficiently excessive that observable harm occurs. Emotional abuse is another example. As was noted earlier, emotional abuse is very difficult to identify and usually is not illegal.

≡Rapid Reference 2.2

Questions That Help Substantiate Allegations

1. Is the witness credible?
2. Does the act described constitute a legislatively defined abusive act?
3. Is there visible evidence to support the allegation?
4. Are there other witnesses who can be questioned regarding the allegation?

3. *Is there visible evidence to support the allegation?* Operators also want to know whether there is visible evidence that maltreatment has occurred. When physical abuse is alleged, for example, the credibility of the report is enhanced if either the act itself or the resulting injuries can be described. In the case of sexual abuse, credibility is strengthened if the act has been observed by the reporter or has been described to the reporter by the victim or another credible witness.

4. *Are there other witnesses who can be questioned regarding the allegation?* Operators often seek to determine whether someone other than the reporter has witnessed the alleged maltreatment. The ability and willingness to provide names both enhances credibility and provides investigators with additional sources of information.

THE STRUCTURE OF AN INVESTIGATION

When an operator has completed a report of an allegation, it is forwarded to an investigator who works in the geographical area from which the allegation was made. The investigator is then required to respond according to the level of urgency assigned to the report. This system often works less effectively in practice than in theory. Often, harried investigators receive more reports than they can reasonably investigate. The process of taking a child into custody can be very time consuming, as can investigations that require multiple interviews or visits to multiple sites. Typically, statutes require that cases be investigated and resolved within a stated period (often within 30 to 45 days of the allegation). When cases are complicated or the evidence is not clear, investigators sometimes find this deadline difficult to meet. The result of the inability to initiate an investigation or to collect sufficient information on an open case is a dangerous backlog of cases in which no investigation or an inadequate investigation has occurred.

Investigations usually require a physical visit to one or more sites. Probably the most frequently visited site is the home of the child who is alleged to be the victim. A home is visited for many reasons, sometimes because it has been identified as the location of the maltreatment, sometimes because parents' perspectives are needed regarding abuse that may have occurred elsewhere, and sometimes to determine whether parents have made adequate efforts to protect the child. If the child is more than 3 years old, interviews with the child alone are usually conducted. Visits may also be made to neighbors' homes, physicians' offices, hospital emergency rooms, schools, churches, and other sites. At these sites investigators conduct interviews, look for physical evidence, observe interactions, and collect information. Based on the information they collect, they make a decision about whether to take the child into custody (DePanfilis & Zuravin, 2001).

In essence, investigators look for *probable cause* to believe that maltreatment has occurred. Although they have the authority to take a child into custody, the final decision about whether the child remains in custody is in the hands of the judge. The investigators present their case in the shelter hearing that was described in Chapter 1. Attorneys for the accused may also present their case. Based on the evidence presented, the judge decides whether enough evidence exists to justify retaining custody.

If the investigator determines that there is sufficient evidence that maltreatment has occurred or that risk of harm exists, he or she may choose to take immediate custody of the child, to make alternate supervisory arrangements (e.g., removal of the child to a grandparent's house), or to provide the family with a referral to a department or agency that will provide supportive services. This decision is based largely on the nature and severity of the maltreatment, the risk of future harm, and current conditions within the home. If, for example, the maltreatment has been active and severe and the perpetrator is currently living in the home, the investigator may elect to remove the child. If, on the other hand, the perpetrator is residing elsewhere in a secure location (e.g., is incarcerated), the investigator may choose to leave the child with the other parent.

Investigations also occur when the accused perpetrator is someone other than the parent. Examples include neighbors, teachers, and workers or residents in foster homes or treatment facilities. In these cases removal from a parent's home may not be an appropriate action. Other measures may be taken to protect the child from further harm. Another important consideration in these cases is whether the abuse constitutes criminal behavior. If so, law enforcement officers may become involved, and the investigator's role may be minimized.

When investigators take custody of a child, they follow the procedures described in their agency's manuals. This process often requires that the investigator transport the child to an agency office, arrange a suitable temporary living arrangement for the child, and transport the child to the temporary home. In the case of physical abuse the investigator may also need to take pictures of injuries or transport the child to an emergency medical facility. In the case of sexual abuse, the child may be taken to an agency where the staff specializes in working with children who have been victimized. After the child has been transported to temporary housing, the investigator must file the necessary documents to bring the case to the attention of the court.

In court the investigator is required to explain and justify his or her decision to the judge. The judge examines the evidence, hears any evidence that may be presented by the accused, and makes a decision about whether there is sufficient evidence to retain the child in custody for an adjudicatory hearing. If the child remains in custody, he or she may be placed in a state-operated or state-funded facility, with a relative or friend of the family, or in a specialized treatment facility. A date is then scheduled for the adjudicatory hearing. The investigator may gather more evidence before the adjudicatory hearing and will once again present evidence supporting the state's case at that hearing. This presentation typically marks the end of an investigator's involvement in the case.

Special—and tragic—circumstances arise when allegations of maltreatment are made against a child welfare worker or a foster parent. Although infrequent, such situations do arise and require special handling. Procedures vary between jurisdictions, but the investigation is typically conducted by an investigator from some other geographical area. The accused may be placed on administrative leave until the situation is resolved. When the allegations are substantiated, the worker may be fired and even prosecuted. Even when the allegations are not supported by the investigation, a cloud of suspicion may remain over the accused that can negatively affect his or her performance and career. It is vital that all child welfare workers ensure that they do not place themselves in situations that appear to be compromising with children in their care.

EVIDENCE THAT MALTREATMENT HAS OCCURRED

It was noted earlier that investigators look for evidence suggesting that maltreatment has occurred. This evidence becomes the basis for the state's case against the perpetrator and for a judge's decision to retain the child in custody. Different kinds of maltreatment tend to create different kinds of evidence. For example, physical abuse tends to produce bruises, cuts, broken bones, burns, and other physical evidence. Neglect may result in *failure to thrive,* in which the child does not appear to be developing normally and may be depressed, disinterested, and detached. Several authors have characterized evidence by the type of abuse that tends to generate it. Although this approach may help investigators focus on evidence related to the type of maltreatment under investigation, they might be so intent on looking for evidence of physical abuse that they miss obvious signs of neglect or sexual abuse. For this reason we use a different categorization scheme. Different types of evidence, also referred to as *indicators* of abuse, are listed as physical, psychological, relational, or environmental.

Physical Evidence of Maltreatment

Physical evidence includes injuries to the body that can be seen with the eye or detected using medical instruments. Visible injuries include bruises, cuts, burns, severely broken bones, missing patches of hair, bilateral blackened eyes, and developmentally inappropriate loss of teeth.

Injuries requiring medical inspection include skull fractures, subdural hematomas, retinal hemorrhages, injury to internal organs in the chest and abdomen, and specific types of bone fractures (Rycus & Hughes, 1998; Schmidt, 1979). Other factors that help to distinguish abusive injuries from accidental injuries include the location of the injury, the shape of the injury, the pattern of the injury, the age of the injury relative to other injuries, and the quantity of injuries (Rycus & Hughes). Rapid Reference 2.3 summarizes physical evidence of maltreatment and describes injuries that require medical intervention for diagnosis.

≡ Rapid Reference 2.3

Physical Evidence of Maltreatment

Visible Injuries

- Bruises
- Cuts
- Burns
- Severely broken bones
- Missing patches of hair
- Bilateral blackened eyes
- Developmentally inappropriate loss of teeth

Injuries Requiring Medical Inspection for Detection

- Skull fractures
- Subdural hematomas
- Retinal hemorrhages
- Injury to internal organs in the chest and abdomen
- Specific types of bone fractures

Bruises are perhaps the most easily recognized indicator of abuse. They are also frequently the result of accidents. Most accidental bruises tend to occur on the bony protruding areas of the body, such as the forehead, chin, arms, and shins (Rycus & Hughes, 1998). Bruises in other *locations* are not necessarily the result of abuse but should be regarded as suspect, particularly when they exist in combination with other indicators. Bruises in certain areas are particularly suspect, including (a) the lower back, buttocks, or upper rear thighs; (b) the ears, cheeks, lips, or neck; (c) the genitals; and (d) the fleshy part of the upper arm.

Bruises sometimes assume the *shape* of the object used, such as a board or a hand. Looping bruises, abrasions, or cuts may be from an extension cord, a rope, or a similar object. Long, straight bruises of various widths may be the product of striking with a belt or strap. Bruises shaped like bite marks should be inspected to determine whether they are child or adult-sized. When in doubt, medical tests are available that can help establish the source of a fresh bite. If the bite is by another child, the issue of whether adequate efforts to protect the victim have been employed must be explored.

Patterns can also be diagnostic. Bruises on the arms, chest, or face in the pattern of fingertips may indicate squeezing and shaking. Marks that circle the neck or wrists may indicate choking or binding. A series of linear marks may indicate repeated blows with a strap or belt.

The *age* and *quantity* of bruises may be instructive. When a child has evidence of multiple injuries, many of which are in various stages of healing, this may indicate an ongoing series of abusive incidents. Although the presence of multiple injuries does not prove that abuse has occurred, it may be a very strong indicator.

Children may experience *cuts* as a result of abusive behavior. As with bruises, cuts may occur accidentally, but the position, shape, pattern, age, and quantity may be a key to their origin. Accidental cuts tend to occur in the parts of the body that protrude, such as fingers, elbows, and knees. Other areas are much more suspect. Cuts on the neck may be the result of strangulation, particularly with a rope, a plastic cord, or some other object. Some abusers have also carved shapes or lines on children's arms and legs. Even when a cut is accidental, the investigator should consider whether allowing the child to be in the position to experience such an injury constitutes neglect. This would be of particular concern if the child had received such injuries repeatedly or has other injuries that tend to be indicative of abuse.

Burns are another common indicator of abuse. As with bruises and cuts, burns may occur accidentally, but the position, shape, pattern, age, and quantity may indicative of their origins. As with cuts, even obviously accidental burns should be scrutinized. If deliberate abuse has not occurred, the investigator should consider whether the burn has resulted from neglect. Abusive burns are most often from contact with flame (e.g., cigarettes, matches, or incense), contact with a hot object (e.g., an iron, radiator, or stove burner), or contact with an excessively hot liquid (e.g., bath or boiling water).

Cigarette burns may occur in many places on the body, typically the hands and arms. Injuries from small burning objects (cigarettes, matches, incense) tend to occur in a shape approximating the shape of the object. For example, cigarette burns tend to be circular. Injuries from larger flames (candles, burning sticks, etc.) usually cover larger areas and may be elongated if the body part was moved during the abusive incident. Flame exposure may produce first-, second-, or third-degree burns. One cigarette burn may be accidental. Several, particularly when they occur at various stages of healing, are virtually always the result of abuse.

Contact with a hot object causes a burn or brand mark in the shape of the object used. Frequent examples include irons, curling irons, stove burners, radiators, knives, keys, or soldering irons. Burns on the head, backs of the hands, or genitals are often the result of maltreatment. Injuries to the insides of the fingers or palm are often generated by accidents while the child is exploring. The severity of a burn is also often an indicator. A more severe burn is more likely the result of abuse because a child who contacts a hot surface accidentally is likely to withdraw from the pain before a particularly severe injury is produced.

Burns from hot liquids such as overheated bath water or boiled water are defined by a line at the point above which the water did not reach. For example, a child that is lowered into a pot of heated water to the depth of the knees will typically be burned only below the knees. Splash marks are frequently absent when the child has been restrained by its abuser. Common examples are burns around the buttocks and genitals, on the legs, and on the hands. Accidental burning is possible when a home's hot water heater is set at an excessive temperature. In these cases records should be checked to determine whether previous incidents have occurred. A follow-up visit to a home might be necessary to determine whether the setting on the heater has been adjusted.

The severity of *broken bones* may be difficult for an investigator to determine unless a limb is severely distorted or a bone protrudes from the skin. Therefore, when any fracture is suspected, the child should immediately be examined by a physician. Certain types of fractures are particularly suspect, including (a) most broken bones in children below the age of 1 year, (b) spiral fractures (the result of an adult's twisting a child's arm, or leg), (c) a chip or break at the end of a bone such as an arm or leg, and (d) broken ribs in infants. As with other injuries, pattern, age, and quantity may be keys to identifying abuse. Repeated breaks in the same area or similar areas and the presence of multiple breaks at various stages of healing are often very strong indicators of abuse. When children are thrown or violently pushed into some hard surface, *skull fractures* may result. Children whose skulls have been fractured may experience intense pain, pressure in the area of the fracture, and blood draining into the eyes and face.

Missing patches of hair often result when a child is pulled, thrown, or lifted by the hair. If the injury is recent, the scalp may be tender to the touch. Although missing hair may be the result of an accident, when it is present along with other suspect injuries the case should be viewed as suspect. An examination by a physician can help to determine the nature of these injuries.

Subdural hematomas, severe blood clots on the outer surface of the brain, often result from hard blows to the head. These clots may occur without any visible evidence such as bruising of the scalp or laceration. Investigators may suspect such an injury, however, if the child displays vomiting, irritability, seizures, or respiratory difficulties.

Bilateral blackened eyes are often the result of frequent slapping of the head in the area of the eyes. Although this condition may result from accidental injury to the nose or skull, heavily swollen eyelids indicate a high probability of abuse. As with other conditions, the presence of other injuries increases the probability that abuse has occurred.

Another common injury in cases of serious physical abuse is *injury to internal organs in the chest and abdomen.* The most frequently damaged organs include the liver, the pancreas, the spleen, and the intestines. Broken bones may also pierce lungs or inflict other injuries. Internal injuries may be difficult to detect, although severe incidents may be characterized by shock, decreased heart rate, dilated pupils, abdominal pain, projectile vomiting, anxiety, and disorientation. When these potentially fatal conditions are suspected, investigators should ensure that the child receives an immediate medical examination.

Failure to thrive is a commonly used term for a condition generated by a lack of adequate nourishment. These children, most often infants, are usually very underweight, comparing very poorly to other children on standardized height and weight measures. They may also have experienced little interaction with adults or other children and may be less socially advanced than is appropriate for their age. Older children may also display the symptoms of failure to thrive, particularly if steps have been taken by the abuser to prevent them from gaining access to food on their own. Investigators should be aware of the possibility that infants experience this problem when investigating allegations of neglect of older children in the same home.

When a child has had a history of medical problems but has received *insufficient medical or dental attention,* this is likely to be a case of neglect. Aside from the possibility of indicators similar to those displayed in failure to thrive, the child may have poorly healed wounds, broken or rotten teeth, scars from previous injuries, or, in severe cases, evidence of broken bones that were never properly set. Children, family members, or neighbors may also report that no medical or dental services have been received. Many neglected children have also not received needed eye and ear (particularly hearing) care.

Child neglect may be characterized by *extreme lack of hygiene.* Infants may have sores or severe rashes produced by infrequently changed diapers. Their clothing or bedding may be caked with the remains of food or vomit. Older children may be streaked with dirt, may have a strong, offensive odor, and may have lice or other body parasites. In severe cases children may have urine stains on their clothing or may have the remains of feces on their bodies or clothing.

Another indicator of neglect is a child that is chronically and significantly clothed in a manner that is inappropriate for weather conditions. For example, the absence of a coat or jacket in very cold weather may constitute neglect, particularly if it is a part of a regular pattern of behavior. Similarly, failing to provide a child with sufficient clothing to protect against sunburn may be an indicator of neglectful behavior.

Developmental delays are often present in both abused and neglected children. These delays may exist across virtually every dimension of functioning, including their physical, cognitive, social, and emotional growth. These delays can often be reversed when the neglect has not been severe and when intervention is timely.

Psychological Evidence of Maltreatment

In addition to physical symptoms of maltreatment, specific psychological conditions may support the supposition that abuse has occurred. Although these are often less powerful as indicators, their strength is enhanced when they are accompanied by questionable injuries or other injuries. Psychological conditions that may be telling in abusive situations may exist in the child, the parents, or siblings. Rapid Reference 2.4 summarizes common psychological indications of maltreatment.

≡Rapid Reference 2.4

Psychological Evidence of Maltreatment

In Children
- Depression
- Anxiety
- Withdrawal
- Detachment
- Hyperawareness
- Overly compliant
- Overly anxious to please
- Adult child
- Fear of or aversion to physical contact
- Craving of attention
- Fits of rage
- Aggressive behavior toward other children and sometimes adults
- Sexually provocative behavior
- Sexual acting out toward other children

In Parents
- Anxiety
- Hostility
- Hesitancy
- Fear
- Explosive outbursts
- Denial
- Overly anxious to please investigator
- Angry, explosive outbursts

In Siblings
- Reluctance to speak
- Fear
- Anxiety
- Uncertainty
- Strong outbursts of emotion

Many of the psychological indicators of maltreatment occur in the abused child. Many of these are simply the short-term consequences of being the victim of maltreatment. Abused children may be depressed or anxious and may appear withdrawn or detached, yet very watchful. They are often very compliant and anxious to please, conditions which, in their fullest expression, produce the so-called adult child who is a caretaker and often a substitute parent. Abused children often experience problems relating to both adults and children, often displaying a fear of or aversion to physical contact. Both abused and neglected children may crave attention and may go to great lengths to get adults to notice them. They may be subject to fits of rage and aggressive behavior toward other children and sometimes adults. Sexually abused children may behave provocatively and may act out sexually toward other children.

Psychological indicators also occur in parents. Many are best observed through their behavior in the presence of investigators. Psychological indicators in parents include anxiety, hostility, hesitancy, fear, explosive outbursts, and denial. Many perpetrators of abuse react to the investigator with anxiety or hostility. They may be overly anxious to please or may engage in angry, explosive outbursts. The nonperpetrating parent is often hesitant as though afraid of saying something revealing and fearful and worried that telling the truth may result in a child's removal or the arrest of the perpetrator. Both the perpetrator and the nonabusing parent often react with denial, claiming to know nothing of either injuries or the situations that produced them

Some psychological indicators of abuse also occur among siblings. Siblings may be reluctant to speak, fearing retribution by the abuser or separation from the abused child. They may display fear, anxiety, uncertainty, and strong outbursts of emotion such as anger or sorrow.

Relational Evidence of Maltreatment

Relational indicators are weaker than physical indicators but are often clearer than psychological evidence. These indicators may be present in the alleged perpetrator's relationship with the child, the nonabusive parent's relationship with the child, the child's relationships with his or her siblings, and the child's relationships with other adults. Common relational evidence of maltreatment is listed in Rapid Reference 2.5.

≡Rapid Reference 2.5

Relational Evidence of Maltreatment

In the Alleged Perpetrator's Relationship with the Child

- Fear
- Avoidance
- Flinching or ducking
- Physically distancing from alleged perpetrator
- Hypervigilance in the presence of the alleged perpetrator
- Constant awareness of the location and activities of the alleged perpetrator
- Denial of knowledge of how injuries occurred
- Denial of any awareness of the injuries
- Strange or unbelievable explanations for injury
- Failure to accompany the child to the hospital

In the Nonabusive Parent's Relationship with the Child

- Protective attitude without supportive action
- Identification of the perpetrator
- Denial of knowledge of how injuries occurred
- Denial of any awareness of the injuries
- Strange or unbelievable explanations for injury
- Delay in seeking treatment

In the Child's Relationship with His or Her Siblings

- Protective attitude toward victim
- Contempt or disregard for victim
- Multiple indicators of maltreatment in all children
- Reluctance to report maltreatment
- Family secrets

In the Child's Relationships with Other Adults

- Reluctance to speak
- Reluctance to seek comfort or help
- Adult child
- Overly pleasing behavior

One of the relationships in which indicators of maltreatment can be seen is the relationship between the alleged perpetrator and the victim. Often the child will show fear and avoidance of the abuser. The victim may flinch or duck when the perpetrator makes sudden movements and may demonstrate a dislike for physical contact, particularly with the perpetrator. Children frequently attempt to distance themselves physically from their abuser and may be hypervigilant, constantly aware of the location and activities of the perpetrator.

One very telling factor in many child abuse investigations is the parent's explanations of how the injuries under investigation occurred. When one parent identifies the other as perpetrator, this is often strong evidence (unless a custody suit is in progress). Parents who deny knowledge of how injuries occurred or deny any awareness of the injuries should be seen as suspect. When the explanation is strange or unbelievable or when an accident described is unlikely given the developmental capacities of the child, investigators may suspect abuse. Any delay in seeking treatment should be viewed with skepticism, as should the failure of a parent who was present at the time of an alleged accident to accompany the child to the hospital. Claims that siblings caused injuries should be considered in the light of the child's developmental capacity to inflict that injury.

Siblings may either demonstrate a protective attitude toward the abused child or treat him or her with contempt or disregard. Abused children are sometimes the family scapegoat, and this status can often be observed in the interactions of the children in that family. When all the children are maltreated, the multiple indicators of maltreatment are often present in all the children. Even though abuse may be chronic and severe, children may be very reluctant to report it. Family secrets, such as physical abuse, sexual abuse, substance abuse, and mental illness, are common in the families of maltreated children.

Indicators of maltreatment are also present in the children's relationships with other adults. They may be very reluctant to speak and may demonstrate a visible reluctance to seek comfort or help. Often, however, the phenomenon of the adult child can be seen most clearly in interactions with strangers such as the investigator. In these cases the child has learned to regard specific behaviors as pleasing to adults and that these behaviors will help the child avoid harm.

Environmental Evidence of Maltreatment

Certain conditions in the child's environment may constitute indicators that maltreatment has occurred. Although the environment can be very telling, this is an area in which investigators must be particularly cautious to distinguish between dangerous conditions and settings that are uncomfortable because of the investigator's personal cultural or socioeconomic background. Many families may not have the financial resources to provide the kinds of comforts to which workers are accustomed. Other families may be from cultures in which cleanliness is not maintained at the level to which the investigator is accustomed, or in which clutter is an accepted part of the culture. The key is to distinguish between the investigator's sensibilities or preferences and conditions that constitute a genuine danger to the child. Conditions that may constitute danger are outlined in Rapid Reference 2.6.

≡Rapid Reference 2.6

Environmental Evidence of Maltreatment

Dilapidated Building Structure

- Rotten flooring
- Sagging supports or ceilings
- Exposed electrical wiring
- Lack of heat
- Flaking lead-based paint
- Presence of substances containing asbestos
- Nonfunctional plumbing

Filthy Living Conditions

- Accumulated garbage
- Rotting food
- Piles of unwashed dishes
- Animal or human feces
- Open pits or wells
- Abandoned tools, equipment, or vehicles

(continued)

Exposure to Dangerous Substances
- Poisons
- Medicines
- Weapons
- Sharp objects
- Drugs and alcohol
- Broken glass

Infestation by Pests
- Rats
- Mice
- Birds
- Roaches
- Other pests

Absence of Food
- No edible food is present
- All or most food is spoiled
- No food has been present over an extended period of time
- Episodes of lack of food have been frequent

Ready Access by Known Perpetrators
- Access by current alleged perpetrator
- Access by past perpetrators
- Access by perpetrators in other cases

Structural conditions in the home that constitute danger might include rotten flooring, sagging supports or ceilings, exposed electrical wiring, lack of heat, flaking lead-based paint, the presence of substances containing asbestos, nonfunctional plumbing, and similar problems. When structural problems are identified, the investigator must make a judgment as to the degree to which the problems threaten the child's well-being. If the problems are moderate and the parents are cooperative, services may be arranged that can correct the problem without removing the child. If the problems are severe or the parents are not willing to cooperate, it may be necessary to take custody of the child.

CAUTION

The investigator must be careful that his or her personal values and cultural norms do not inappropriately influence the decision, particularly with regard to the home environment. Factors such as culture or socioeconomic status may make cleanliness, the availability of food, and orderliness vary in the homes visited. Investigators should remember that the most important factor is whether the child is endangered, not whether their sensibilities are offended.

Filthy living conditions may also be sufficiently hazardous to constitute a reason for removal. Mounds of accumulated garbage, rotting food, piles of unwashed dishes, the presence of animal or human feces, and similar conditions constitute a clear danger of disease and are attractive to a variety of animals and pests. Investigators also consider the conditions of the property surrounding the residence. Open pits or wells, piles of garbage, and abandoned tools, equipment, or vehicles may threaten a child's safety.

Another situation that increases risk to a child is exposure to dangerous substances such as poisons, medicines, weapons, sharp objects, drugs, alcohol, and broken glass. Poisons, medicines, weapons, and sharp objects should be stored out of reach of a child and in child-proof containers. Drugs and alcohol should also be in a place where children cannot access them. Broken glass, plastic, or similar substances should be collected and disposed of properly. When an investigator recognizes that these procedures have not been followed, he or she must consider the way in which they contribute to the child's overall level of risk. If parents are uncooperative with regard to correcting the problems, the risk is heightened considerably.

Infestation by pests is another common problem that confronts investigators. The problem is compounded by the difficulty involved in determining the point at which the presence of rats, mice, birds, roaches, and other pests reaches a dangerous level. A few roaches in a home may not be dangerous and can easily be eliminated with proper treatment. An occasional mouse or two in a rural home is not uncommon and can easily be eliminated with traps or poison. However, investigators sometimes encounter homes where the infestation is severe as indicated by the frequent appearance of roaches, the presence of mouse droppings, and other evidence of a significant problem. Severe infestation places all family members at risk of disease.

The absence of food in a home can also be an indicator of a harmful environment. Its usefulness as an indicator is influenced by the severity, duration, and frequency of the problem. When no edible food whatsoever is present, or when the little that is present is spoiled, investigators may consider how the children have been and are to be fed. When it is known that no food has been present over an extended period of time or that episodes of lack of food have been frequent, the risk is compounded.

Another problem that investigators must consider is the degree to which access to the child is available to known perpetrators. One source of danger is the perpetrator who has been accused in the current investigation. Other past perpetrators may also have easy access to the child's environment and may constitute a danger.

ASSESSING RISK

Assessing the degree of risk to a child can be an exceptionally difficult process (Lyons, Doueck, & Wodarski, 1996). When injuries are present and witnesses can identify the perpetrator, the level of risk is clear. When the injuries are questionable, witnesses are unclear, and the conditions in which the child lives are undesirable but not dangerous, the decision can be much more difficult. In the last instance, the investigator must transition from making a clear determination of whether risk has occurred to determining the degree to which risk of future harm exists. In some jurisdictions a sufficient level of risk alone may constitute grounds for removal of the child.

When investigators assess risk, they consider several questions (see Rapid Reference 2.7 for a summary):

1. *Are indicators present?* The first step in assessing risk involves determining which indicators of risk exist for the child. Ideally, this is a comprehensive examination of all dimensions and all risk factors. The presence of a single risk factor may be less threatening to the child's well-being than would the presence of many. Similarly, although the child may be healthy, the presence of multiple risk factors may be sufficient cause for action on the part of the investigator.

≡Rapid Reference 2.7

Questions Investigators Should Consider When Assessing Risk

1. Are indicators present?
2. How significant are the indicators?
3. How severe are the indicators?
4. How many indicators are present?
5. In what ways may the indicators interact to enhance risk?
6. To what degree are parents willing and able to cooperate to reduce risk?

2. *How significant are the indicators?* After the indicators have been identified, their significance should be evaluated. Significant indicators represent a more serious threat to a child's well-being. Less significant indicators represent a lesser degree of danger. Significant indicators include such things as evidence of injury that is clearly from abuse and extreme filth in the environment. Because a young child's accusation of a parent is almost always credible, this would also be regarded as a significant indicator. When highly significant indicators are present and no other arrangement can be made to ensure the child's safety, investigators often initiate the removal of the child.

3. *How severe are the indicators?* When a single risk indicator or a few indicators are present in sufficient severity, the situation may warrant immediate intervention. Examples include severe injuries that are clearly the result of maltreatment or the presence of injuries that are less suggestive of abuse but where relational and environmental indicators are also present. When indicators are severe, the investigator is often compelled to take immediate action.

4. *How many indicators are present?* Risk is compounded by the presence of multiple indicators. When a large number of indicators are present, risk is increased, and the probability that the investigator will take action should increase accordingly.

5. *In what ways may the indicators interact to enhance risk?* Some indicators increase the probability that other conditions in the home will lead to injury. For example, the presence of prescription medication

stored within a child's reach creates a level of danger. If that medication is not in childproof containers and parental supervision is lax, the probability of accidental ingestion increases.

6. *To what degree are parents willing and able to cooperate to reduce risk?* Sometimes investigators find homes in which the conditions are far from optimal but the parents are very willing to cooperate in order to make the environment safer for their children. When parents are willing to take immediate steps to improve conditions, investigators are sometimes able to avoid removing the child by ensuring that services to help the family make the corrections are in place.

Some jurisdictions use risk assessment instruments. *Risk assessment instruments* are pen-and-paper questionnaires that investigators complete to help them. Some allow investigators to assign a number representing the level of risk in each of several dimensions of the child's life. These numbers then become the basis for determining the degree to which the child is endangered. A selection of risk assessment instruments can be found in Rapid Reference 2.8.

≡Rapid Reference 2.8

Selected Risk Assessment Instruments

Child Abuse Potential Inventory (Milner, Gold, Ayoub, & Jacewitz, 1984). This 160-item self-report inventory, completed by a parent, is designed as a screening device to differentiate physical abusers from nonabusers.

Childhood Level of Living Scale (Polansky, Chalmers, Buttenwieser, & Williams, 1978). This 99-item behavior-rating scale assesses neglect of children age 7 and under.

Child Well-Being Scales (Magura & Mosas, 1986). These 43 behavior-rating scales are a multidimensional measure of child maltreatment situations specifically designed for use as an outcome measure in child protective services programs.

Family Risk Scales (Magura & Mosas, 1986). These 26 behavior-rating scales were designed to identify a full range of situations predictive of near-term child placement so that preventive services can be offered and changed as indicated.

Home Observation for Measurement of the Environment Inventory (Bradley & Caldwell, 1977). This 100-item observation-interview procedure assesses the quality of stimulation of a child's early environment.

ALTERNATIVES TO REMOVAL

Removing a child from his or her family is only one of several options available to investigators who determine that either maltreatment or risk of maltreatment exists. Many jurisdictions are required to make every effort to leave a child in an environment that is as close to normal as possible so long as the danger is removed or neutralized. Certainly, it is desirable to minimize the disruption that a child experiences. Although it is easy (and justified) to be indignant at the conditions a maltreated child experiences, it is important to remember that being removed from one's home by a stranger and taken to the home of another stranger is usually very traumatic for a child. For this reason, investigators often attempt to find ways either to provide a referral to services that will allow the child to stay with his or her parents or arrange for the child to be placed with a caretaker who is either related to or a close friend of the family.

When conditions in the home permit, an investigator may be able to allow the child to remain in the home but ensure that services are put in place that will correct the deficiencies that endanger the child. If, for instance, the perpetrator normally resides in the home but is currently incarcerated, it might not be necessary to remove the child. If the maltreatment has occurred because a parent suffers from mental retardation or medical problems, the presence of a relative or neighbor who is willing to stay in the home or make frequent visits may help avoid removal.

If the child's safety cannot be ensured in the home, the investigator may seek an alternative living arrangement with a relative or friend of the family. If this alternative is chosen, the investigator must be reasonably sure that the new caretaker will not return the child to its home or permit the alleged perpetrator unsupervised access to the child.

Sometimes, when risk is perceived to exist but is not at a sufficient level to warrant removal, the investigator may recommend that the family receive specialized services to reduce the level of risk. Agencies that provide housekeeping, parent training, family counseling, or other services may be asked to visit the home.

TAKING THE CHILD INTO CUSTODY

The process of receiving a child into custody varies among jurisdictions. In some areas investigators who do not believe that assuming custody of the child will provoke a parent into a dangerous act may simply take the child with them in their own vehicle. The investigator then takes the child to an agency field office or to an emergency room or sexual abuse assessment center if such is deemed necessary. From that location the child is transported to a shelter, which may be a residential facility or a foster home. Some jurisdictions have assessment centers where children who have recently been taken in to custody can be evaluated by professionals from different disciplines.

In some jurisdictions investigators make the decision as to whether the state should take the child into custody, but a law enforcement officer must actually remove the child. When this is the arrangement, the investigator must call for a law enforcement officer to come to the scene to assume custody. The requirement of involving law enforcement may be waived if the situation is believed to be life-threatening for the child.

In some jurisdictions the investigator may actually be an employee of a law enforcement agency that has contracted with the child welfare agency to provide investigative services. These investigators may or may not be sworn law enforcement officers and may or may not have the authority to assume custody.

Regardless of who actually assumes custody of the child, transportation to various sites such as a shelter home, medical facilities, or an assessment center may be done by the investigator or, at some point, may be assigned to an employee whose primary duty is the transportation of children. Some jurisdictions, in order to minimize the amount of time investigators are out of the field, have also used volunteers in this capacity. Others find that the investigator may be able to gain additional information from the child during transportation, and they ask that the investigator remain with the child until he or she is placed in a shelter.

DON'T FORGET

Many jurisdictions require that investigators choose the intervention that is likely to be the least traumatic for the victim. This may involve placing supportive services in the home, removing the child to the home of a relative or friend, or placing the child in a state-operated shelter.

Preparing for Court

Investigators must also prepare for the series of hearings that will determine whether the court will support the decision to take the child into custody. They prepare their cases by writing a narrative describing what they learned, saw, and experienced during the investigation. They may take photographs of injuries or of conditions in the home and may take statements from witnesses. Ultimately, they will have to appear before a judge to explain and justify their decision.

Special Cases of Maltreatment

Much of this chapter was written with the assumption that a parent or parents were the perpetrators of maltreatment. In fact, although maltreatment is most frequently committed by parents, many other persons in other settings may be perpetrators. A few of those are discussed here to provide a sense of how the investigative process proceeds if the alleged perpetrator is someone other than a family member.

When the alleged perpetrator is a nonbiological caretaker or guardian, the process is usually not very different from that just described. Similar kinds of assessments are conducted, and similar decisions are made. All four dimensions of indicators must be considered and the level of risk determined. Just as with biological parents, a decision must then be made regarding whether the child will be removed or left in the home.

If the alleged abuser is a part of a service organization such as an educational or religious institution, removal from the home may not be necessary. Unless the parents have collaborated in the maltreatment or have knowingly failed to protect the child, simply guaranteeing that the child will not continue to be in the presence of the alleged perpetrator is likely to be sufficient. Aside from interviews with the child and parents, the majority of the investigation is likely to occur away from the child and outside the home.

DON'T FORGET

Special situations require special handling. When investigators encounter unusual allegations or conditions, they should act cautiously, giving priority to the safety of the child.

The alleged perpetrator may also be a nonresident family member, a neighbor, or a family friend. Again, in these cases it may not be necessary to remove the child if the investigator can be reasonably certain that the child will be protected from future exposure to the abuser.

In the topsy-turvy world of child welfare, unusual situations are constantly presenting themselves in which decisions must be made with little guidance from policy or precedent. Many child welfare agencies are structured so as to permit investigators to utilize the expertise of supervisors when unusual situations arise. A high level of turnover and the heavy caseload may mean that supervisors are inexperienced themselves or that their duties make them unavailable when a decision needs to be made. A few examples of cases that were once uncommon but are becoming increasingly frequent are child prostitution, Munchausen by proxy (or Munchausen syndrome by proxy), and child-on-child sexual abuse. These are discussed briefly as examples of unusual situations in which investigators must often make quick judgments.

Investigators may encounter situations in which a parent or some other person with influence over a child is charging a fee to other adults who are having sex with the child. Child prostitution is not only abuse but also a criminal offense. Investigators who encounter these situations should be concerned for the safety and well-being of the child, concerned for their own safety, and aware of the need to involve law enforcement officers.

Munchausen by proxy is an unusual condition in which a caretaker, often the mother, deliberately causes a child to be ill in order to generate attention for herself. Some experts dispute that this disorder exists, but investigators occasionally encounter cases with the characteristics that typify this problem. Munchausen-by-proxy cases typically require long periods of intensive observation or reconstruction of a case from medical records. These cases often are reported by physicians or other medical personnel simply because they are the ones who are in a position to observe the behaviors and relationships that tend to characterize Munchausen. Munchausen victims often have a long history of apparently inexplicable illnesses and relapses. Careful investigation can link the onset of those illnesses to specific activities by the perpetrator. For example, perpetrators have been known to mix feces with medicines or administer overdoses of a medication. Further, when the victim is removed from the care of the perpetrator, his or her health often begins immediately to improve, and relapses cease to occur. Perpetrators also often have an almost hypnotic effect on family members and close friends so that, even with strong evidence to the contrary, they continue to insist on the perpetrator's innocence. Investigators who encounter Munchausen cases must rely heavily on the expertise of physicians, attorneys, psychologists, and other professionals to build their cases. Agencies involved in Munchausen cases also find that hiring the services of an expert in the disorder to serve as a consultant is critical to their work.

Child-on-child sexual abuse has become relatively common in child welfare cases. It may occur within the family or by another child outside the family (Lindholm, 1986). Disturbingly, it also often happens to children in foster care. Investigators who encounter these cases often do so through the reports of adult caretakers who have become aware of the problem, perhaps by interrupting an incident. They frequently discover that the perpetrator has also been sexually abused. Intervention includes moving the victim or perpetrator (as well as other potential victims) to alternative housing where further abuse will not occur, providing counseling for both the victim and the perpetrator, and investigating to determine whether efforts to protect by caretakers have been reasonable.

Because unusual situations arise in protective investigations and no support may be available to aid in the decision, it is wise to apply a few basic principles to guide decision making. Rapid Reference 2.9 lists these principles. The examples of unusual investigations just described serve as illustrations for each principle.

≡Rapid Reference 2.9

Guidelines for Making Decision in Unusual Cases

1. Err on the side of protection of the child.
2. Document carefully.
3. Avoid contact with or comment to the press.
4. Avoid unstructured discussion with other professionals.
5. Report situations and decisions to a supervisor or someone in authority as quickly and accurately as possible.

CAUTION

Remember to always err on the side of the child's protection.

1. *Err on the side of protection of the child.* In an unusual situation it is best to make the protection of the child top priority. This may not, however, involve removal of the child. In a suspected Munchausen-by-proxy case, immediate removal of a child may be counterproductive because evidence to support the removal may be scant and difficult to access. Investigators would do well, however, to alert their supervisors, agency attorneys, and medical personnel of the situation and seek their advice as to how to proceed. When there is clear evidence of child-on-child sexual abuse, however, the best course is often the immediate removal of either the perpetrator or the victim.

2. *Document carefully.* It is always important that the investigator carefully document all relevant observations and interactions, but this is particularly important in unusual cases. One example of the importance of this principle is seen in the child prostitution example. Because a case of this nature is very likely to become criminal, the observations of the investigator may be needed to build a criminal case.

3. *Avoid contact with or comment to the press and others.* Unusual cases sometimes come to the attention of the press. In these cases the investigator may be approached by reporters who are seeking information about the case. Often the reporters are very skilled at extracting comments from even the most unwilling. Although many journalists are responsible, others have been known to take innocent comments out of context, thereby misrepresenting the person being interviewed. An investigation into child prostitution or a Munchausen case can be seriously damaged by a single, apparently harmless comment. Investigators should ignore the queries of reporters or respond with no more than a "no comment."

4. *Avoid informal discussion with other professionals.* A common way to deal with the stress of an intensive day of investigations is in casual conversation with one's fellow workers. These conversations often include the stories of some of the day's investigatory work. Although these discussions can be very beneficial for many reasons as long as confidentiality is observed, discussion of unusual or high-profile cases may result in a leakage of information to persons outside the agency. Investigators

should avoid including details about unusual cases in informal discussions with coworkers and other professionals.

5. *Report situations and decisions to a supervisor or someone in authority as quickly and accurately as possible.* Unusual cases should be reported to those at higher levels as quickly as possible. Involving administrative personnel can enable investigators to access resources and experience not otherwise available to them. It also helps administrators to prepare for questions from the press, parents, law enforcement, legislators, and others who may be interested.

CHAPTER SUMMARY

The first step in the child welfare process is the investigation. After receiving a report of an allegation of maltreatment, a worker conducts an investigation to determine whether there is evidence to support the allegation. The worker looks for indicators that maltreatment has occurred or is at risk of occurring. If the investigator believes the evidence to be sufficient, he or she initiates action that may range from the recommendation of supportive services through removal of the child. Children who are taken into custody may be taken to a shelter, an emergency room, or a center that specializes in the assessment of sexual abuse. The investigator then prepares for a series of court appearances in which he or she will be required to justify the decision to take the child into custody.

 TEST YOURSELF

1. **The agency in charge of investigating allegations may be either public or private.** True or False?

2. **Maltreatment may be either active or passive.** True or False?

3. **Sexual abuse occurs only between adults and children.** True or False?

4. **Some jurisdictions consider *risk* to be a sufficient criterion for intervention.** True or False?

5. **Allegations of maltreatment are categorized according to their perceived level of severity.** True or False?

(continued)

6. Failure to thrive is a condition in which

(a) A child does not appear to be developing properly across multiple life dimensions

(b) A child develops a series of strange and inexplicable illnesses

(c) A child is beaten severely over a period of years and experiences arrested emotional development

(d) A child fails to develop cognitively at an age-appropriate rate

7. Four characteristics of bruises cab help investigators determine whether they are the result of abuse. These characteristics include

(a) Coloration, spotting, size, and pattern

(b) Age, size, coloration, and spotting

(c) Shape, quantity, size, and coloration

(d) Shape, pattern, age, and quantity

8. In most jurisdictions spanking by parents is regarded as

(a) An example of child abuse that warrants state action

(b) Permissible as long as it is not so severe that the child is injured

(c) The right of a parent regardless of severity

(d) Legal for any person who is responsible for a child's well-being at any moment

9. Which of the following should be regarded as a very strong indicator of maltreatment?

(a) When bruises are larger than the size of a baseball

(b) When a parent who has not been accused accuses the other parent

(c) When alcohol is present in the home

(d) When the home is dirty, disorderly, and cluttered with books, papers, and toys

10. A child who appears to be hypervigilant and overly anxious to please may show the characteristics of

(a) Abandonment

(b) Hyperactivity

(c) The adult child

(d) Conduct disorder

Answers. 1. True; 2. True; 3. False; 4. True; 5. True; 6. a; 7. d; 8. b; 9. b; 10. c.

Three

ESSENTIALS OF CHILD AND FAMILY ASSESSMENT

When children are taken into state custody, one of the earliest responsibilities of the child welfare agency is to conduct an assessment of the case's essential persons and social systems. This assessment becomes the basis of virtually every decision made after adjudication. Ideally, the assessment considers every aspect of the child's life but focuses primarily on the strengths and needs of the children and their families. The primary goal is the identification of the problems that have caused or contributed to the maltreatment and the strengths that can be built upon to prevent its recurrence. Another important goal is to recognize specific needs a child may have such as psychological, medical, dental, or educational (Dulmus & Wodarski, 2002). This provides a basis for planning ways in which these needs can be met. The assessment is the precursor to the case plan.

Assessment is typically conducted by an employee of a child welfare agency, although specialized evaluation or diagnosis may be left to specialists. Often the worker is also the person who will supervise the children while they are in care. The assessment usually follows a standardized format, using an interview guide selected by the agency.

TARGETS OF THE ASSESSMENT

The assessment may target one or several persons and systems (Dulmus & Wodarski, 1996). The decision about who will be included depends on the level of involvement of each individual and group in the case. Rapid Reference 3.1 lists possible targets for assessment. The child who has been taken into custody virtually always receives some form of assessment. Others who may be included are the biological or source family, the host family, and a residential facility. The term *biological family* is used to describe the family into

53

===*Rapid Reference 3.1*

Possible Targets of the Assessment

- The individual child
- The biological or source family
- The host family
- A residential facility

which the child was born. *Source family* is used here to indicate either a biological family or a family that functions legally and pragmatically as the biological family for the child even though he or she may have been born into some other family. It is intended to include any family from which a child might be taken into custody. The term *host family* is used to designate a family other than a professional foster family with whom the child resides while in state custody. Foster families do not usually receive assessment because they are known to the child welfare agency. Examples might include a family that is biologically related to the source family or one that is composed of their friends. Residential facilities are considered briefly because of the possibility that a child may be placed in a setting with which workers have been previously unfamiliar.

The Individual Child

The child taken into custody should always receive a thorough and comprehensive assessment to determine what his or her strengths and needs may be. In many homes where children are maltreated, multiple physical, mental, and emotional needs are overlooked. The child welfare agency is responsible not only for providing housing for the child but also for assuring that the needs of the child are met as well. The assessment begins the process of recognizing those needs. The term *begins* is used here because the assessment should be an ongoing process for the child. Even though the initial assessment may be thorough, some problems may not be evident until the child is older or until he or she has spent some time in custody. One example is a developmental delay that cannot become obvious until that developmental stage has been reached. Ideally, child welfare workers should have ongoing, frequent contact with children in custody and should be alert for developing problems that require intervention. In reality workers are often overburdened with heavy caseloads and are unable to have sufficient contact with children to ensure that assessment is ongoing.

The Biological or Source Family

If the court intends to attempt to reunify the child with his or her source family, that family must also receive a thorough and comprehensive assessment (Suarez, Smokowski, & Wodarski, 1996; Walton, 2002). The problems that generated the maltreatment must be identified, and a plan must be developed to correct those problems. The unutilized assets of the family, such as relatives who are willing to be supportive, should also be identified and included in the plan. If the court does not intend to attempt reunification, some assessment with the source family may still be useful. For example, the presence of a biological predisposition to a mental illness or alcoholism in a family may be very useful in developing a plan for the child. Without obtaining this information from the source family, workers may have no way of knowing that such conditions exist. Reunification may not be the goal in several circumstances, such as if the parents choose voluntarily to relinquish their rights, if the parent has a long history of severe maltreatment of other children, if the maltreatment of the current child has been particularly severe, or if a single parent is going to be incarcerated for an extended period.

Host families also require assessment. This is not the case when a child is placed with a licensed foster family whom the child welfare agency employs and hopefully knows well. It is necessary, however, when the child is to be placed with a relative or friend of the family who is unknown to the agency. This assessment should also consider strengths and weaknesses with a focus on determining how these factors may affect the child's well-being and what intervention may be needed to support the family.

Children may be placed in a *residential facility* immediately following adjudication. This situation may arise when they have severe medical or psychiatric needs or when they have been involved in delinquent activity. Often the facility will be known to the child welfare agency. Sometimes it may not. If the facility is not known and the agency has discretion about the location of the placement (if the child is delinquent or if the judge has the right to select a placement, the agency may not have discretion), an assessment visit should be made to the facility. The visit should include a tour of the facility, an examination of its sleeping quarters, an inspection of its kitchen and dining area, an examination of its license and credentials, and an interview with its executive and clinical directors. The worker should attempt to ascertain whether the sleeping arrangements are safe (e.g., whether the child is likely to be secure from maltreatment by other residents), whether the facility is adequately maintained and is clean, and what its working philosophies and practices are in the management and treatment of children. Ideally, the facility should provide a safe, comfortable environment in which the issues for which the child is being placed there can be effectively addressed.

SITES OF THE ASSESSMENT

Different components of the assessment may be conducted in different places, as described in Rapid Reference 3.2. The location should depend on several factors, including who needs to be assessed, what equipment will be required, and what clinical advantages may be gained by site selection.

Assessments of families are often best conducted in the family's home. Visits to the home allow the practitioner to talk with the family in its natural environment where the practitioner can see not only the home but also the interaction of family members in that setting. Although family members are likely to present as positively as possible even in their home, they are more likely to interact more normally than they would in an office. Further, if an assessment requires several visits, the practitioner will have multiple opportunities to view the home environment to determine its suitability. Assessments in the home are usually desirable for both source and host homes. An assessment in which only the home is inspected is sometimes referred to as a *home study.*

Rapid Reference 3.2

Possible Sites of the Assessment

- In the host home
- In the source home
- At a temporary shelter
- At a medical facility
- In a mental health center or office
- In a substance abuse treatment center or office
- In school
- At an agency assessment center

Assessments, particularly of a child in custody, may be conducted at a temporary shelter. The term *shelter* refers to the place in which the child resides before being officially placed in a foster home. A shelter may be a group home, an individual home, or a medical facility. It may actually be the foster home in which the child will eventually be placed. A discussion of placement alternatives sounds as though the arrangements are very structured, with children moving smoothly from one setting to another. In reality the distinctions are much less clear. A child may remain in a shelter long after the order has been given to place him or her in foster care. In the rush to find a place for a child to sleep, practitioners may simply call the list of foster parents, asking whether they can keep a child for a night or two. If that parent agrees to a short-term stay, the child may be shifted from one short-term residence to another in a process sometimes referred to as *bouncing* from home to home. Eventually, if children land in homes that are willing to keep them for longer periods, that may become the foster home by default. Practitioners often visit one of these homes to interview the child as a part of their assessment.

Assessment may also take place in an emergency room or a physician's office. Although there is rarely time for a full assessment in either setting, practitioners often find that they must get answers from the child in these settings that later become a part of the overall assessment. Further, the medical evaluation performed at the facility may provide important information that will affect the case plan.

Evaluations that are a part of assessment are sometimes conducted at mental health centers or in the office of a private mental health practitioner. There may be questions as to whether the child, a member of the source family, or a member of the host family has a mental health problem that will require treatment. Examples might include conduct disorder or attention-deficit/hyperactivity disorder in children and bipolar disorder in adults. Any of these conditions might contribute to or be the root of maltreatment. Recognizing and treating them would be an important component of a successful treatment plan.

Substance abuse evaluation may also be necessary as a part of an assessment. As with mental health, substance abuse evaluations typically occur in a treatment center or office. The evaluation may include a psychosocial assessment, an interview specific to substance abuse, and urinalysis. If the assessor discovers a substance abuse problem, he or she will report it to the child welfare practitioner, who should ensure that the problem is addressed in the case plan. Substance abuse assessments may be conducted for both children and adults.

Specialized evaluations may also be conducted in schools or in centers operated by school systems. Such evaluations usually focus on issues related to learning and may include vision and hearing tests as well as diagnostic testing to identify learning disorders such as dyslexia or processing disorder.

Some jurisdictions have a central office at which assessments are conducted over a period of several days. Professionals may come to the center to do testing, or children may be transported to their offices. Often, assessments include triage, in which practitioners from several disciplines review and discuss the case to determine who will provide what services.

COMPONENTS OF THE ASSESSMENT

Assessments may be as simple as a home study and a single interview with a child or may be very complicated, including a home study, a psychosocial study of the members of both source and host families, and various evaluations by different professionals. These individual studies and evaluations may be thought of as individual components, so that when all have been conducted and compiled, the final product is the assessment.

Determining Who Will Be Assessed

The decision as to who will be assessed is likely to rest in the hands of the child welfare worker, a group of professionals, or members of the judiciary. In some jurisdictions the child welfare worker, usually someone assigned to the case from the residential care unit, conducts a psychosocial study and makes recommendations as to other evaluations that he or she believes should be performed. In other areas groups of professionals assemble in cross-disciplinary teams to review information presented to them by the caseworker and make recommendations regarding evaluations. In some jurisdictions judges may order specific types of evaluations. Where they are unable to give such orders, some choose to make such strong recommendations that caseworkers feel compelled to comply.

The decision as to who will be assessed and what components of an assessment they will receive depends on several factors. In order to make informed decisions, caseworkers should ask several questions and generate a list of the answers. The list can then be used to guide assessment planning. Rapid Reference 3.3 lists important questions that should always be asked.

≡Rapid Reference 3.3

Questions That Should Be Asked to Guide Assessment Planning

1. What conditions do I know the child has or experiences that may be barriers to effective functioning?
2. What conditions do I suspect the child has or experiences that may be barriers to effective functioning?
3. Where can these conditions be assessed most effectively?
4. What conditions do I know the source family has or experiences that have caused or contributed to maltreatment and must be corrected before reunification can occur?
5. What conditions do I suspect the source family has or experiences that have caused or contributed to maltreatment and must be corrected before reunification can occur?
6. Where can these conditions be assessed most effectively?
7. What conditions do I know may exist in the potential host family that need to be addressed in order for this child to experience a successful placement?
8. What conditions do I suspect may exist in the potential host family that need to be addressed in order for this child to experience a successful placement?
9. Where can these conditions be assessed most effectively?

1. *What conditions do I know the child has or experiences that may be barriers to effective functioning?* The caseworker may know that specific problems exist for several reasons. Parents or teachers may report that the child has been evaluated and that a problem exists. Caseworkers may also have access to records that identify conditions.

2. *What conditions do I suspect the child has or experiences that may be barriers to effective functioning?* Neighbors or family friends may report that a problematic condition exists or that they suspect it exists. Alternatively, the caseworker may suspect a problem because of observation of or interaction with the child.

3. *Where can these conditions be assessed most effectively?* Options for obtaining assessment or evaluation are often limited. In jurisdictions where there is only one mental health center, for example, mental health evaluations will probably have to be conducted there. Where additional options are available, the worker should consider issues such

as the competence of the agencies with the child's specific problem or age group, the sensitivity of the agencies to the child's culture, and the speed with which the evaluation can be conducted.

4. *What conditions do I know the source family has or experiences that have caused or contributed to maltreatment and must be corrected before reunification can occur?* If the goal is reunification, problem conditions in the source family must be identified and addressed. Caseworkers may identify these problems through interviews with and observation of the family, conversations with significant others, discussions with professionals who have worked with the family, and other sources.

5. *What conditions do I suspect the source family has or experiences that have caused or contributed to maltreatment and must be corrected before reunification can occur?* There may be times when the caseworker may be unable to confirm that a problem condition exists but strongly suspects that it does. Evaluation is almost always appropriate in these situations.

6. *Where can these conditions be assessed most effectively?* Similar questions should be considered in response to this question as were asked in response to Question 3 above.

7. *What conditions do I know may exist in the potential host family that need to be addressed in order for this child to experience a successful placement?* Although this is an important question to ask, if the answer involves many problems or particularly severe problems, the child should probably not be placed with this potential host. Unfortunately, a limited repertoire of potential placements may limit the options of even the most dedicated worker. In some jurisdictions placements are very limited and may even be as dangerous as the source family. In these situations the worker may wish to consider putting interventions in place for the proposed source family.

8. *What conditions do I suspect may exist in the potential host family that need to be addressed in order for this child to experience a successful placement?* This question should be answered similarly to Question 7. Unfortunately, the choice of placement is sometimes a matter of the lesser of two bad situations. The child may be better with a proposed host willing to receive intervention than with some other host.

9. *Where can these conditions be assessed most effectively?* This question is particularly important because it is important to prevent the child

from experiencing additional maltreatment and to avoid bouncing to other homes. Again, the same processes should be used to answer this question as were used for Questions 3 and 6.

Effective assessment is critical to a positive outcome, yet workers may experience significant barriers to its successful completion. The barriers may include resistance by administrators, disagreement among professionals, turf wars between agencies, and budgetary problems. These kinds of issues often prevent caseworkers from obtaining all the components of an assessment that they believe to be necessary.

Assessment of Individual Functioning

The first component of an effective assessment involves assessment of individuals. At a minimum this requires an assessment of the child who has been maltreated. It may also need to include assessment of various members of the source or host families.

Dimensions of the Assessment

Comprehensive assessment of individual functioning includes several dimensions of the person's life. These dimensions include (but are not necessarily limited to) the physical, psychological, social, and cognitive. Information may be obtained from records (e.g., physical or psychological examinations), direct interviewing (using a guided interview questionnaire or standardized instrument), or pen-and-paper questionnaires completed by the person being assessed.

Indicators of a Need for Further Evaluation

Often, assessments are initially conducted as a sort of a scan in which the overall life dimensions are briefly explored. In the process of the scan, practitioners may discover conditions that indicate the likelihood that noteworthy problems or strengths exist in those dimensions. When such indicators are encountered, the assessor knows that more in-depth information should be collected. One example might be when initial questions indicate that a child is lagging behind in school. This would suggest that physical functions such as vision and hearing should be tested to ensure that there are no problems that interfere with learning. If no physical problems are identified, practitioners might need to consider evaluation for developmental disabilities, problems with cognitive development, or lack of support for education in the home. Similarly, if particularly aggressive behavior is observed, diagnostic activity by a mental health provider may be needed.

It is important that child welfare workers not focus only on problems and weaknesses. Individuals also often have considerable assets that can be accessed and activated during an intervention. These assets, often called strengths, should be identified in the assessment so that they can be incorporated into the case plan. Strengths may include a high level of intelligence, a strong social support system, or a particularly good set of social skills. Assessment should include questions directed at identification of assets in these and other areas.

The Process of Assessment

The process of assessment of individuals usually includes direct conversation with or observation of the child, review of professional records, interviews with significant others, and conversations with professionals such as teachers or physicians. It usually begins with the completion of a psychosocial assessment form and often requires the inclusion of other documents prepared by consulting professionals.

Assessment of Family Functioning

Dimensions of the Assessment

Practitioners who conduct family assessments need to examine a number of dimensions of family life. Important areas include management style, communication patterns, disciplinary style, financial problems, and potential for violence. It is particularly important to identify all persons who are members of the family being assessed. Many families, particularly those of nondominant cultures, include biological relatives, relatives by marriage, or family friends as members of the extended family. These persons may need to be included in the case planning process and may constitute a significant resource in the intervention.

> DON'T FORGET
>
> Assessments of child and family strengths are essential components of a comprehensive assessment.

Indicators of a Need for Further Evaluation

Practitioners who are conducting family assessments should be alert for certain conditions that indicate the need for further evaluation. Examples include high levels of family conflict, authoritarian or permissive parenting styles, violence in the home, the obvious absence of physical resources, and family isolation. For example, in families where the father or mother is clearly dominant, children may form alliances with the nondominant parent as a protective measure. Both the dominant management style and the opposing alliances can be dysfunctional and can raise stress levels in the family, enhancing the probability that maltreatment of the children may occur. All this must be weighed also against cultural considerations. In many cultures the father is (at least apparently) the head of the household and can be very dominant. Practitioners must be particularly careful in these cases not to impose their own values on the family. Family isolation is another indicator of the need for further evaluation. If a family appears to have little outside social support, the reasons for this isolation may need to be ascertained during assessment and addressed in the case plan.

As with individual assessment, it is critical to include assets and strengths when assessing families. Families may have deep reservoirs of social support, a member with unusually strong problem-solving abilities, or a member with unusual and marketable job skills that have not been utilized. Family strengths can be used to build family competence, minimizing the probability of further child maltreatment.

The Process of Assessment

When further evaluation is indicated, several instruments for family assessment in specific areas are available. A list of some of these instruments is included in Rapid Reference 3.4.

Medical and Dental Assessment

Dimensions of the Assessment

Medical and dental assessment is best left in the hands of professionals trained in that dimension. As with other dimensions, however, practitioners must be aware of indicators that may alert them to the need for referral. Although these needs may have been considered to some extent during the

≡Rapid Reference 3.4

Selected Family Assessment Instruments

Conflict Tactics Scales (Straus, 1979). This 19-item self-report inventory is widely used to assess conflict among family member.

Family Assessment Form (McCroskey, Nishimoto, & Subramanian, 1991). This instrument assesses the family's physical, social, and economic environment; psychosocial history of caregivers; personal characteristics of caregivers; child-rearing skills; caregiver-to-child interactions; developmental status of children; and overall psychosocial functioning of the family from an ecological perspective.

Index of Family Relations (Hudson, 1982a). This 25-item self-report inventory measures the extent, severity, or magnitude of problems that family members have in their relationships with one another.

Inventory of Family Feelings (Lowman, 1980). This 38-item self-report inventory assesses the overall degree of attachment between each pair of family members.

Family Assessment Screening Inventory (FASI; Gabor, Thomlison, & Hudson, 1994). This questionnaire is designed to obtain information about a wide range of family strengths, resources, and problem areas.

Index of Parental Attitudes (Hudson, 1982b). This 25-item self-report inventory can be used for a child of any age. It is rated on a 1 to 5 continuum that measures extent and severity of parent-child relationship problems as perceived by the parent.

Family Assessment Device (FAD; Epstein, Baldwin, & Bishop, 1983). The FAD is a 60-item self-report measure that was developed as a screening device to operationalize the factors from the McMaster Model of Family Functioning. The six subscales correspond to the theoretical dimensions in the model: (a) problem solving, (b) communication, (c) roles, (d) affective responsiveness (the ability of family members to experience appropriate affect over a range of stimuli), (e) affective involvement (the extent to which family members express interest in and value each other's activities), and (f) behavior control (the way the family expresses and maintains standards of behavior).

assessment of maltreatment, workers at that stage may have focused only on conditions that rise to the level of abuse or neglect. During the development of the case plan, practitioners need to identify other conditions that may have been missed due to the limited focus of the prior assessment.

Medical needs may be varied and may, in some cases, be severe. Generally, practitioners should look for injuries that may have been missed by protective investigators, illnesses (both acute and chronic), and problems with vision or hearing. Dental needs may be assessed by observation and by asking questions about dental history and current distress. Ideally, any child taken into custody who does not have a consistent record of medical and dental examination should receive those services within the first few days of entering custody.

Indicators of a Need for Further Evaluation

Several conditions may indicate the need for further medical evaluation. These include complaints by an older child or crying by an infant, flat affect, excessive inactivity, excessive activity, persistent cough or nasal discharge, tugging at an ear, and general failure to thrive. Conditions that may indicate the need for dental evaluation include complaints of pain or crying, chronically bad breath, difficulty eating or chewing, and discoloration of the tooth enamel. Dental and medical evaluation are both highly specialized. Child welfare practitioners should not engage in diagnosis in these areas but should refer the child for specialized examination when they suspect a condition.

The Process of Assessment

Although medical and dental evaluations are best left to professionals with specialized training, careful observation and carefully worded questions asked as a part of the psychosocial or family assessment can help practitioners recognize the presence of indicators.

Educational Assessment

Dimensions of the Assessment

Educational assessment may include examination of physical, cognitive, psychological, substance use, and social dimensions. Generally, anything that may interfere with children's learning processes is considered during educational assessment. Physical issues may include problems with vision, hearing, undernourishment, or hyperactivity. Cognitive problems may include developmental delays, dyslexia, and difficulties with motor skills. Psychological issues may involve conduct disorder, oppositional/defiant disorder, mood disorders, and the beginnings of more serious disorders described in Axis I of the *Diagnostic and Statistical Manual of Mental Disorders–Fourth Edition, Text Revision (DSM-IV-TR;* American Psychiatric Association [APA], 2000). Psychological evaluation is described in greater detail in the next section. Substance abuse evaluation would consider whether the use of alcohol or other drugs were interfering in the child's education. This form of evaluation is described in greater depth in a later section. Social evaluation involves looking at the social skills and interactions of the child to identify problems that may interfere with the development of social support and positive relationships with classmates or teachers.

Although educational evaluation often focuses on deficiencies, it is also likely that some strengths will be discovered during the process. In fact, practitioners should be alert for strengths and should consider ways to use them in the case plan. For example, a child with a hearing problem may also have a particularly high level of intelligence, an asset that should be very helpful in correcting problems in the educational process.

Indicators of a Need for Further Evaluation

Indicators for the physical, psychological, and substance abuse dimensions are discussed in other sections of this chapter. In addition, practitioners should be alert for failing grades, being a year or more behind in school, truancy, fighting, disobedience, disrespect for authority, problems relating to classmates, bullying, and being bullied.

The Process of Assessment

Educational evaluation usually begins with a referral to a school nurse, counselor, social worker, or psychologist. Physical causes should be ruled out or corrected before proceeding to other dimensions. Frequently, problems in multiple dimensions require referral to several different professionals.

Individual or family assessment might lead to a referral to a professional who specializes in a specific dimension. In these cases, professionals may use any of several instruments for educational assessment.

Mental Health Assessment

Dimensions of the Assessment

Mental health evaluation may be necessary for the child in custody, the source family, or both. Mental health refers to the absence of specific mental and emotional disorders that affect individual and family function and contribute to the probability of ongoing abuse. These disorders are described in greater detail in the *DSM-IV-TR* (APA, 2000). Identification and treatment of psychological disorders can be critical to the case plan. For instance, a parent who suffers from bipolar disorder is likely to experience strong mood swings. At times the parent might be extraordinarily depressed, unable to respond to children's needs or to discipline them. At other times the same parent might be highly animated, speaking in rapid bursts, and given to fits of rage. Clearly, this sort of erratic behavior could create stress in a home and contribute to maltreatment. Identification, however, can lead to successful treatment. Many who have bipolar disorder can stabilize their moods with appropriate medication. In fact, treatment can eliminate or diminish the effects of many mental illnesses.

Indicators of a Need for Further Evaluation

As with medical and dental evaluation, mental health evaluation is best left to trained professionals. Child welfare practitioners should be alert for the presence of indicators that mental health problems exist. These indicators include bizarre behavior, explosive temperament, difficulties in maintaining relationships, sleep problems, over- or undereating, difficulty in getting or maintaining employment, lack of motivation, and inability to concentrate. Generally, when attitudes or behaviors are well outside the norm (and cannot be explained by cultural factors), a mental health evaluation may be in order.

The Process of Assessment

Multiple mental health screens as assessment instruments are available to assist child welfare workers. Such instruments allow the worker to gather additional information to determine if further evaluation is necessary by a mental health professional. A list of some of these instruments is included in Rapid Reference 3.5.

Substance Abuse Assessment

Dimensions of the Assessment

Substance abuse is included in the *DSM-IV-TR* (APA, 2000), but it is discussed separately here because it is so often seen as a separate issue in the

≡Rapid Reference 3.5

Selected Child Mental Health Assessment Instruments

Child Behavior Checklist–Revised (CBCL; Achenbach, 1991) is a 118-item checklist for parents to evaluate the behavior of their child ages 4 through 18 years.

Children's Depression Inventory (CDI; Kovacs, 1981) contains 27 items to measure levels of depression.

Children's Behavior Rating Scale (CBRS; Hudson, 1994a) is a 20-item rapid assessment instrument for parents to complete to identify problem behaviors in their child.

Reynolds Adolescent Depression Scale (RADS; Reynolds, 1992) is a 30-item assessment tool used to identify depression in youths ages 13 through 18 years.

Multidimensional Adolescent Assessment Scale (MAAS; Hudson, 1996) is a 177-item questionnaire in which questions are divided among 16 subscales measuring a variety of mental health concerns.

treatment community. Substance abuse refers to the use of alcohol or other substances to the point that the user's overall functioning is impaired. Substance use or abuse is frequently a factor in child maltreatment. In order to identify the need for further evaluation or treatment, child welfare workers need to consider (a) the substance or substances being used, (b) the amount of the substance that is being used, (c) the frequency with which the substance is being used, (d) the degree of impairment the individual experiences from using the substance, (e) whether the substance being used is legal, and (f) whether activity that might endanger the child is generated around the family by the use of the substance.

Indicators of a Need for Further Evaluation

The primary indicator of the need for further evaluation for the use of any substance is the case of alcohol or over-the-counter medications. If indicated, this should lead to questions about quantity of use, frequency of use, and the effects of use. The use of illegal substances adds another level of concern. Those who use illegal substances may be subjected to arrest or to harm from the persons from whom the substances are purchased. If the person being interviewed reports frequent use of any substance, or if there is any indication that impairment occurs as a result of the use, the individual should be referred for a complete substance abuse evaluation. Often, the identification and treatment of a substance abuse problem can be a central component in an effective case plan.

The Process of Assessment

Questions in the substance abuse assessment typically focus on the six areas just identified: presence of use, quantity used, frequency of use, degree of impairment, legality of the substance, and degree of danger generated by the use of the substance. When further evaluation is indicated, several instruments for substance abuse assessment are available. A list of some of these instruments is included in Rapid Reference 3.6. As with medical, dental, and mental health assessment, in-depth evaluation of substance abuse problems is best left to those with specialized training in that field.

Legal History Assessment

Dimensions of the Assessment

Knowledge of legal history may be important for many reasons. When the child in custody has a history, workers will need to be aware of related activity in the courts or in the juvenile justice system. When parents or significant others have engaged in criminal activity, this may affect the stability of the home or the level of safety in the home. The case plan will need to include and accommodate these conditions. When jurisdictional laws permit, it may be advisable to check into the history of nonbiological parents who reside in or frequently visit the home.

Rapid Reference 3.6

Selected Substance Abuse Assessment Instruments

CAGE (Ewing, 1984) is a mnemonic for four questions that are used to screen for alcohol problems.

Index of Alcohol Involvement (IAI; Hudson, 1994b) is a 25-item rapid assessment instrument to assess alcohol use.

Index of Drug Involvement (IDI; Hudson, 1994c) is a 25-item rapid assessment instrument to assess drug use.

Substance Abuse Subtle Screening Inventory (SASSI; Miller, 1988) contains 86 indirectly worded questions on alcohol and substance abuse.

Indicators of a Need for Further Evaluation

The presence of a legal history may be very important to the case plan, may be neutral, or may be completely unimportant. When the child has a history, factors such as the probability of running away or committing violent acts in the home should be considered. When a parent or significant other has a history, the degree to which that record presents a danger to the child should be considered. Violent crimes, substance abuse, and domestic violence should raise particular concerns. Certainly any history of abuse of other children should also be considered whether that is a part of a criminal history or the records of a child welfare agency.

The Process of Assessment

In some jurisdictions it may also be possible to obtain official records (sometimes known as *face sheets*) for adults who are being assessed. Ideally, the information collected at the initial assessment will both inform the intervention and serve as a foundation for future assessment. It is unlikely that workers will learn everything they need to know from the initial contacts. A hearing problem may be discovered in an otherwise healthy child several months or even years after the child is taken into custody. A parent or significant other may be discovered to have a record of child maltreatment in another state long after the initial data have been gathered. Practitioners may find it helpful to develop a checklist for each case that includes each assessment component that they suspect may be necessary. This will help to ensure that important areas are not forgotten or overlooked. Workers might also add a section to this basic checklist in which they list areas that may require assessment in the future. This will help to ensure greater continuity if the case passes into the hands of another worker.

CHAPTER SUMMARY

Assessment is vital to successful case planning, a topic that is discussed in greater depth in the following chapters. It is from the assessment that basic strengths and needs are identified and interventions are devised to enhance those strengths and address those weaknesses. A good assessment may require evaluation of multiple dimensions of the lives of several people or groups. An assessment planning checklist can help to ensure that all the needed areas are included.

TEST YOURSELF

1. **The primary goal of assessment is to identify the problems that have caused or contributed to the maltreatment and the strengths that can be built upon to prevent its recurrence.** True or False?

2. **Foster families are typically assessed each time a new child is placed in the home.** True or False?

3. **Assessment of the child should be an ongoing process.** True or False?

4. **No investigation of a licensed residential facility is necessary before placing a child in its care.** True or False?

5. **The assessment process often begins with a child welfare worker's completion of a psychosocial evaluation.** True or False?

6. **During assessment *triage* refers to**

   (a) The identification of a suitable foster home for a child who has been taken into custody

   (b) A process unique to educational assessment in which a child's physical, mental, and emotional needs are considered as they relate to the learning process

   (c) The identification of three alternative placements from which a best fit can be identified for the child

   (d) A process in which practitioners from several disciplines review and discuss the case to determine who will provide what services

7. **Comprehensive assessment of individual functioning includes, at a minimum,**

   (a) The physical, psychological, social, and cognitive dimensions of the individual's life

   (b) The social competency of each of the systems with which the individual interacts

   (c) Evaluation of all family members for substance abuse and mental health problems

   (d) Identification of all factors that may place a child at risk of further abuse

(continued)

8. Family assessment should include

(a) Only persons biologically related to the child

(b) Both persons biologically related to the child and anyone who in a serious romantic relationship with the parent

(c) Anyone identified by the family as a member of the family

(d) Paternal grandparents if the family is Hispanic

9. Educational assessment should include

(a) Any area of a child's life that may impair or improve educational performance

(b) Only physical and cognitive conditions suspected to impair functioning

(c) A completed Minnesota Multiphasic Personality Inventory for each child

(d) A careful nutritional analysis of each child's diet

10. Substance abuse evaluation usually focuses on which of the following areas?

(a) Presence of use, quantity of use, frequency of use, and presence of addiction

(b) Degree of effect on family, likelihood of future arrest, cultural issues, and perceived motivation for treatment

(c) Presence of use, quantity used, frequency of use, degree of impairment, legality of the substance, and degree of danger generated by the use of the substance

(d) Presence of use, quantity used, degree of effect on family, perceived motivation for treatment, frequency of use, and cultural factors

Answers. 1. True; 2. False; 3. True; 4. False; 5. True; 6. d; 7. a; 8. c; 9. a; 10. c.

Four

ESSENTIALS OF CASE PLANNING

Ideally, the next step after the completion of the initial assessment is the completion of a case plan (Holt, 2000). The case plan is a written document that describes the steps that the child, source family, host family, and child welfare agency must take to improve the child's condition and to move the child in the direction of reunification or termination of parental rights. Case plans usually are prepared by an employee of a child welfare agency and then submitted to the court for its approval.

Although the initial assessment should be complete by the time the case plan is prepared, practical considerations such as the timing of court appearances, the availability of professional staff, and the size of case loads often force child welfare practitioners to develop a plan before all assessment data are in. Given the extraordinary pressures faced by child welfare workers, a good understanding of the essentials of case planning is imperative. The format of these documents varies somewhat between jurisdictions, but quality plans have similar components and are developed in similar ways. This chapter describes the essentials of effective case planning, including a discussion of the basic rules and guidelines workers should adhere to, the core components that should be included, the processes involved in creation and modification of a plan, and three sample plans.

BASIC GUIDELINES FOR CASE PLANNING

One of the most important principles of case planning is that the plan should be *based on the characteristics of the child and the family that were uncovered during the assessment*. A proper assessment will have revealed a great deal about their history and current condition. The practitioner who prepares the case plan should examine the assessment to identify relevant weaknesses, strengths, and needs (Cowger & Snively, 2002). The case plan should correct or compensate for the weaknesses, optimize the strengths, and address the needs. In essence, the case plan identifies relevant conditions, describes their natures and sources, develops a plan for addressing or utilizing them, and outlines a strategic plan for the process.

A second basic principle of case planning is that the practitioner should *collaborate with the child and family as the plan is developed*. This, of course, may be practical in some cases and impractical or impossible in others. For example, the child welfare worker may discover a family with substantial personal and social resources that needs little more than a referral for financial assistance and some basic classes in parenting skills. In other situations there may be no source family at all (e.g., where a substance-abusing mother has abandoned the child), and the child may be an infant or sufficiently impaired that collaboration is impossible. Many cases will fall somewhere between these extremes. Practitioners should concentrate early interaction with the family on determining the degree to which collaborative planning is possible. Collaboration has many benefits: (a) It maximizes the interest and commitment of the participants; (b) it models the problem-solving and decision-making processes; and (c) it ensures that the participants understand what they must do to complete the process.

A third principle of case planning is that *the weaknesses and needs of the child and family must be prioritized*. Prioritization is important for several reasons. First, it is likely that some problems may be more central to the conditions that produced the maltreatment than other problems. These core problems may need to be addressed before the others can improve. Second, it may be important to identify a problem that can be easily resolved as a high

Putting It Into Practice

Imagine that a family displays not only a lack of communication but also poor communication skills. Family meetings would still need to be scheduled and monitored, but classes in communication skills might also need to be planned. This would allow the family to use any basic skills it had but also to access community resources to enhance its own strengths.

priority. This can give the family a sense of accomplishment and the confidence it needs to move on to more difficult problems. Additionally, limited external resources (e.g., agency or community programs or funding) may make it difficult or impossible to address all problems. In these cases it may be critical to target those problems where the greatest benefit can be realized in the shortest period of time.

DON'T FORGET

Incorporating strengths into the intervention empowers children and family.

Not only must problems be identified and prioritized, but *they must also be clearly defined*. Defining a problem refers to preparing a written description that accurately and comprehensively describes it. The definition should also be written in behavioral terms, that is, so that the problem can be observed to determine whether it is improving, remaining the same, or worsening. For instance, a problem statement including only the comment that stress and tension are high would not be as useful as a statement that included observable manifestations of the problem. To strengthen the statement, a practitioner might note the frequency with which arguments occur, the presence and frequency of physical threats, or the number of inappropriate resolutions to arguments that occur during a given period.

Another basic priority in case planning is *the identification and incorporation of individual and family strengths into the plan*. Incorporating strengths into the intervention empowers children and families, teaches them alternative ways of thinking, encourages them to access and utilize their resources, reduces their dependence on external resources, and develops self-esteem and self-efficacy. Strengths may exist on an individual, family, or social-system level. Individual strengths may exist in the child in custody, siblings, parents, and extended family. For example, a parent whose explosive temper has led to maltreatment may be able to learn to call a member of the extended family who is skilled in deescalation when his temper begins to rise. Family strengths may include particularly strong relationships between family members, financial resources, high levels of family tradition and pride, and deep commitment to the family by its members. Family pride can be a particularly strong resource when it can be used as a source of motivation for parents and siblings.

Assets with the social system may include neighbors, teachers, recreation personnel, community programs or centers, and similar resources. These can be accessed as sources of child care, centers for tutoring or mentoring, and sites at which strong vocational or avocational interests can be encouraged.

A sixth basic priority in case planning is the *development of measurable and attainable goals and objectives*. Goals are the long-term accomplishments that signal successful completion of the case plan. Objectives are the short-term, more easily accomplished steps that lead to the accomplishment of goals. Both goals and objectives must be measurable; that is, there must be a way to determine the degree to which they have been met. They must also be attainable; in other words, they must be something that the participants can reasonably be expected to accomplish within the allotted time (Garvin, 2002). An example of a goal in a treatment plan for a mother with a history of active substance abuse might be, "Ms. Smith will remain free of the use of illegal substances for at least a six-month period." Objectives to reach that goal might include, "Ms. Smith will regularly (missing no more than one session per month) attend individual therapy sessions at the Community Mental Health Center. Her therapist must report sufficient progress toward dealing with issues related to the use of substances before reunification can occur" and "Ms. Smith will regularly (missing no more than one meeting per month) attend Narcotics Anonymous meetings." The goal of abstinence for a six-month period is reasonable and hopefully attainable. It is sufficiently important that if Ms. Smith cannot accomplish it, she should probably not have custody of her children. It is also measurable in that properly conducted urinanalysis can offer a reasonable degree of assurance that the goal has been met. Similarly, the objectives are attainable (barring a significant illness or similar major event, she should be able to attend both the therapy sessions and the meetings) and measurable. Attendance at therapy could be measured by requesting weekly reports from her therapists. The policies of twelve-step groups regarding anonymity might preclude receiving reports from a sponsor or group member, forcing the practitioner to rely on Ms. Smith's own report of her attendance. This is considered a form of measurement, although it is clearly less reliable than the report of a professional or other outside source. In such cases it is best to have both multiple objectives (in which others can be more accurately observed) and ongoing monitoring of progress toward goals.

A good case plan also *specifies who will do what by when.* Goals are accomplished through objectives, and objectives are accomplished through tasks (Wodarski, Rapp-Paglicci, Dulmus, & Jongsma,

DON'T FORGET

Goals must be observable, measurable, and attainable.

2001). As with goals and objectives, tasks must be measurable and must also include a statement of who is responsible for performing them and the time by which they will have been accomplished. Imagine, for example, that Ms. Smith is willing to attend therapy sessions but is unable to provide her own transportation. A task related to the objective of regular attendance of sessions might read, "The case manager will provide vouchers for bus transportation to and from therapy sessions by the first day of each month for each month Ms. Smith is required to attend sessions."

It is vital that case plans be written in a language that the family will understand. They will be required to comply with the plan and should be able to comprehend it as well as explain it back to the case manager. Where cognitive impairment prevents understanding, the practitioner must offer a clear explanation and ensure that some system is in place to provide reminders and allow for questions to be answered. One of the best ways to do this is to discuss the case plan with all participants during regularly scheduled visits.

The ninth basic principle of successful case planning is *to be sensitive to cultural differences.* This is a critical yet often neglected factor. Cultural differences are discussed in greater depth in Chapter 10, but a few comments are in order here to heighten the reader's awareness of the matter. Examples of cultural issues that might affect case planning include differences in the ways in which individuals perceive appropriate levels of corporal punishment and the tendency of some groups to be overly anxious to comply with authority figures. In the first example, some cultures support the use of forms of punishment that are regarded as extreme in this society. Parents from those cultures may require education or even therapy to understand and accept the restrictions of American culture. In the example of those who could be overly anxious to comply with authority, some Southeast Asian families might quietly accept the mandates of a case plan without participating in its development. Although on the surface this might appear to be desirable, in reality it might prevent the family from developing the kind of commitment to the plan that can be generated through collaboration and might inhibit them from developing useful insight into the nature of their problems.

A tenth principle of case planning is *to write a plan the court will accept.* Although this may seem obvious, poorly conceived and written plans are a very real problem for some child welfare workers. Judges often have little patience with incompetence. When the logic of a plan is clear and sound and the plan is written in clear language that uses adequate legal terminology, judges are more likely to approve it. Over time, as practitioners present a series of well-conceived and well-written plans, judges develop respect for individual workers and will both trust them and help them with difficult decisions. Workers who present poor plans or plans in which the writing is too informal may find the courtroom a very difficult place indeed. The logic of the plan is enhanced by following the steps for the development of goals, objectives, and tasks discussed earlier. The language of a plan can be strengthened by using the sample plans included at the end of this chapter or by reviewing well-written plans developed within one's own jurisdiction. Rapid Reference 4.1 summarizes the basic guidelines for case planning.

≡Rapid Reference 4.1

Basic Guidelines for Case Planning

- Base the case plan on the assessment.
- Collaborate with the child and the family.
- Prioritize the needs of the child and the family.
- Clearly define the problems in terms that are observable and measurable.
- Identify the strengths the child and family may utilize to help themselves.
- Identify goals and objectives that can be measured and that are reasonable given time, resource, and cultural constraints.
- Specify who is responsible for completing what part of the plan by what date.
- Write in a language that the family will understand.
- Be sensitive to cultural differences.
- Write a plan that the court will accept.

FORMAT OF A CASE PLAN

Case plans occur in at least two general types of formats (see Rapid Reference 4.2). The *integrated format* incorporates goals, objectives, tasks, accountability, and due dates into integrated statements. The *discrete format* lists goals and objectives separately (or discrete) from tasks, the identification of accountable parties, and completion dates. Although both formats are useful, it is important that practitioners be aware of the format used in their jurisdictions and comply with that format as closely as possible. It is also important to note that even within these categories the format may vary between jurisdictions.

Many case plans begin with problem definitions. Although some simply begin with goals and objectives, it is often helpful to have a ready description of the problems that they are intended to address. Problem definitions may include a description of the conditions that prompted the decision to take custody of the child as well as the conditions within the family that contribute to the condition. Problem definitions may also include some of the observable indicators of the problem. Examples of problem definitions are provided in the sample case plans at the end of this chapter.

When a discrete format is used, the components are typically separated into two or three sections. If there are three sections, these typically include (a) statements of the goals for the case, (b) statements of the objectives for the case, and (c) statements that assign tasks to specific individuals and groups, including the date by which they should be completed. If the discrete case plan has two sections, one typically combines goals and objectives, and the other describes tasks, accountability, and the date of completion.

Discrete case plans have the advantage of being comprehensive and are much more likely to provide a clear link among problem, goal, objective, and task. If they are not well written, however, they can be unwieldy and difficult to follow. In addition, caseworkers who are not properly trained may have difficulty distinguishing among goals, objectives, and tasks. Examples of discrete case plans are included in the sample cases at the end of this chapter.

When a case plan is integrated, goals, objectives, and tasks are not separated. Rather, they are combined into a series of statements. These statements may include the goals and objectives or may simply assume that they are understood and begin with the tasks that must be completed. The statements

Rapid Reference 4.2

Types of Case Plan Formats

Discrete: Goals, objectives, and tasks are presented separately from one another.

1. Goals, objectives, and tasks are included in separate sections.
2. Goals and objectives are grouped together but are presented separately from tasks.

Integrated: Goals, objectives, and tasks are combined into a series of statements.

are written in the imperative; that is, they instruct the person responsible for completing the task that it must be done.

Integrated case plans are often much briefer and more concise. When well written, they provide clear, unambiguous behavioral guidelines for all participants. A potential weakness is that the link among goals, objectives, and tasks may be lost because it may be difficult to state clearly in a single statement. An example of an integrated case plan is included among the sample plans at the end of this chapter.

DEVELOPMENT OF THE CASE PLAN

Case plans should be developed for individual children and families. After some time practitioners may begin to experience cases with similar characteristics. Although it is possible to learn from similar cases, it is important not to assume that similar characteristics make cases identical. For example, while the problems experienced by two families may be similar, their assets, such as family income, may vary. Similarly, families with similar problems may have different responses to case plans because of cultural differences between them. It is also important to remember that problems may appear similar but, in fact, have very different root causes. Interventions that address the core of one family's problems may miss the core of another's.

Interactions with the families should also be individualized. One family, for example, may respond particularly well to a very informal style of interaction. Others may require a more formal approach. The intervention described in the case plan should grow out of the caseworker's growing understanding of the family. Similarly, as the family's understanding of its problems increases, their insight should influence the direction of the plan.

The plan should be developed to maximize the use of the family's internal strengths. This requires

that its own resources be employed without any additional external support than is actually required. Ideally, some of the problems (e.g., lack of communication) might be addressed by scheduling regular family meetings (assuming that communication skills are strong). In this situation the plan would require that the meetings be scheduled and that the case manager monitor their progress, but no additional external resources would be required. In other cases more intensive external involvement might be necessary. It is important to remember that in order for a family to use its own resources, it may need to be aware that the resources exist and must have some confidence that they can be used. In such cases the practitioner must help family members identify small, obtainable objectives that can be easily reached to help them build confidence in their own abilities.

The case plan must also include mechanisms to ensure that the resources needed by the family are accessible. Accessibility may require transportation, child care, money, and other resources. When these services are needed, a description of what they are and how they will be accessed should be included in the plan. For example, a task statement might be phrased as follows: "Ms. Smith will attend weekly parenting skills meetings at XYZ Community Mental Health Center. She will be provided with bus vouchers by the case manager, Ms. Collins, to facilitate her transportation to the center."

The practitioner must also ensure that resources included in the plan are currently operating and that they continue to be available throughout the duration of the plan. Unfortunately, social service programs sometimes lose their funding or key personnel and may vanish with little notice to their clients. If a case plan includes resources that have ceased to operate, it may be weeks before the caseworker discovers that no services have been received. The problem is complicated in jurisdictions where judges must approve specific service providers. This requires an additional hearing in which the worker can present the alternative to the court. Similarly, programs may cease to operate during the course of a case plan. Practitioners should monitor services through ongoing contact with families to ensure that they are still available. When it is known that the ongoing existence of services is threatened, the caseworker should maintain a dialogue with program staff to gain personal knowledge of its status.

Case plans should be as comprehensive as possible. This means that the maximum number of problems should be addressed. Practitioners often face many barriers in developing comprehensive interventions. In some cases, services simply may not be available to address specific needs. In other situations the family may be incapable of addressing a broad range of issues simultaneously. In these cases the plan may require some foundational work before it is modified to address broader and deeper issues. The importance of comprehensiveness and the presence of so many barriers to achieving it underscores the need for a collaborative effort in developing the plan. For example, it is important to ask family members whether they believe tasks, objectives, and goals are attainable and, should they respond negatively, to determine what adjustments, if any, are appropriate.

≡ Rapid Reference 4.3

Principles for Developing a Case Plan

- Case plans should be individualized.
- Interactions with the families should also be individualized.
- The plan should be developed to maximize the use of the family's internal strengths.
- The case plan must also include mechanisms to ensure that resources are accessible.
- Resources must be currently operating and must be available throughout the duration of the plan. Case plans should be as comprehensive as possible.
- Plans should also be developed such that future modification is possible.

Plans should also be developed such that future modification is possible. Families may fail to achieve some goals within the allotted time. In many of these cases it may be desirable to allow more time or to try a different approach to dealing with that specific problem. Plans should be written in such a way that, with the court's approval, modifications can be made to facilitate the family's success. Rapid Reference 4.3 summarizes these basic principles.

MODIFICATION OF THE CASE PLAN

Case plans may be modified for many reasons. In most jurisdictions this requires the approval of the court and is often initiated at a hearing. Occasions that may prompt modification include (a) when the family has done better than expected and has reached stated goals ahead of schedule, (b) when the family has done worse than expected and it appears that reaching stated goals will be impossible, (c) when additional problems or strengths have been discovered that either require or permit revision, (d) when goals have been met but other conditions have arisen that require intervention, and (e) when it appears that individuals who had been excluded from the original plan require intervention for the plan to be successful.

Modification should not be regarded as an indication that the original plan was inadequate. In fact, the ongoing process of assessment often uncovers conditions that require at least some adjustment of the plan. Often, the decision as to whether the adjustment can be made informally or whether it will require a return to court is dependent on the statutes governing the disposition of children in a given jurisdiction. In some jurisdictions, for example, judges are permitted to determine what kind of intervention a child will receive (substance abuse, mental health, etc.) but cannot choose the specific agency or program at which the services will be delivered. In other areas judges must approve not only intervention type, but also the agency. When a judge's approval is required, a formal approval by the court is required. This must take place in a scheduled hearing because communication to and by the judge about a case in any setting other than court is prohibited.

Depending on the jurisdiction, modification of the case plan may be initiated by the caseworker, the court, the child's attorney, or the family's attorney, typically through a legal document submitted to the judge requesting a status hearing (as with other legal terminology, this term may vary across jurisdictions). If the judge chooses to grant the hearing, notices are issued to all parties as to the hearing's date, time, and purpose. At the hearing those who agree with the need for modification present their reasoning. Those who oppose it submit their case. The judge then rule as to whether the modifications should be adopted.

CONTENT OF THE CASE PLAN

Case plans typically include content that addresses six basic areas: disposition, assessment, intervention, monitoring, supportive services, and outcome measurement (see Rapid Reference 4.4). These content areas are usually written into the task statements described earlier in the section on format.

Disposition refers to the living arrangements the child will experience during the course of the case plan. There are several alternatives, and these may vary between jurisdictions. Common alternatives include return to the source home with mandatory supervision, placement with the biological family, placement with nonbiological extended family, placement in a foster home, placement in a specialized foster home, placement in a residential facility, and placement in an independent living program (see Rapid Reference 4.5). These placement alternatives are discussed in greater detail in Chapter 5.

Assessment is often a part of the case plan. For example, some type of evaluation may have been deemed necessary during the original assessment but could not be completed prior to the dispositional hearing. Alternatively, assessment may be included because a need for follow-up evaluation was anticipated after certain services had been delivered.

The tasks that the case plan delineates constitute the *intervention*. The intervention is designed to facilitate reunification or make alternative permanent living arrangements for the child. In addition,

Rapid Reference 4.4

Content of a Case Plan

- Disposition
- Assessment
- Intervention
- Monitoring
- Supportive services
- Outcome measurement

≡*Rapid Reference 4.5*

Placement Alternatives in Case Planning

- Return to the source home with mandatory supervision
- Placement with the biological family
- Placement with nonbiological extended family
- Placement in a foster home
- Placement in a specialized foster home
- Placement in a residential facility
- Placement in an independent living program

interventions typically address problems that may exist in other dimensions of the child's life. These dimensions would include those identified in the assessment described in Chapter 3.

The case plan also includes a description of the mechanism that will be used for *monitoring* the progress of the plan's participants. This may be as simple as requiring regular visits from the case manager or much more complex. More complex monitoring mechanism could include such things as ongoing evaluations by medical or mental health personnel, regular urinalysis, or scheduled tutoring sessions.

Case plans also list the sources of the *supportive services* that will need to be in place to provide optimal probability of success. Supportive services include such things as financial assistance, transportation, child care, and homemaking services. Supportive services should be clearly linked through the task statements to the objectives and goals they support. For example, when the cleanliness of the home has been identified as a factor contributing to risk, a task statement might read, "The case manager will ensure that Helpful Homemakers Service will provide both housecleaning and home maintenance training services weekly for 6 weeks to improve the level of cleanliness in the home and to ensure that the skills are in place to maintain that level of cleanliness."

Provisions for *outcome measurement* should also be incorporated into the plan. Outcome measures refer to the behavior, attitude, skill, or knowledge that can be observed to determine whether the plan's goals and objectives have been achieved. For example, where basic child care skills and knowledge are lacking, the plan might require parents to demonstrate that they can change diapers or properly prepare formula for an infant. When safe conditions within the home have been an issue, the plan might require parents to demonstrate a knowledge of basic safety procedures and to submit to regular inspections of the home.

SUPERVISION OF THE CASE PLAN

After a case plan has been developed and approved, it must be supervised. This means that some person or group of persons, frequently the worker from the child welfare agency who developed the plan, must work with participants to help them comply with its mandates. This process (summarized in Rapid Reference 4.6) may involve monitoring, communication, support, correction, advocacy, referral, and similar activities.

Monitoring refers to observation of the behavior of all participants to ensure that efforts are being made to comply with the plan. Monitoring often occurs through regular visits to homes, schools, and businesses; through the administration of periodic evaluations or tests; and through conversations with professionals who provide services to plan participants.

Effective *communication* is essential to the success of any plan. Often, however, there are communication problems among the participants and the agencies with which they interact. The case manager is responsible for identifying such miscommunications and clarifying what was intended to the satisfaction of each party. Frequent examples of communication problems include (a) a failure on the part of the host family to understand some of the expectations of the court and (b) a lack of understanding on the part of a family member as to the procedures and purpose for an evaluative test.

The practitioner often finds the need to provide *support and encouragement* to those who are trying to follow a case plan. Many families

Rapid Reference 4.6

Activities Required for Case Plan Supervision

- Monitoring
- Communication
- Support
- Correction
- Advocacy
- Referral

are dealing with lifelong emotional and behavioral patterns that can be very difficult to change. Others may have deficits in self-esteem that cause them to become very discouraged at the slightest failure. Although many of these issues should be dealt with in therapy with a professional, encouraging words and supportive conversation can also be very beneficial. Occasions for such interactions frequently arise during monitoring visits.

Case managers also find that they sometimes need to *correct* plan participants for attitudes and behaviors that threaten the success of the plan. Correction is most appropriate when the terms of a plan have not yet been violated but it appears likely that violation is imminent. For example, if a plan requires abstinence from illegal substances and a participant begins to express a lack of willingness to continue to comply, the case manager may be forced to address the issue.

Another important function of case managers who supervise plans is *advocacy*. There may be times when plan participants experience barriers to service that can be corrected through some action on the part of practitioners. For example, a phone call to a school principal may motivate a teacher who is balking at taking a foster child into class. Similarly, a request for expedited services from a transportation agency may allow a family to begin to receive services much earlier than if standard procedures were followed.

Case managers also make *referrals* for additional services. When needs are discovered that require additional services, practitioners may choose to refer plan participants to additional programs. Workers should be careful not to violate statutory or court mandates when making such referrals.

SAMPLE CASE PLANS

Clearly, case planning can be a complex and challenging task. The task is easier when a practitioner has a clear picture of what is expected. One of the best ways to facilitate this is to provide sample case plans from the jurisdiction in which the practitioner will be working. A second possibility is to provide a group of sample plans that includes at least some of the characteristics of the plans in that jurisdiction. This section includes three case plans that provide examples of both discrete and integrated plans as well as a series of questions that should be considered when a plan for reunification is developed.

Putting It Into Practice

Sample Case Plan 1: Child with Special Needs

The first sample is a discrete plan in which goals and objectives are combined in one section and tasks are listed in a separate section. It begins with a problem statement, including a list of the conditions that either exist because of or contribute to the special need. It is also written with the assumption that an overall goal, defined in a previous case plan, is the reunification of Melissa with her biological mother. As with all the examples in this book, practitioners must keep in mind that the court may have slightly different expectations for a case plan in each jurisdiction. Special needs include such conditions as developmental delays, learning disabilities, conditions such as attention-deficit/activity disorder, and various kinds of cognitive impairments. These conditions enhance the risk that the child will experience educational problems and subsequent behavioral problems. When these conditions can be recognized and addressed in preschool children, the probability of the child's educational success is greatly improved. The caseworker may encounter children in which the special need has been diagnosed or recognized, but more often may suspect its presence due to one or more of the following characteristics:

1. Clear evidence of a lack of age-appropriate social and intellectual skills, such as that demonstrated by lack of conversational capacities, vocabulary, and an overall lack of age-appropriate knowledge and interests
2. Difficulties in relating to other children of the same age group
3. Inability or lack of desire to participate in age-appropriate activities
4. Lack of reaction to or inappropriate reaction to attempts at interaction or conversation
5. Inability to maintain attention for an appropriate period of time
6. Uncontrollable acting out in school or social settings
7. Absence of diagnosis or formal recognition of the problem
8. Lack of sufficient social and educational support to help to compensate for the problem

Problem statement

Melissa lacks age-appropriate social skills such as the ability to interact successfully with children her own age and the inability to converse with adults as a 5-year-old would normally interact. She appears to be more comfortable with younger children and has what appears to be the vocabulary of a 3-year-old. She is more comfortable interacting with younger children than with children of her own age group. She appears to lack much of the knowledge and many of the interests common among children of her age and seems to have difficulty concentrating on any single task for more than a few seconds at a time. Melissa has received no formal educational or psychological testing.

Goals and Objectives

Goal 1. Determine whether some special need exists and identify that need through evaluation by a qualified professional or professionals.

Objective 1a. Identify a qualified medical professional to determine whether some special need exists because of a medical condition.
Objective 1b. Identify a qualified medical professional to determine whether some special need exists because of psychological causes.
Objective 1c. Should no special need be identified, provide ongoing social skill development and educational opportunities that will allow Melissa to use her own resources to reach age-appropriate levels.

Goal 2. If a special need is identified, ensure that proper treatment is received and provide services that will enhance the child's functioning and improve the probability of educational success.

Objective 2a. Obtain referrals from the professional who identifies the special need.
Objective 2b. Obtain additional relevant referrals from other professionals who participated in the evaluation.
Objective 2c. Identify a means of payment for the professional services that will be provided.
Objective 2d. Identify a method of transportation for Melissa to access the services.
Objective 2e. Work with the service provider to identify suitable outcome measures to determine the degree to which Melissa has progressed during the intervention.

Goal 3. Provide education, training, and support for issues related to the identified special need to Melissa's biological and foster parents.

Objective 3a. Identify the types of services needed.
Objective 3b. Identify a provider for each type of service.
Objective 3c. Identify a source of payment for each service.
Objective 3d. Refer each participant to the appropriate provider.
Objective 3e. Work with the service provider to identify suitable outcome measures to determine the degree to which each participant has progressed during the intervention.

Goal 4. Ensure that all participants are able to make reasonable progress toward their goals.

Objective 4a. Monitor the progress of all participants on a weekly basis.
Objective 4b. Provide encouragement and additional services to assist participants wherever necessary.

(continued)

Task Statements

1. The case manager shall schedule an appointment for Melissa within one week of the hearing in which a physician or nurse practitioner shall conduct an evaluation for special needs.

2. The case manager shall schedule an appointment for Melissa within one week of the hearing in which a qualified mental health professional shall conduct an evaluation for special needs.

3. If special needs are identified, the case manager shall within one week of the completion of the evaluation consult with the physician, nurse practitioner, and/or mental health professional to determine whether Melissa is already receiving services to address the condition and whether those services appear to be adequate.

4. If Melissa is not receiving services or the services being received are not adequate, the case manager shall make a referral within three days to the appropriate agency or agencies that can provide services.

5. Once the referral has been made, the case manager shall within two weeks of the referral
   a. Obtain all signatures necessary to ensure that services may be delivered
   b. Facilitate the transfer of all the necessary records to and from the provider
   c. Arrange transportation to the location at which services will be delivered
   d. Arrange financial remuneration for the provider where necessary
   e. Meet with the provider or a representative from the provider's office to identify outcome measures that can be used to evaluate the Melissa's progress

6. Through monthly visits with Melissa the case manager shall
   a. Ensure that assessment and service delivery occur in a regular manner
   b. Facilitate communication between the provider and the child's caregiver

7. On an ongoing basis the case manager shall
   a. Communicate the provider's recommendations to the court where necessary
   b. Adapt the case plan to accommodate recommendations made by the provider

8. If Melissa is found to have a special need within one month of that finding, the case manager shall arrange an appointment for Ms. Smith with a qualified mental health professional to determine whether she has psychological or educational needs related to that need.

9. If Ms. Smith is found to require mental health or educational services regarding Melissa's special need, the case manager shall

a. Arrange an appointment for Ms. Smith with a suitable provider within two weeks
b. Obtain all signatures necessary to ensure that services may be delivered
c. Facilitate the transfer of all the necessary records to and from the provider
d. Arrange transportation to the location at which services will be delivered
e. Arrange financial remuneration for the provider where necessary
f. Meet with the provider or a representative from the provider's office to identify outcome

10. Through monthly visits with Ms. Smith the case manager shall
   a. Ensure that assessment and service delivery occur in a regular manner
   b. Facilitate communication between the provider and Ms. Smith

11. On an ongoing basis the case manager shall
   a. Communicate the provider's recommendations to the court where necessary
   b. Adapt the case plan to accommodate recommendations made by the provider

Putting It Into Practice

Sample Case Plan 2: Sexual Abuse by A Caretaker

The following treatment plan is an example of a discrete type in which goals, objectives, and tasks are separated into individual sections. Despite this separation, the three sections should be clearly and logically related so that the reader can easily discern how they are related. This sample is an example of a plan that might be written for a child who has experienced sexual abuse by a biological parent.

Definitions of sexual abuse are similar across many jurisdictions. The Tennessee State Code 37-1-602 (2001), for example, includes rape, sexual battery, assault with intent to commit rape or sexual battery, incest, sexual exploitation of a minor, touching, fondling, oral stimulation, and oral, vaginal, or anal intercourse. Researchers have identified numerous severe short- and long-term effects on its survivors. Short-term effects include depression, anxiety, school problems, and acting-out behaviors. Long-term effects include posttraumatic stress disorder, various affective disorders, substance abuse,

(continued)

and difficulties with social adjustment. Although sexual abuse often has severe effects regardless of the relationship between victim and perpetrator, children who are abused by caretakers, particularly family members, are likely to be more strongly affected than are those abused by others. In children, certain psychological and behavior indicators may be present when a child has been abused. These include but are not limited to

1. Psychological maladjustment, as indicated by depression, anxiety, phobias, guilt, low self-esteem, feelings of betrayal, feelings of having betrayed the perpetrator, and nightmares
2. Behavioral difficulties, such as excessive aggression or withdrawal, age-inappropriate sexual behavior, isolating conduct, self-mutilation, fire starting, cruelty to animals, or suicidal ideation
3. Relational problems, such as excessive fear of or attraction to the perpetrator, inability to form positive relationships with others, unusual levels of distrust of others, excessive fear of individuals of one gender, age-inappropriate sexual behavior, social isolation, and fighting
4. Academic issues, including poor grades, truancy, inattention in academic settings, fighting at school, and withdrawal from social situations
5. Age-inappropriate interest in or fear of sexuality as evidenced by sexually graphic drawings or play, inappropriate touching of peers and others, sexual aggression toward others, excessive and age-inappropriate promiscuity, unusually high levels of fear about being associated or alone with members of one gender

Caseworkers working with children who have been sexually abused by caretakers face a variety of problems. Generally, those problems fall into four categories: (a) the need to ensure the psychological well-being of the child, (b) the need to protect the child from further harm, (c) the need to enhance the awareness and skills of nonperpetrating caregivers, and (d) the need to treat the perpetrating caregiver. This section considers the first two categories. Categories c and d would need to be addressed if plans for the child included a return to the source home.

Problem Statement

Juanita is a 14-year-old female who resided with her biological parents until being taken into custody. She was taken into custody after reporting a 5-year history of sexual abuse in which both her father and mother participated. She has displayed psychological problems including depression, anxiety, guilt, and low self-esteem. Behavioral problems include an inability to relate well to nonperpetrating male family members and peers, isolation, and suicidal ideation. She has poor grades in school and is in danger of failing her current grade. Because of the severity of the abuse and the involvement of both parents as perpetrators, it has been determined that Juanita will not be returned to the custody of either biological parent.

Goals

1. Protect Juanita from future incidents of sexual abuse through creating a safe living environment and providing suitable psychological and psychoeducational services.
2. Identify additional issues related to the abuse through ongoing assessment, evaluation, and diagnosis.
3. Provide services that will help Juanita deal with present and future psychological issues related to the abuse.
4. Provide services that will help Juanita deal with present and future behavioral issues related to the abuse.
5. Provide services that will help Juanita deal with present and future relational issues related to the abuse.
6. Provide services that will help Juanita deal with present and future academic issues related to the abuse.

Objectives

1. Identify a safe and supportive living environment for Juanita in which she will be protected from future incidents of abuse and will have adequate services available to help her deal with her issues from her history of abuse.
2. As a result of the psychological and psychoeducational services, Juanita will be able to
   a. Discuss her abuse with qualified professionals and demonstrate an understanding that the abuse was not her fault
   b. Identify, explore, and cope with her emotions regarding the incidents of abuse
   c. Identify, explore, and cope with her emotions regarding both the offending and nonoffending caretakers
   d. Identify appropriate sexual behaviors including an understanding of the acts to which she has a right to consent or choose not to consent
   e. Role-play specific strategies related to the prevention of future sexual abuse
3. Provide ongoing assessment and evaluation to identify additional relevant needs and issues, as well as to identify additional perpetrators.
4. Provide medical services as needed.
5. Provide tutoring services to help Juanita improve her grades and complete the work necessary to successfully completing her current grade in school.

(continued)

6. Identify social, extracurricular, and after-school programs that can help Juanita develop a positive attitude toward school and education.

Tasks

1. The case manager shall within one week of the hearing facilitate Juanita's placement in a qualified therapeutic foster home where the parents have been trained to deal with issues related to a history of sexual abuse and where wraparound services are available on both a regular and an on-call basis.

2. The case manager shall within two weeks of the hearing arrange an appointment with a physician or nurse practitioner to further evaluate any need Juanita may have for medical treatment related to her history of abuse.

3. The case manager shall within two weeks of the hearing arrange an appointment with a qualified mental health practitioner to initiate psychological and psychoeducational services for Juanita. The responsibilities of the practitioner will include ongoing evaluation for additional relevant needs and issues, as well as the identification of additional perpetrators.

4. The case manager shall within two weeks of the hearing arrange for tutoring services for Juanita and shall work with school board officials to identify social, extra-curricular, and after-school programs that can help her develop a positive attitude toward school and education.

5. For each agency or provider the case manager shall
   a. Obtain all signatures necessary to ensure that services may be delivered
   b. Facilitate the transfer of all the necessary records to and from the provider
   c. Arrange transportation to the location at which services will be delivered
   d. Follow up to ensure that assessment and service delivery occur
   e. Facilitate communication between the provider and the foster parents
   f. Communicate the provider's recommendations to the court where necessary
   g. Adapt the case plan to accommodate recommendations made by the provider

6. The case manager shall make monthly visits to the foster home to monitor Juanita's progress and level of adjustment.

7. The case manager shall make monthly inquiries of agencies and mental health providers to determine professionals' perceptions of Juanita's progress.

Putting It Into Practice

Sample Case Plan 3: Caretaker Demonstrating Use of Excessive Corporal Punishment

The following is an example of an integrated case plan in which goals, objectives, and tasks are incorporated into single statements. It is a plan for a child whose parents have used excessive corporal punishment and where it is the court's intention to attempt reunification with those parents.

Most jurisdictions permit parents to use corporal punishment, such as spanking, but consider it abusive if it is administered in an excessive manner. Excess is defined differently in various jurisdictions, but it usually includes actions that cause physical injury such as bruises, lacerations, sprained muscles, and broken bones. Indicators may include

1. Physical injuries, particularly to the buttocks, lower back, upper legs, and arms that cannot be explained by normal injuries experienced during the course of childhood
2. An unusually high frequency of injuries, such as bruises or lacerations, on the buttocks, lower back, upper legs, or arms
3. Unusually high levels of fear or aggression in children
4. Presence of an authoritative parental disciplinary and family management style
5. Explosive emotional behavior by parents or children
6. Reluctance of parents to discuss disciplinary practices

Caseworkers who are assigned children who have experienced excessive corporal punishment must consider a number of factors, including the physical and emotional needs of the child, appropriate training and treatment for the offending parent, and appropriate training and treatment for the nonoffending parent. Parents who have recently immigrated from countries where severe corporal punishment is the norm may require culturally sensitive intervention.

Problem Statement

Billy is an 8-year-old Caucasian male who was taken into state custody because of injuries received during incidents of excessive corporal punishment by his biological parents. Billy had severe bruises and lacerations as a result of being beaten with a belt by his father, William. His mother, Amanda, is also reported to have beaten Billy across the neck and back with a broomstick. Billy shows signs of long-term abuse, having wounds and scars in various

(continued)

stages of healing that appear to have been inflicted over a period of several years. When questioned about the injuries, Billy's parents explained that he needs severe punishment because he "can be difficult" and that the extreme appearance of the injuries is because he "marks up easily."

Case Plan

1. The case manager will ensure Billy's physical safety through placement in a foster home until intervention with the parents permits his safe return to their home. The case manager will identify such a home within three days of this hearing and have Billy placed there within two weeks of this hearing.

2. Within one week of the assessment the case manager will identify resources that can address Billy's physical, emotional, and psychological needs.
   a. If Billy is already receiving services, the case manager will contact the provider to determine whether the services being provided are adequate.
   b. If Billy is not receiving services or the services being received are not adequate, the case manager shall make a referral to the appropriate agency that can provide services.

3. Once referrals have been made, the case manager shall
   a. Obtain all signatures necessary to ensure that services may be delivered
   b. Facilitate the transfer of all the necessary records to and from the provider
   c. Arrange transportation to the location at which services will be delivered
   d. Follow up to ensure that assessment and service delivery occur
   e. Facilitate communication between the provider and the foster parent
   f. Communicate the provider's recommendations to the court where necessary
   g. Adapt the case plan to accommodate recommendations made by the provider

4. Within two weeks of the hearing the case manager will identify resources that can address the parent's issues regarding excessive corporal punishment.
   a. If William and Amanda are receiving services, the case manager will contact the program to determine whether the services being provided are adequate.
   b. If the parents are not receiving services or the services being received are not adequate, the case manager shall make a referral to the appropriate agency that can provide services. Services provided by the agency shall include disciplinary techniques, anger management, family management, and interpersonal skills.

5. Once referrals have been made, the case manager shall
   a. Obtain all signatures necessary to ensure that services may be delivered
   b. Facilitate the transfer of all the necessary records to and from the provider
   c. Arrange transportation to the location at which services will be delivered
   d. Follow up to ensure that assessment and service delivery occur
   e. Facilitate communication between the provider and the parents
   f. Communicate the provider's recommendations to the court where necessary
   g. Adapt the case plan to accommodate recommendations made by the provider
6. William and Amanda must demonstrate specific knowledge and competencies within specified time periods, such as
   a. Within three weeks they will be able to describe the stages of child development as well as the behaviors and processes that are typical of each stage
   b. Within four weeks they will be able to identify at least two alternatives to physical discipline in response to specific scenarios proposed by the caseworker
   c. Within six weeks they will be able to prepare an agenda for a family meeting and describe the purposes for such a meeting
   d. Within eight weeks they will be able to demonstrate the use of effective anger management techniques in response to sample scenarios that require parental discipline

Putting It Into Practice

Sample Case Plan 4: Reunification Criteria

The case plan in this sample is presented as a series of questions that should receive satisfactory answers before children who have been removed from their homes because of maltreatment should be returned to their parents. Appropriate answers to these questions constitute the criteria for reunification.

The primary intent of child welfare legislation in most jurisdictions is reunification of children with their families. In order for caseworkers to recommend and judges to order that reunification should occur, however, they must feel reasonably certain that the child will be safe from future incidents of abuse, neglect, or abandonment. The case plan, properly constructed and implemented, should provide reasonable insurance that the conditions that caused

(continued)

or contributed to the abuse have been addressed. Reunification criteria, then, should be the natural outgrowth of the case plan. Criteria should normally be expressed in no more than one or two sentences and should identify specific behavioral or attitudinal changes that have occurred with respect to various members of the family system. Each of the sections provides guidelines for developing criteria for children, caretakers, the family, and other social systems.

Criteria Related to the Child

1. Does the child express a desire to return to the custody of the caretaker?
2. Has the child made sufficient recovery from any medical problems to permit reunification?
3. Has the child made sufficient recovery from any psychological problems to permit reunification?
4. Is reunification therapeutically indicated for the child?
5. Does the child (if age-appropriate) exhibit sufficient awareness of the nature of abusive behavior to permit reunification?
6. Have adequate supports, such as psychological services or educational programming, been put in place to allow the child to continue to progress and grow?

Criteria Related to the Offender

1. Does reunification with the offender appear to be in the best interest of the child?
2. Does the offender express a desire for reunification?
3. Does the offender express a desire for reunification in appropriate terms?
4. Has the offender completed all components of the case plan successfully?
5. Has the offender taken responsibility for the past abuse and for refraining from abusive behavior in the future?
6. Has a relapse prevention plan been put in place for the offender, and does he or she display a willingness to comply with it?

Criteria Related to a NonOffending Caretaker

1. Does reunification with the nonoffending caretaker appear to be in the best interests of the child?
2. Does the nonoffending caretaker express a desire for reunification?
3. Does the nonoffending caretaker understand his or her responsibility in the past abuse and understand how to prevent future abuse?
4. Has the nonoffending caretaker completed all the components of the case plan successfully?
5. Can the nonoffending caretaker understand and verbalize the family safety plan that has been put into place to avoid further abuse?
6. Has the nonoffending caretaker dealt with his or her own issues related to the abuse?

Criteria Related to the Family

1. Are there issues remaining within the family that need to be dealt with before reunification can occur?
2. Have other family members complied sufficiently with the terms of the case plan?
3. Do all members of the family understand their role in the family safety plan, and can they express it in an age-appropriate fashion?
4. Are other members of the family sufficiently protected from the potential for abuse?
5. Have other members of the family dealt with their own issues regarding the abuse?

Criteria Related to Other Social Systems

1. Have other social systems (e.g., extended family, neighbors, friends) been recruited to support the family in an appropriate manner?
2. Have other social systems (e.g., school, church, social service providers) been accessed so that ongoing services for special needs will be available?
3. Have other social systems (e.g., income maintenance programs, medical providers, and housing programs) been accessed to ensure that the physical needs of the child and family will be met following reunification?

 TEST YOURSELF

1. **Ideally, the next step after the completion of the initial assessment is the completion of a case plan.** True or False?

2. **The formats of case plans are identical between jurisdictions.** True or False?

3. **Practitioners should concentrate early interaction with the family on determining the degree to which collaborative planning is possible.** True or False?

4. **One of the basic priorities in case planning is the identification and incorporation of individual and family strengths into the plan.** True or False?

5. **Although it is important that goals be measurable, the case manager need not be concerned about whether objectives are measurable.** True or False?

(continued)

6. When a case plan is integrated,

(a) Goals, objectives, and tasks are combined in a single series of statements

(b) The caseworker can feel assured that the plan is inferior to a discrete plan

(c) The caseworker can feel assured that the plan is superior to a discrete plan

(d) Goals, objectives, and tasks are presented in separate sections of the plan

7. A case plan is typically modified

(a) After private communication with the judge about a case

(b) At the discretion of the caseworker alone

(c) Through a legal document submitted to the judge requesting a status hearing

(d) At regular intervals (in most jurisdictions three to six months)

8. *Disposition* refers to

(a) The attitude of the court toward a given case and its principal participants

(b) The living arrangements the child will experience during the course of the case plan

(c) A temporary living arrangement made for children immediately before adoption

(d) The way in which a case manager approaches the supervision of a specific case plan

9. When practitioners experience similar cases, it is important to remember that

(a) Any similarities are important indicators of identical underlying causes

(b) Protective investigators can be overzealous and remove children unnecessarily

(c) Each case requires a discrete case plan so that similar issues can be addressed

(d) Each family is unique and may require individualized intervention

10. Cultural differences are

(a) Relatively insignificant in the development of a case plan

(b) Critical in the development of a case plan

(c) Easy to understand and consider in case planning

(d) Irrelevant given the clarity of the law regarding maltreatment

Answers. 1. True; 2. False; 3. True; 4. True; 5. False; 6. a; 7. c; 8. b; 9. d; 10. b.

Five

ESSENTIALS OF FOSTER CARE

Foster care refers to the substitution of some alternative parent, parents, or institutional provider for the source parents of a child who has been removed from the source home as a result of maltreatment. The foster home may be a short-term, long-term, or permanent arrangement. Some short-term stays are planned, as in cases where the source family needs only brief intervention before the child can be returned. Other short-term stays are the result of less propitious decisions, such as a desperate midnight search to find a child a place to sleep. Often, such a placement may work for a day or a week but may lead to additional short-term placements before a more stable home can be found. Many long-term placements are with relatives or friends of the source family (Terling, 2001). Some kinship arrangements, for example, become permanent. Others may be the result of a skillful or fortuitous match between child and foster parents. Placements with nonfamily members are few, often the result of careful matching of a child for whom no reunification is planned with parents who are seeking to adopt.

Foster homes are intended to provide a safe, stable living environment that simulates a family as closely as possible. This is done with several goals, including (a) to minimize the child's trauma, (b) to ensure that the child is free from further harm, (c) to provide an environment in which the child's issues related to maltreatment can be dealt with, and (d) to facilitate a suitable long-term outcome (reunification, foster care, or adoption). In reality, the foster care system in many jurisdictions is replete with problems. For example, children may bounce from home to home in a pattern that denies them the stability they so desperately need. Alternatively, they may be placed in a home that is desperately overcrowded, denying them the individual support and intervention that they require. Some children benefit from their stay in the system. Others enter it damaged and exit more damaged than they were upon entry.

Good case managers cannot save all children from their families and from the problems in the system, but they can do a great deal to improve the potential of the children whom they serve. One of the keys to success lies in identifying an appropriate placement for the children and providing the needed support to both the child and the foster parent. Successful identification and support requires a good assessment, a carefully developed case plan, and a thorough understanding of the foster care system.

THE CHALLENGES OF FOSTER CARE

The foster care system includes individuals, couples, and institutions that have agreed to provide living arrangements for a child in state custody. The agreement may be for a single child or for many. Families range from relatives or family friends who have agreed to care only for children they know to professional parents who may house hundreds of different children over decades of foster parenthood. Institutions include such organizations as small shelters run by a staff of hired employees, large privately owned psychiatric institutions, and state-operated facilities designed to address foster children with special problems such as delinquency or substance abuse.

Most foster parents or institutional providers are compensated by the state for the expenses they incur. Foster parents usually receive a small monthly stipend for each child. Private institutional providers may be compensated either on a per-case basis or through contracts for a specific number of slots or beds. Some private agencies also maintain individual foster homes for which they receive state money and may raise additional dollars from private sources.

Although foster parents and agencies usually receive compensation for their expenses, the amount, particularly for individual homes, is often inadequate. Agencies are often forced to supplement state payments with public insurance or philanthropic contributions. Some parents who care for their relatives (e.g., a grandmother who cares for her grandchildren) receive no state assistance whatsoever in some jurisdictions.

Being a foster parent can also be very challenging. Those in individual homes open their doors to children from a wide variety of settings, cultures, and environments. Many are troubled emotionally. Some suffer from mental and emotional disorders. Others have medical problems either complicated or generated by years of neglect or physical abuse. Some of the children have had little supervision and come from homes where there have been no rules. Interactional styles are likely to vary between foster child and foster family. For example, a child may come from a home where shouting and conflict were common. The foster home may have established more peaceful methods of communication.

Although it would be nice to think that the transition from source home to foster home would be made as easy as possible for both child and family, the event is often very traumatic. In many jurisdictions parents may receive phone calls from caseworkers at any hour of the day or night asking them to consider keeping a child at least temporarily. A "yes" response may mean that new children, recently removed from their homes, may arrive within minutes. The children are likely to be frightened, worried, angry, or experiencing any other of a variety of strong emotions. Parents may find themselves needing to spend hours feeding and comforting a child before anyone in the home can sleep or go about their usual business.

STRUCTURE AND PLACEMENT DECISIONS IN THE FOSTER CARE SYSTEM

These and other challenges of foster parenting make an understanding of the structure of the system critical for the caseworker. Fundamentally, a worker making placement decisions should have an understanding of the structure of the system, that is, what kinds of homes are available and where they are located geographically. In addition, the practitioner seeking a placement should have some knowledge of the needs of the child being placed and an awareness of the conditions in each home (e.g., the number of children placed in each home, the kinds of problems the children and parents may be experiencing, and a history of the success of each home with children placed there in emergency situations).

The Structure of the System

Similarities and differences exist in the structure of the system of care between jurisdictions. Because it would be impossible to discuss all the differences in the space available in this book, this section focuses on similarities. It notes general categories of differences and allows readers to determine what form those take in their own jurisdictions. The structure of the system can be conceptualized in terms of the type of home. For the purposes of this book, the following types of foster homes are identified (see Rapid Reference 5.1): (a) traditional, (b) relative care, (c) kinship care, (d) therapeutic, (e) medical, (f) shelter, (g) respite, (h) residential, (i) psychiatric, and (j) juvenile justice. Each of these types of homes can be operated either by the state or by a private agency funded through state sources.

Traditional homes are those that receive levels of training (training is discussed in a later section) to deal with issues that are common among children who enter care. Parents for these homes complete a process of recruitment, training, and licensure that prepares them for and identifies them as a home that can deliver this level of care to children. Foster parents in these homes have many of the same rights and responsibilities as biological parents, but they also operate under certain restrictions. For example, they may impose discipline on a child (but usually not corporal punishment); they may make certain minor medical decisions but must obtain state approval for others; and they may make some decisions about a child's education (e.g., whether to allow a child to participate in an extracurricular activity) but cannot make

Rapid Reference 5.1

Types of Foster Homes

- Traditional
- Relative care
- Kinship care
- Therapeutic
- Medical
- Shelter
- Respite
- Residential
- Psychiatric
- Juvenile justice

others (e.g., changing schools) without state or judicial input. Their basic responsibilities include providing shelter, food, clothing, transportation, supervision, and emotional support to the children in their care. They are supported through these processes by the case manager, funding from state and federal sources, and often by a foster parent support group. State and federal sources provide a variety of services such as medical and dental services or insurance, counseling, psychoeducation, training, transportation, educational services, recreational services, and other related services.

The term *relative home* is used in many different ways across the various jurisdictions and in the many publications about foster care. It is sometimes used interchangeably with *kinship care*. In this book it is used in a very specific way. It refers to persons who are biologically related to children who have been removed from their homes but receive less support from the child welfare system than do other state caregivers. In some jurisdictions, for example, relatives may assume custody of a child with no support other than an occasional visit from a caseworker. In others they may get some services, such as transportation assistance or government medical insurance.

In some areas relatives who care for children under state supervision receive all the support that is given to nonrelated foster parents. In others, new programs have been developed to provide specialized support such as case planning through mediation. In this book these types of arrangements are referred to as *kinship homes* (Geen & Berrick, 2002). At the time of this writing several jurisdictions were piloting kinship care programs and comparing their levels of effectiveness to more traditional services (Ehrle & Geen, 2002; Leos, Bess, & Geen, 2002; Scannapieco & Heger, 2002; Testa & Slack, 2002).

Another type of home is often referred to as *therapeutic*. Therapeutic homes are traditional in structure; that is, they are typically located in a single-family home with a parent or parents who are contracted with the child welfare agency to provide the services that are included in traditional homes. In addition, however, the parents receive specialized training to deal with specific problems children may have, including psychiatric issues, social skills deficits, and learning disorders. Intensive services sometimes referred to as *wrap-around* are also provided on a 24-hour basis. Wraparound includes such services as counseling, psychiatric services, crisis intervention, and others (McGinty, McCammon & Koeppen, 2001). These homes typically house fewer children and are often operated by a private provider. Therapeutic homes are often used for children whose particularly high levels of need constitute some sort of risk to themselves or to other members of the home. In these cases the risk is considered too great for placement in a traditional home yet is not sufficient to justify placement in an institutional facility.

Medical homes house children who have medical needs that are severe enough to warrant special attention but not to require hospitalization. These homes may be single family or may include several children, particularly if the children are infants. Foster parents are specially trained, and professional medical assistance is often readily available. Placement in medical foster homes may be required by conditions such as heart or lung problems, diabetes, fetal alcohol syndrome, and human immunodeficiency virus.

Some children require short-term living arrangements while a longer term home is being located. The homes in which these children are placed are sometimes referred to as *shelter homes*. Shelter homes may be single family or institutional and may be either publicly or privately operated. A traditional home can sometimes serve as a shelter. Additionally, institutional homes may have beds that are used for shelter as well as those that are reserved for long-term residents.

Homes that are open to children on a short-term basis to provide parents with a break from their duties are known as *respite homes*. These are often single-family homes where families do not wish to make a long-term commitment to caring for foster children but are willing to host them for a few days. Additionally, state workers, private agency employees, and volunteers sometimes provide respite services in which they will take a child on an outing but return the child to the home within a few hours.

Foster children may also be placed in *institutional* settings. Some institutional homes are specialized, serving children with such conditions as severe psychological problems, mental retardation, a history of sexual abuse as the perpetrator, and a history of delinquent behavior. Some institutions, due in large part to overcrowding of the system, have become homes for children who might best be placed in traditional or therapeutic homes.

Children placed in *psychiatric* institutions typically have severe psychological problems that cause them to become suicidal, violent, or delusional or to have some other condition that makes them either unmanageable in a more traditional environment or an ongoing threat to self or others. The intent of the placement is to stabilize the problem through psychoeducation, medication, counseling, and social skills training. Psychiatric institutions often house children in clusters of 8 to10 bedrooms that share a common area. The common area then connects to the rest of the facility, which includes a recreational area, cafeteria, treatment areas, and staff offices. Children often earn rights and additional freedoms by demonstrating appropriate behavior over specific periods in a system known as a *token economy*. When their behaviors have stabilized, they may be moved to a less restrictive environment.

Other *specialized institutions* may house and treat children with more specific problems. Two examples of such problems are those who work with persons with mental retardation and those who treat children with a history of sexually abusing other children. The choice of these two examples should not be seen as suggesting that these two conditions are in any way similar or connected. Rather, they have been chosen because they illustrate two very different types of specialized institutions. Institutions that care for children who experience mental retardation focus on providing a safe, secure environment where the children can gain the skills and knowledge to live as successfully as possible as adults. Emphasis is on physical safety, education, and skill development. Institutions that deal with children who have sexually abused other children focus on confinement and treatment. The environment is typically more restrictive and structured. Emphasis is placed on protecting the children from one another and the community from the children, as well as on treatment of their problem.

Children in state custody because of maltreatment are sometimes also involved with the *juvenile justice* system. These are most frequently older children who have committed crimes ranging from low-level status offenses (such as truancy, drinking, or running away from home) to violent offenses and property crimes. Typically, these children are housed in facilities that are rated in terms of their level of security, with increasing levels of security being indicated by a larger number. For example, a relatively insecure institution for status offenders would be identified as a Level 1 facility, and a high-security facility for chronically violent teens would be identified as Level 5. Juvenile justice facilities focus on dealing with the children's issues that have contributed to their behavior. This often involves family members who may make visits to the facility for family therapy sessions or may receive treatment at some other site (e.g., at home or in a counselor's office).

Older children who will not be reunified with their families and who are unlikely or unwilling to be adopted may participate in a specialized form of foster care known as *independent living*. Middle to late adolescents who participate in this program live semi-independently in supervised clusters of apartments and receive training in knowledge and skills that will allow them to function successfully as adults. Independent living program are discussed in greater depth in Chapter 9.

Knowledge of the Needs of the Child

In order to find a proper match of child and home, the practitioner needs a thorough understanding of the needs of the child. Many of these needs should have been identified in the assessment. Certainly factors like mental and physical health, educational deficits, social skills deficiencies, cognitive limitations, and similar conditions suggest the need for special placement.

In fact, many of the characteristics of the child identified during assessment should help the practitioner make critical decisions about both the type of home children will be placed in and the specific home that will be the best fit. A chart illustrating the kinds of characteristics that might suggest that a child should be placed in a particular type of home is included in Rapid Reference 5.2.

When it is possible to do so, child welfare workers should also consider other characteristics of individual children before choosing a placement (see Rapid Reference 5.3). It is important to note that this step is often impractical because of heavy workloads and overcrowded homes, but it can greatly improve the success of the placement.

The *age* of the child can be particularly important when a placement alternative is chosen. Some foster parents are particularly good with young children. Others excel with adolescents. When possible, practitioners should match children with parents who are particularly strong with their age group. When more than one child is placed in a home, the age mix should also be considered. There are strengths and dangers associated with having children of various ages in the home. In a best-case scenario older children can provide limited supervision, mentoring, and healthy social relationships. In a worst-case scenario they may be the source of additional abuse or neglect. Caseworkers should exercise caution when placing older and younger children together in the same home, particularly when crowding or parental responsibilities mean that activities in the home will be difficult to supervise.

≡Rapid Reference 5.2

Conditions That Suggest Placement in Specific Types of Foster Homes

Type of Home	Criteria for Placement
Traditional	Child has been placed in state custody.
Relative	Child has been placed in state custody.
	Relatives are willing to provide a home with minimal support.
	There is no kinship foster care program or home available.
Kinship care	Child has been placed in state custody.
	Relatives are both willing and suitable to care for the child.
Therapeutic	Child has been placed in state custody.
	Child has psychological, emotional, or cognitive problems too severe for a traditional home.
	Child's problems are not sufficient to require an institutional placement.
Medical	Child has been placed in state custody.
	Child has medical problems too severe for a traditional home.
	Child's problems are not sufficient to require hospitalization.
Shelter	Child has been placed in state custody.
	No suitable long-term placement has been located.
Respite	Child has been placed in state custody.
	Foster parents need a brief period of relief from responsibilities.
	Child needs a brief period in an alternative setting.
Residential	Child has been placed in state custody.
	Child has some special condition that cannot be addressed in other settings.
Psychiatric	Child has been placed in state custody.
	Child has some special condition that cannot be addressed in other settings.
Juvenile justice	Child has been placed in state custody.
	Child has been assigned to some placement by the court because of delinquent activity.

Rapid Reference 5.3

Additional Child Characteristics to Consider When Choosing a Placement

- Age
- Gender
- Culture
- Personality traits
- Interactive styles
- Special circumstances
  - Health conditions
  - Mental and emotional conditions
  - Attachment issues
  - Learning disabilities
  - Keeping siblings together

Gender is a second important characteristic to be considered. Some parents may do better with boys than girls or vice versa. Some homes are also able to accommodate children of both genders while others are not. Certainly, issues related to history of abuse should be considered when placing boys and girls in the same foster home.

Practitioners may also wish to consider how *culture* may affect relationships within a foster home. These issues are discussed in greater depth in Chapter 10. It is important to note here, however, that the overall cultural sensitivity of foster parents or of an institution has the potential to influence children in powerful ways. Imagine, for example, a female child of Southeast Asian descent whose family has recently immigrated placed with a male from a traditional Hispanic family and a female who had recently immigrated from Africa. Further imagine that these children were placed in the home of a middle-class, two-parent American family of European descent. Given this combination, there would be significant potential for conflict in several areas. For example, many Hispanic and Southeast Asian families are patriarchal; that is, much of the authority and decision making are in the hands of a father or grandfather. Some African cultures are matriarchal, with substantial power resting in the hands of the mother or grandmother. The conflict between looking primarily to a mother for guidance and primarily to a father for guidance can be substantial. Contact between cultures can be very beneficial, but coupled with the experience of abuse, the trauma of removal from a home, and the stress of adapting to a new environment, it can be very difficult. A culturally sensitive foster home can make a potential negative into a positive by using the occasion to teach children to value their own cultures and appreciate those of others.

Another important aspect of effective child placement has to do with the *interactive style* of the child. For example, children who are particularly shy may struggle in the homes of parents who are not particularly responsive to their emotional needs. Similarly, a child who finds assertion difficult may not express important needs when placed in a home with several more demanding children.

Many kinds of *special circumstances* may also affect placement decisions. If a case is high profile (i.e., has come to the attention of the media or an important politician), parents who can deal with the pressures that may present must be carefully selected. In other cases, the biological parents may be particularly aggressive in their attempts to regain custody of the child. They may be hostile and threatening toward the foster parents. Obviously, careful selection of the right family is very important in such circumstances.

Knowledge of Conditions in the Home

In addition to the needs and characteristics of the child, practitioners should also consider conditions within the proposed foster home when making a placement decision. Rapid Reference 5.4 lists these characteristics. One important factor is the *capability of the parents* in each home. Even though parents and personnel in the various types of foster homes are selected and trained at similar levels, differences typically remain in degree of competence from home to home and from parent to parent. Certain parents may also be particularly skilled in working with children of a specific age group, gender, or culture. Some parents may be very challenged by working with high-demand teens, while others may find that working with those children is the most desirable.

≡Rapid Reference 5.4

Characteristics Within the Home to Consider When Choosing a Placement

- Capability of the parents
- Effects on other children in the home
- The number of children placed in the home
- The kinds of problems the children and parents may be experiencing
- The history of the home with children placed there in emergency situations

Practitioners should also consider the effects of a new resident on other children already in the home. A peaceful environment may be destabilized by the arrival of a disruptive new child. Children who have overcome specific challenges may be a help to a new arrival struggling with a similar issue or may be drawn back into old problems through the influence of a new resident.

The number of children placed in each home is also an important issue. In some cases this means no more than counting bed space. In other situations it means considering the degree to which an additional child may affect a foster family that is functioning very effectively. At times the addition of a single child has no major effect on a family. At other times it may totally disrupt a previously positive and stable environment.

It can also be helpful to have an awareness of the kinds of *problems the children and parents may be experiencing* in a home at the time of a potential placement. Otherwise, very strong and stable homes can be affected by personal problems and tragedies. Illness or death among the biological families of the foster parents can distract their attention and sap their emotional energy causing children in the home to receive less support and supervision than is typical. Changes at work such as promotions, demotions, and terminations can also produce stress, affecting the way in which parents interact with their foster children. Similarly, when children in a home are struggling with school, interpersonal relationships, identity issues, and other issues, placing an additional child in that environment may have negative consequences for everyone.

When a child must be placed in a home on an emergency basis (which, unfortunately, may be all too often), the *history of the homes* being considered with children placed in emergency situations should also be considered. Some parents do well with midnight phone calls and early morning arrivals. Others find this so disruptive that the home functions poorly for weeks after the new arrival. Still others may grow tired of emergency placements and conclude that they no longer want to be foster parents. Caseworkers should be aware of these possibilities and govern their placement activities accordingly.

Rapid Reference 5.5

Responsibilities of Foster Care Case Managers

- Overall supervision of the case
- Liaison to the court
- Linkage to additional services
- Coordination of resources

It is important to have as much information as possible when arranging placements. In fact, however, the worker often lacks this basic information or may be forced by extreme overcrowding in many homes to make placements that are less than appropriate. In these cases the support of the case manager may be critical to the success of the placement. The responsibilities of the case manager are outlined in Rapid Reference 5.5 and are described later in this chapter. As a foundation for understanding the relationship of case manager to foster parent, the processes of recruitment and training of foster parents are discussed first.

RECRUITMENT AND TRAINING OF FOSTER PARENTS

Locating appropriate families to serve as foster parents can be a challenging task (Rhoades, Orme, & Buehler, 2001). Although it is rewarding work, it is also very demanding. Foster parents face the task of helping children for whom others have created problems. At best, children are likely to be traumatized by the removal from their homes. At worst, they come with an assortment of physical and psychological problems worsened by the removal process. The children need love, attention, help, and support. They may respond well to their new environment, or they may act in angry, aggressive ways. Parents who are willing and able to cope with these contingencies are rare.

When willing parents are found, child welfare workers must ensure that they are sincere, reasonably balanced emotionally, and represent no danger to the children. Sometimes well-meaning people have problems of their own that prevent them from being able to be effective foster parents. In other cases they may be predators who want to use the status of foster parent to take advantage of children. Both types of applicants must be identified and excluded so that children are not placed in their care (Cox, Buehler, & Orme, 2002).

The process of recruiting foster parents includes four basic steps. These steps are (a) locate, (b) screen, (c) inform, and (d) commit. *Locating* potential foster parents is a challenge in itself. Many jurisdictions have either individuals or groups of individuals whose primary responsibility is locating parents through advertising and outreach. Many use newspaper ads, radio spots, and even television commercials. Some use billboards and personal appearances at community groups such as churches or rotary clubs. Some jurisdictions have found that private agencies are more successful at recruiting foster parents and have begun to privatize foster care, that is, to provide funding to agencies that then recruit, train, and support foster parents. Another very valuable method of recruiting foster parents is through referrals from current families. In other cases relatives or family friends may become foster parents to care for a child brought into custody.

The means of processing applicants for foster parenting varies across jurisdictions. Many have a process similar to the one that is discussed here. The recruiting agency publicizes a phone number that prospective parents can call. During business hours the number is usually answered. When personnel are not available to respond, an answering machine asks that the caller leave a name and number. Child welfare workers return the call and ask the caller a series of questions that prequalify them. If the answers are consistent with the qualities the agency desires, an appointment is arranged for the potential parents to meet with child welfare practitioners who are trained to screen applicants.

The second step in recruitment involves *screening* applicants who have passed the telephone interview. During an interview a trained practitioner attempts to determine whether the necessary emotional stability and the required level of safety exist in a potential home. If the interview creates a positive impression, applicants are approved to progress to the next step.

A more formal background screen is also included at some phase of the recruitment and training process. In some areas it is done very early in the process. In others it occurs during the training period. Formal screening includes a search of police records and available child welfare records to determine whether potential parents have committed some offense that might affect their effectiveness as parents. Often, they are asked about history of offense either on a written application or in an oral interview. Certain categories of offense, particularly offenses from many years earlier, may not disqualify them. Others, such as violent crimes or prior incidents of child abuse, may disqualify them automatically. Honesty may also be a factor in the decision to include or exclude applicants. Those who lie about prior offenses, no matter how insignificant, may be excluded because they have lied. One of the significant problems in background screening is the availability of records. Law enforcement records tend to be fairly accurate and comprehensive. Child welfare records are often poorly kept or nonexistent. To make matters worse, different computer programs are used in many jurisdictions, so accessing records is sometimes difficult or impossible. Many jurisdictions ask potential foster parents to furnish personal references from persons they have known in other states, even if they resided in that state many years earlier. This is done in the hope that if the prospective parent has a history of child maltreatment in that state, it will be known to one of the references.

The third step of recruitment involves *informing* potential parents of the demands and responsibilities of foster parenting. This may be done through a letter or a phone call inviting them to attend training. They may also be asked to an additional interview in which the process of becoming a parent and the responsibilities involved in assuming that role are discussed.

The final step in the recruitment of foster parents involves asking them to commit to a training program. This may be done by signing and returning a letter, by signing a document at the end of an interview, or by simply asking prospective parents whether they are willing to participate.

After potential foster parents have been recruited, they must be *trained*. Actually, in many jurisdictions the training process also serves as a screening mechanism. During the course of training, a process that may last for several weeks, the trainees may come to understand things about foster parenting that will cause them to withdraw from the program. Similarly, trainers may realize that parents are not really suitable for the role and may ask them to discontinue training and exit the program.

Training typically involves a standardized curriculum taught by persons who specialize in preparing foster parents. The curriculum often includes training in such areas as child and home management, parenting skills, stress management, child development, child psychology, and special strategies for dealing with issues commonly experienced by children in care. Prospective parents also receive instruction regarding the policies that will govern the operation of their home and the kind of support they can expect to receive. Parents who have been selected for therapeutic or other specialized homes may receive additional training to deal with issues unique to that environment.

Prospective parents who have completed training are typically *licensed* before having children placed in their home. Licensure involves a comprehensive review of all the documents and information generated during the recruitment and training of prospective parents. If acceptable standards are met, the child welfare agency issues a license that approves the home to receive children.

THE ROLE OF THE CASE MANAGER

Foster parents are promised certain kinds of support. Some of this support is financial (e.g., a monthly stipend, government medical and dental services, or compensation for approved psychological or psychiatric assistance). Other support may include regular visits from a caseworker; the potential for further training, education, and psychological services; and participation in foster parent support groups. The availability of most of these services is dependent on the effective operation of the case manager (Mather & Hull, 2002).

Case managers have many responsibilities in the care of foster children. Although their roles may vary somewhat between jurisdictions and types of homes, their functions can be seen as belonging in one of several categories. These categories include supervision of the case, liaison with the court, support of the foster parents, advocacy for the child, linkage to additional services, and coordination of resources.

Case managers are responsible for *overall supervision* of the case. Supervision requires regular visits to the home that include visits with both children and foster parents. The visits are intended to accomplish several things with regard to both children and parents. Case managers need to know how well the children are adjusting to their new environment, how effectively the problems identified during assessment are being addressed, to what degree their strengths are being utilized, and what progress they are making toward the goals identified in the case plan. Regarding the foster parents, the practitioner should determine whether they are in need of resources to support either themselves or the children in their care. If needs are identified, the caseworker must identify resources to meet those needs, provide a referral to the resources, and arrange transportation or financial assistance where it is needed.

Case managers also supervise the activities of parents from the source family. Their intent is similar to that for foster children. They need to know whether the problems that were identified in assessment are being addressed, whether the parent's strengths are being developed and utilized, and what progress the parents are making toward case plan goals. Where barriers exist to the parent's success, the case manager must help them identify ways to remove or circumvent the barriers.

Caseworkers face many challenges to fulfilling their responsibilities of supervision. Often they have very large caseloads, making regular visitation and extensive interaction with all parties difficult. When they discover needs, their efforts may be impaired by limited resources. That is, there may be no agency available to provide the needed services, or the agency may be so overcrowded that accessing services is impossible. One of the greatest challenges of case management is in determining how much change has really occurred. Although the court ultimately decides whether children will be reunified with their parents, the case manager is, in a very real sense, its eyes and ears. Judges are unlikely to have any contact with children or parents other than in the courtroom. They rely on the case manager for reports of visits, test results, progress reports, and overall perceptions of change in both child and parent. In many situations the case manager's recommendation has the greatest weight in determining whether reunification can occur. This responsibility means that practitioners must be very careful to be accurate and impartial both in observing and reporting. They must observe carefully, trying to eliminate personal and cultural biases. They must allow for both successes and failures, recognizing, for example, that one positive urinalysis result from a parent struggling with substance abuse may not constitute an overall failure in the case plan. They must also report their conclusions clearly, without bias or emotion, and in a language that is acceptable to the court.

Practitioners also provide *liaison to the court;* that is, they communicate with the court regarding the status of children, measures that have been or must be taken to improve their condition, and the progress of both the child and the source family toward the goals of the case plan. They must read and interpret reports, provide written summaries, and report results and perceptions to the court.

Case managers must also *advocate* for the children in their care. This may require that they speak on behalf of the children with a teacher or school administrator, urge an agency to provide counseling on an expedited basis, or engage in some other similar activity. Children and families in the child welfare system interact with agencies and individuals in many other social service systems, such as the educational, mental health, and substance abuse treatment systems. There are frequently barriers to service within and between these systems that children and families struggle to overcome. Practitioners can often help them through the process through their advocacy. Sometimes (perhaps often), similar barriers may exist within the child welfare system itself. Once again, prompt and effective action by a practitioner can often help clients overcome these barriers.

Case managers also provide their clients with *linkage to additional services.* Often as a child or family progresses through a case plan, the need for some other service becomes clear. For example, parents from source families may uncover memories of abuse they experienced as children that were not identified during assessment. Practitioners should be aware of possible resources for dealing with such issues and be able to refer these parents to those resources.

Case managers are often required to *coordinate resources* on behalf of their clients. This means that they must help children and families plan which resources to access at what point, how they will access those resources, at what point the need for the resources will end, and whether additional resources are needed to maintain or further the gains made from working with each resource. For example, when the case plan notes educational problems and requires that a child have glasses to improve the ability to see in the classroom, the child may also need tutoring. The case manager would ensure that the child sees an optometrist and then is referred to a tutoring service. Even after reaching the appropriate grade level, the child might need some sort of ongoing help that is less intensive than tutoring but more substantial than classroom work. The case manager would need to locate and help arrange this service.

Clearly, case managers require specialized knowledge in several dimensions. For example, they need to have a good working knowledge of what resources are available and how they can be accessed. Further, they need a good basic understanding of the child welfare system and the way the system works (one of the goals of this book). Additionally, their work is facilitated by a broad, general knowledge of the kinds of problems foster children, foster families, and source families experience.

ISSUES FOR CHILDREN IN FOSTER CARE

As was indicated in Chapter 3, children who enter foster care may experience a broad range of problems that may have been induced by abuse or may occur naturally as a result of biological or social factors. Listing all these problems would likely require a multivolume series of books rather than one section of a chapter in a single book. This section, therefore, focuses on three of the more fundamental and frequent problems that are produced by a history of abuse.

Some of the more common problems children experience include *poor self-esteem, depression,* and *anxiety.* For these children the years of neglect, abuse, and verbal assault have taken a toll on the way they see themselves, the world, and their future. They may doubt their ability to succeed or even to be loved. Many also experience a strong *distrust of adults or older children.* They may lack age-appropriate social skills and, as a result, may find it difficult to relate to both adults and peers.

Attachment disorder refers to a condition many maltreated children experience as a result of frequent, extended, or traumatic separation from their primary caregivers during early childhood. It manifests as a lack of ability to form meaningful relationships, fear and avoidance of intimacy and efforts from others to offer or build intimacy, superficiality in relationships, extreme distrust of others, a deep desire to control others, and sometimes an explosive temper. In more extreme cases it may also include destructive behavior and cruelty toward animals or other people (Cline, 1992; Levy & Orlans, 1995; Rycus & Hughes, 1998). Obviously, children who suffer from attachment disorder may struggle to adapt to a foster home and may stretch the patience and resources of unaware parents. Many children with this condition can be successfully treated given professional help and a dedicated foster family.

Separation trauma is also an issue for some children. Children who are removed from homes in which they have been maltreated are suddenly taken from a familiar world and placed in an environment of unknowns. Despite the abuse they may have experienced in their source home, they are likely to have had some form of support there, whether from parents who both loved and harmed, siblings who shared their world, extended family, neighbors, or friends. Many react to this event in a way that Rycus and Hughes (1998) have compared to the grieving process. They use the stages of grieving, identified by Kubler-Ross (1969), to describe what children who are traumatized by separation may experience. These stages are (a) shock/denial, (b) anger/protest, (c) bargaining, (d) depression, and (e) resolution. Both foster parents and caseworkers should be aware of the likelihood that children may experience some or all of these stages and that their behavior may be affected as a result. Once again, a supportive home and professional help are critical to helping a child through this process.

ISSUES FOR MEMBERS OF SOURCE FAMILIES

The members of source families may also have substantial problems. In addition to the issues that produced maltreatment, they often experience difficulties with employment, unstable or unsafe housing, educational deficiencies, weak problem-solving and decision-making skills, anger control, and communication problems. Parents may be angry that their children have been removed and resentful of representatives from the agency that did so. They may also experience guilt for their abusive behavior or shame that they have been exposed. They may deny that any problem exists and insist on some alternative explanation for the difficulties their children have experienced.

Because not every child in a home where maltreatment occurs always experiences the maltreatment, siblings of children who have experienced maltreatment may not be taken into custody. Siblings may experience a range of emotions related to the removal. They may be angry at either their parents or at the child welfare agency. They may be afraid that they, too, will be removed, or they may wish that they had been taken with their brother or sister. They may also experience many of the symptoms of separation trauma and attachment disorder. The case manager must be aware of and address these and other issues because problems among siblings can contribute to the overall level of stress and dysfunction in a home, increasing the probability that maltreatment will recur.

ISSUES FOR FOSTER PARENTS

Foster parents may experience a number of issues when children enter their homes. Many of these have been mentioned in other sections of this chapter. In addition to the emotional strain of having a new, possibly troubled child arrive suddenly in their home, they may experience several other problems.

These include lack of expertise for children with specific kinds of problems, overload or burnout, and lack of support from the case manager.

Despite efforts during assessment to identify problems that suggest placement in a therapeutic or psychiatric environment, some children with severe problems are placed in traditional foster homes. The reason may be that the problems were not identified during assessment, that no space was available in the appropriate environment, or that insufficient funding prevented placement in a more costly home. These conditions may result in foster parents who *lack expertise with specific problems* experienced by the children placed in their care. This can greatly increase stress within the home, resulting in unsuccessful experiences for the parents and possibly causing them to reconsider their role in the program.

Foster parents may also experience *overload or burnout*. This may be the result of inappropriate placements, too many children in the home, or lack of support from the child welfare agency. Burnout can sometimes be alleviated with an infusion of supportive services, relocation of children who have been inappropriately placed, and reduction of the total census of the home. In extreme cases foster parents may need psychotherapeutic services or time without children in the home.

Foster parents are sometimes frustrated by *inaccessibility of resources*. Although they are promised regular stipends, medical and dental services for the children, and other important support, foster parents may have difficulty actually accessing those services. One example of this problem occurs when parents who have recently received a new child into their home experience difficulties in obtaining a Medicaid card. If a child is ill, they will be forced to pay for these expenses themselves or deny treatment to the child. Once again, many of these problems can be averted by active advocacy and involvement on the part of the case manager.

CHAPTER SUMMARY

The foster care system is both vast and complex, and it varies among states and even among jurisdictions in individual states. This chapter provides a good foundation for understanding individual systems. Practitioners though must determine what difference may exist in their own locations.

TEST YOURSELF

1. **The foster home may be a short-term, long-term, or permanent arrangement.** True or False?

2. **Foster homes are intended to provide a safe, stable living environment that simulates a family as closely as possible.** True or False?

3. **The term *foster home* refers only to single-family homes.** True or False?

4. **The level of support received by parents who care for children of their relatives is consistent across jurisdictions.** True or False?

5. **Therapeutic homes exist to provide specialized services to children with severe medical needs.** True or False?

6. **Children become involved with the *juvenile justice* system because**

   (a) They have committed status offenses

   (b) They have committed delinquent offenses

   (c) They have committed both status and delinquent offenses

   (d) They have had difficulty adjusting to a traditional home

7. **High profile cases**

   (a) Always require a very high level of cultural sensitivity

   (b) Require placement in an institutional environment

   (c) Require no special treatment when a home is selected

   (d) Require that foster parents be carefully selected

8. **The process of recruiting foster parents includes four basic steps:**

   (a) Locate, screen, inform, and commit

   (b) Advertise, advise, alert, and equip

   (c) Recruit, train, license, and assign

   (d) Locate, screen, train, and commit

9. **In their role as liaison to the court, case managers must**

   (a) Communicate with the court regarding the status of children

   (b) Make legal decisions about children's custody arrangements

   (c) Offer opinions regarding the legality of parental status

   (d) Advocate for the rights of the source family

10. Understanding cultural differences is

   (a) Unimportant in the selection of a foster home

   (b) Critical in the selection of some placements

   (c) Something that is natural to many caseworkers

   (d) Unimportant in presentations to the court

Answers. 1. True; 2. True; 3. False; 4. False; 5. False; 6. c; 7. d; 8. a; 9. a; 10. b.

Six

ESSENTIALS OF SPECIALIZED CARE

The last chapter gave an overview of the various types of foster homes. This chapter discusses four of those types in greater depth: therapeutic, psychiatric, medical, and kinship. As has been mentioned about much of the child welfare system, the names and structure of these homes may vary among jurisdictions. Therapeutic homes may house children with severe psychological problems in one area but limit their residents to those who have milder disturbances in others. Psychiatric and medical homes may be single-family or institutional and may be operated by the state or by private agencies. Acceptance criteria for psychiatric placements may vary among jurisdictions or even within jurisdictions. For example, one home may accept sex offenders or those who have acted out violently. Others may exclude either or both groups. Practitioners may also find these guidelines to be somewhat soft if an institution's census is low or if the state agency (which may provide millions of dollars per year in funding) is in desperate need of a placement for a child.

Homes in which children reside with relatives may be called relative care, kinship homes, or some more generic name such as protective services. These kinship homes may be operated by the state or by a private agency. They may be funded or nonfunded and may receive a variety of services from the state or no support whatsoever. The differences in the structure of the system in various parts of the country is perhaps no more evident than it is in foster care. These differences makes understanding the overall structure of the child welfare system critical to an understanding of foster care.

THE STRUCTURE OF THE SYSTEM

Although the child welfare system might be categorized in many different ways, one of the most useful ways of understanding today's system is to begin with the separation of public from private. Public refers to those services operated by state employees. Private refers to services operated by private agencies. These agencies may be for profit or not for profit. They may be funded totally with state dollars, totally with private dollars, or with some combination of state and private money. The pattern over the last several years has been to shift service provision away from state agencies, transferring direct service to private agencies. Typically, state agencies are then downsized, retaining only the staff needed to provide funding and monitoring activities.

Privatization, as this process is termed, has occurred at virtually every point in the system. Protective investigation services have been transferred to private programs or law enforcement agencies. Case managers may be employed by the state or by contracted private agencies. Adoption and independent living may be either public or private as well. To further complicate the situation, various jurisdictions are at different stages of the process. Some are almost entirely privatized and others only partially, while still others remain largely public.

With respect to foster care, the service delivery system has similarities and differences between public and private agencies. For example, the management structure tends to be similar in both types of agencies. Several direct service workers typically answer to a single supervisor. Several supervisors in turn answer to a higher administrator who may be one of several who answer to yet another. In a state bureaucracy this hierarchy may contain many levels. When services have been privatized, particularly regionally within states, there are likely to be fewer levels of management. Bureaucracy has the advantages of stability and continuity. Private agencies often have greater flexibility and stronger communication between direct service workers and higher level administrators.

It is important to understand the distribution of private and public services within a foster care system because the location of resources has a great deal to do with how they can be accessed. Where the system is highly privatized and the services are scattered across a broad range of agencies, it is critically important that the case manager maintain a current list of the programs that are available for children and families with specific kinds of needs.

THERAPEUTIC FOSTER HOMES

Therapeutic homes (also known as treatment homes) are often privately operated. These agencies contract with the state for the cost of services, then hire foster parents, a case manager, and additional agencies to provide the services. The homes may be from any socioeconomic range. Therapeutic homes serve children with significant developmental, behavioral, and psychological problems. Many children placed in these homes have experienced extreme maltreatment over extended periods of time. Before therapeutic homes were developed, these children might have been placed in psychiatric institutions. Through the combined efforts of the foster parents, the case manager, and supportive agencies, they are often able to live successfully in a homelike environment.

Role of the Foster Parent

One of the goals of most therapeutic programs is to keep children in natural, homelike environments while also providing the intensive services needed to help them cope with their problems. By living in a home, the children are able to experience many of the normal socialization processes experienced by other children. Foster parents and siblings provide an environment that is similar to that of a conventional home. The children are often able to attend public schools, participate in sports, and join community recreational programs. Their lives vary as little as possible from the experiences of other, less troubled children.

Therapeutic foster parents receive special training to deal with a broad range of issues the children may experience. They receive education regarding the problems that the children for whom they will care are likely to experience. They are given information about psychopharmacological medications, their uses and side effects. They are taught to recognize potential points of intervention, to note and track behavioral antecedents, to administer basic techniques of behavioral modification, and to provide specific therapeutic interventions. They are taught principles of effective communication, successful environmental structuring, and effectual family management. They are prepared as much as possible to participate as both foster parents and paraprofessional workers.

In addition to their work with the child, therapeutic foster parents also interact with case managers and other professionals to ensure that children's daily needs are met and that they receive the services they need to deal with their more difficult issues. For instance, foster parents are involved in their children's education as biological parents would be. They supervise homework, interact with teachers, and may participate as would biological parents in their children's extracurricular activities. In addition to activities typical of most parents, however, therapeutic parents also are an important source of information for the child welfare case manager and a critical point of contact for agencies that provide services to the home. They are to a great extent the eyes and ears of the professional workers in monitoring the progress and well-being of the children in care.

Role of the Case Manager

Case managers who work with therapeutic homes play a critical role in the care of the children (see Rapid Reference 6.1). They are often the point of contact through which parents can reach agencies that provide supportive services, medical personnel, financial resources, and the court. They should also be a source of support for the parents and should be able to refer them to additional sources of support when they are needed.

Case managers should visit the home at least once per month (more often if that is the expectation in their jurisdiction) and should be continually available to receive phone calls from the home or the agencies that provide services. They should be in frequent contact with these outside agencies and should ensure that communication between them is effective. The case manager may also need to be active as an advocate. Children who are appropriate for placement in therapeutic homes often experience problems in other life dimensions. For

≡Rapid Reference 6.1

Role of the Caseworker With Therapeutic Homes

- Visit the home consistently
- Be continually available to receive phone calls
- Be in frequent contact with wraparound agencies
- Be active as an advocate
- Provide additional referrals
- Liaison with the court

example, a child may act out in a classroom where the teacher is either untrained or too busy to deal with issues presented by the child. This might result in an attempt by the teacher or the school administration to have the child removed from school. In such cases the case manager may need to intervene to ensure that the child is provided an alternative source for educational services.

Role of Outside Agencies

In many jurisdictions an agency or group of agencies may contract to provide services that are beyond what might be expected of foster parents. These services are typically therapeutic and are related in some way to the problem that resulted in the child's placement in the home. They are often intended to be comprehensive; that is, they are intended to address every aspect of the problem. They are often referred to as *wraparound* because they wrap around the services provided by the therapeutic home.

Wraparound services may include professional assessment and evaluation, counseling, psychiatric services, psychoeducation, tutoring, and other services. The need for these services is often recognized in an assessment conducted by one of the wraparound agencies or some other professional (such as a physician or private mental health practitioner). In many jurisdictions the wraparound agency must obtain permission from the child welfare agency, the court, or both before providing the needed services.

A Typical Day in a Therapeutic Home

A typical day in a therapeutic foster home is very much like a typical day in many homes where children reside with biological parents. The family might rise early for breakfast and to prepare for work and school. The children might dress in their bedrooms while a parent or parents prepares breakfast. At breakfast, they might talk about what they expect their days to be like, about some upcoming event at school, or about a planned family outing. The children might walk to the bus stop while the parents drive or take the bus to work.

The children might return in the late afternoon, met at home by a parent who has returned early from work. They might play at the neighborhood park, have dinner, complete homework, watch television, and be off to bed.

If at some point a child appears to be escalating emotionally or psychologically, a parent might step in with therapeutic techniques. On other days the play time at the park might be replaced with a visit from the case manager or an in-home session with a therapist from a wraparound agency.

This scenario might be seen as somewhat middle class, and one might reasonably argue that because families (foster and otherwise) vary so much in their behaviors and habits, there is no such thing as a typical day for any family. Although it is certainly true that families are different and behave differently, it is also true that even very divergent habits between families vary significantly from the activities in an institution. This section has been included to help illustrate the differences between a family home and the two types of institutional settings that are discussed later in this chapter. The clear differences in the environments of family homes and institutional settings illustrate the great value of the family foster home for providing a child with a more normal environment, hopefully minimizing trauma and promoting normal processes of socialization.

Criteria for Referral to Therapeutic Care

Children are typically referred to a therapeutic home after they are recognized to have a significant developmental, behavioral, or psychological problem. This may occur when they first enter custody or after disruptions in a traditional home. Others enter therapeutic care as they enter late childhood or adolescence and their problems become more evident. Typically, they are not referred from a traditional setting to therapeutic care (sometimes termed a higher level of care) until multiple incidents or one very extreme incident has made it clear that the child is not likely to be successful in a traditional home. The primary criterion for referral to a therapeutic home is that the child experiences developmental, emotional, or psychological problems that cannot be successfully addressed in a traditional setting. Signs of these problems include diagnosis with a specific disorder or persistent problems in one or more of the following areas: anger management, school problems, truancy, defiant or oppositional behavior, substance abuse, running away, and other status or delinquent behaviors.

Although therapeutic homes can clearly be very beneficial, there are significant challenges involved in operating them. One such challenge is the limited availability of suitable parents. Recruiting traditional foster parents can be very difficult. Locating and recruiting parents who are willing and able to face the additional difficulties involved in caring for children with more difficult problems is even more daunting. If an agency chooses to move successful traditional parents into a therapeutic role, it runs the risk that they will not work well in the therapeutic environment, perhaps resulting in frustration and the loss of a home. Yet another challenge is budgetary. Although therapeutic homes are less expensive to operate than traditional homes, they are far more costly than traditional homes. The extra cost involved may cause financially strapped agencies to balk at the creation of therapeutic homes.

Therapeutic homes are an important part of an overall continuum of care. Many states require that troubled children be placed in the "least restrictive environment," that is, an environment in which the children's ability to move about is as unconstrained and natural as possible. Therapeutic homes provide many children who might otherwise be assigned to a psychiatric placement with a more natural, less restrictive alternative.

Criteria for Referral to a Psychiatric Institution

Unfortunately, some children have problems that are simply too difficult to be managed in a therapeutic home. This may result in their placement in a psychiatric institution. Typically, every effort is made to avoid such a decision, but it is sometimes inevitable. Criteria for referral to a psychiatric institution are summarized in Rapid Reference 6.2.

PSYCHIATRIC INSTITUTIONS

Psychiatric institutions for juveniles may be operated either by the state or by a private agency. They are usually relatively large (often housing more than

---

≡ *Rapid Reference 6.2*

Criteria for Referral to a Psychiatric Institution

1. Danger to self and/or others
2. Unmanageable behavior
3. Uncontrollable psychotic episodes
4. Severe levels of cognitive impairment that precludes living in a more traditional home

100 residents) and are designed to allow their operators to maximize efficiency and cost-effectiveness through planned use of common areas and smaller units that include the primary living areas. They have extremely structured milieus, very rigid rules, and highly monitored environments. Staff are divided into several groups. Daily service workers, sometimes referred to as techs, oversee and direct the children's daily activities. Therapists, often with master's- or doctoral-level training, provide counseling and psychoeducation. Psychiatrists oversee counseling activities and prescribe medication. A nursing staff often attends to medical needs and dispenses medication. Administrative staff oversee and conduct daily operations such as management, maintenance, and food preparation.

Psychiatric institutions are structured to maximize security for staff, residents, and the community. Units often contain several bedrooms that may include beds and desks. The bedrooms often open into a common area that contains couches, chairs, tables, a television, and some games and books. Each unit, composed of a group of bedrooms and their common area, can be locked to prevent anyone in the unit from leaving or anyone from outside accessing it. Access may be gained through use of a key or an electronic pass card or by being buzzed in by someone who is monitoring the entrance electronically. Residents sleep, study, and spend some recreational time in their units. They leave the units for other activities, such as classes, dining, therapy, recreation, religious activities, and occasional field trips.

Children may leave their units for specific purposes only. Individually, they may need to attend therapy sessions, meet with administrators, or see physicians. They may also leave in groups for dining, religious activities, or recreational activities. Individuals who exit the unit are often accompanied by a staff member. Groups may be accompanied by one or more staff and often must follow prescribed procedures, such as walking single file and in alphabetical order.

Psychiatric institutions often house children other than those from foster care. Children may come from private homes, from the juvenile justice system, and from other sources. Regardless of their source, they are most often older children and adolescents whose disorders have manifested to the point that they cannot live successfully in a regular home environment.

Children typically attend school within the institution. They leave their units for classes and often return there to do homework. A computer area is often available for word processing, Internet access, and other computer-related activities. Those who require tutoring may receive it from a staff member or a specialist from the school system who comes to the facility to provide instruction.

Many psychiatric institutions use token economies in which greater levels of freedom and responsibility may be earned through continuous appropriate behavior. Residents are awarded points when they accomplish certain goals. When they have accumulated a sufficient number of points, they move to a higher level, meaning that they gain greater freedom and often greater benefits. For example, one institution in Florida allows those who have achieved the highest level to live in private rooms with a personal television and to have extensive freedom of movement within the facility.

Goals for residents of psychiatric facilities vary. Some may be able to stabilize their conditions, deal with their problems, and return to a foster home or their biological family. Others whose problems are more severe are unlikely to leave the institution until they have reached the upper age limit for foster children in their jurisdiction.

Role of the Agency Staff

Rapid Reference 6.3 lists the various services that the staff provides to residents of psychiatric facilities.

Daily service workers (DSWs) supervise and direct the everyday activities of the residents. They ensure that residents are awake in the morning, supervise their movements throughout the day, do paraprofessional-level intervention and counseling, and provide some psychoeducation. DSWs have more direct contact with residents than any other category of employee and can be a rich source of information about the condition and progress of children in care.

Another group of workers provides professional counseling and therapy. Usually master's-level social workers, psychologists, or mental health practitioners, these workers may be either employees of the institution or contractors who work either specific hours or specific clients. They may do individual or group therapy and may also provide psychoeducation. When child welfare practitioners need professional perspectives on the progress of their clients, the counseling and therapy staff is often their best source of information. There may also be a clinical supervisor who oversees the activities of the clinical staff.

≡*Rapid Reference 6.3*

Categories of Staff in Psychiatric Facilities

- Daily service
- Counseling and therapy
- Psychiatric
- Medical
- Educational
- Operational

Psychiatrists constitute another group of staff. There may be a single staff psychiatrist who works full-time for the facility or a group of part-time contractors who review charts and prescribe medication. Full-time personnel are likely to take a more active role in the supervision of clinical staff and may replace the clinical supervisor in some instances. Part-time staff may participate in *staffings,* the meetings in which clinical personnel discuss the status and progress of individual residents, but they are less likely to supervise staff.

Medical personnel are the third group. In large institutions there may be full-time physicians or nurse practitioners. In midsized to smaller facilities there are likely to be part-time nurses or nurse practitioners. When no full-time physician is on staff, children may be transported to a private office for medical consultations. Staff nurses treat minor conditions and administer medication prescribed by physicians and psychiatrists.

A fourth group of personnel is composed of educational professionals. Again, the nature of this group may vary among facilities. In some, educators may be employees of the facility. In others, they are employees of the local school board assigned to work with the children in the institution. Educational personnel teach daily classes and provide tutoring services to help residents improve their educational performance.

The final group of facility personnel is operational. Administrators supervise the staff members who conduct daily business such as accounting, marketing, community liaison, personnel management, food preparation and service, fund-raising, and purchasing. Many of the administrative personnel may come from backgrounds outside the social service field.

Role of the Case Manager

The case manager's role with children in psychiatric institutions is often less intense than in traditional or therapeutic homes. Visits may be less frequent, and many supervisory activities may take place through telephone conferences. This is in large part because psychiatric institutions are often geographically remote from practitioners' normal work area, and frequent travel may detract from their ability to supervise other homes. Despite geographical challenges, practitioners should maintain frequent contact with the child, institution, and source family. These visits provide the basis for their other activities, which differ very little from those described for case managers earlier in this chapter.

Role of Outside Agencies

The role of outside agencies is typically minimized in psychiatric facilities. Most necessary services are provided by staff. Examples of the kinds of services that might be received elsewhere include medical, dental, and special psychiatric or psychological consultation. Some facilities may contract with outside organizations for food service and maintenance.

A Typical Day in a Psychiatric Home

As with all types of homes, daily activities vary among psychiatric institutions. It will be helpful here, however, to describe the kinds of things that residents often do in order to contrast their activities with those in other settings.

Children typically arise at a regular time and may be awakened by a common alarm, a broadcast announcement, or a visit from a staff member. They are given a set amount of time to prepare for the day and then are taken as a group for breakfast. After breakfast they might have individual or group therapy sessions for an hour before beginning school. School might last until midday, at which time they might return to their units to clean up for lunch. After a brief break, they would then proceed to the cafeteria.

Following lunch, the residents might return to their units for a brief break. The group might do homework or watch television while individuals are taken for brief meetings with clinical personnel. Afternoon would likely bring more school time followed by recreation, dinner, study time, and bed at a prescribed hour. All activities would be closely monitored by staff members, and movement between activities would be in groups following procedures established in the agency's policy and procedures manual. Any violation of the policies might result in sanctions for a child. Consistent obedience would result in some kind of positive benefit.

Criteria for Release

Children whose conditions are believed to be sufficiently stabilized that they will be able to succeed in an outside environment may be released from psychiatric care. Judgment about their degree of stability is often left to the psychiatrist, who makes the decision based on the frequency, intensity, and duration of problem episodes. Children may be released to their biological parents or to a traditional foster home or may be stepped down to a therapeutic home or some lower security facility.

MEDICAL FOSTER HOMES

Medical foster homes are intended to provide an environment that is as natural as possible for children who suffer from severe medical problems. Children in these homes may range from infancy to late adolescence and may experience a broad range of medical problems. Sometimes parents of single-family homes decide to foster many infants in a single location. As children grow older, this arrangement is less frequent because of the added complexity of caring for older children.

Role of the Foster Parent

Medical foster parents have all the responsibilities of traditional parents plus the added responsibility of the paraprofessional medical care of the children. These responsibilities may include such activities as administering medication, managing equipment, and changing dressings or bandages. In addition, they must provide emotional support and crisis intervention services to children whose mental health may be affected by their illness. Medical foster parents often receive general training about working with children who are ill and specific training about the illnesses experienced by the children for whom they care.

Role of Outside Agencies

Medical foster homes often receive support from outside agencies. Sometimes the services are similar to those offered to other foster homes. However, medical homes may also be visited by nurse practitioners, nurses' aids, medical equipment companies, and various kinds of therapists. If children are unable to leave the home, they may also receive educational visits from school system personnel. Foster parents may also participate in support groups and receive periodic training from other agencies.

A Typical Day in a Medical Home

As with other homes, a so-called typical day may vary substantially among medical homes. In homes where the children are primarily infants, the foster parents may develop a fairly strict schedule and follow it closely. In a home for infants this might involve breakfast and feeding followed by administration of medication, play time with each infant, nap time, lunch, and an afternoon very much like the morning.

When the children are older, a great deal of the daily activity depends on their mobility and energy level. When health permits, they may attend school or spend some time with a foster parent at a local park. Often, however, as their illness progresses, they are able to spend less time outside the home.

As with therapeutic homes, medical foster homes are intended to provide an environment that is as normal as possible for children to live in. As a result, children who are both old enough and mobile enough to watch television, play in the home or outside, or visit neighbors or community parks may do so.

Criteria for Placement

Children are placed in a medical foster home when their medical needs are perceived to be too great for a traditional setting but insufficient to require hospitalization. These criteria may arise from a variety of disease or physical conditions. In some jurisdictions children may need a physician's approval for placement in a medical home. In others the decision may be made by a multi-disciplinary committee. Some areas also require the approval of the court.

Criteria for Referral to a Hospital

Children are referred to a hospital or facility that can provide more intensive care when their needs exceed the capacities of their medical foster home or its caregivers. Although the condition that requires transfer to a more care-intensive environment is likely to be severe, it is not always life-threatening. Children are sometimes hospitalized until their condition is stable and then are returned to the home.

KINSHIP FOSTER HOMES

Children have been placed in the homes of willing relatives for many years. This form of placement, often referred to as kinship care or relative care, has many advantages. Experts have noted that placement with relatives can minimize the trauma of removal, accommodate cultural needs, and help ease the burden on the foster care system (Child Welfare League of America, 1994; Ellis, Ellis, & Galey, 2002; Ingram, 1996). The history of success in relative care has been erratic, however, perhaps in large part because of the broad variation in the level of support provided in different jurisdictions. This book uses two terms to designate categories of care: *relative care* and *kinship care*. Relative care refers to programs designed to provide little or no support from child welfare workers. Kinship care is used to indicate programs in which child welfare workers, either public or private, provide substantial support to the family (Geen & Berrick, 2002). It is also important to note that this is not a common way of using these terms. They are used in many different ways in the scientific literature, sometimes almost interchangeably. Rapid Reference 6.4 defines some of the similarities and differences between these types of care.

Relative care programs are probably less numerous than they were a few years ago. In response to a push from professional and academic circles, increasing numbers of states have placed greater emphasis on kinship care. Historically, however, many children have been placed in the homes of

≡ *Rapid Reference 6.4*

Types and Characteristics of Homes That Care for Children of Relatives

Relative Care

The caregivers are relatives of the child in custody.

The home receives no financial assistance from the child welfare agency.

The home receives little or no visitation or support from a child welfare case manager.

The home does not receive services from other agencies paid by the child welfare agency.

The court may not be involved in the placement decision.

Kinship Care

The caregivers are relatives of the child in custody.

The home receives financial assistance from the child welfare agency.

The home receives regular visitation or support from a child welfare case manager.

The home may receive services from other agencies paid by the child welfare agency.

The court is involved in the placement decision.

relatives, sometimes with the approval of the court, sometimes without, and often with no more than cursory attention to support by the state.

Placement with relatives has sometimes been a form of early intervention that protective investigators have used to remove children from homes in which they experienced maltreatment without taking them into formal custody. In these cases investigators might learn of the existence of willing relatives during investigational interviews, visit the homes of those relatives and interview them to ensure that both the environment and prospective caregivers are suitable, and ultimately leave the child in what they judged to be a safer environment. The workers might refer the family to informal, nonmandatory sources of support and might or might not put state supervision in place.

Obviously, a system this informal has many flaws. Perhaps most prominent is the possibility that the relatives might simply return the children to the source home without any services being provided or protective mechanisms put in place. This would, of course, do little to protect a child. Another flaw is the lack of any observational system to monitor service provision or progress. A final, equally dangerous flaw is the lack of financial, emotional, and professional support for these relative caregivers. With no funds to support the extra expenses generated for the household and no means of insuring that the family's psychological and emotional needs are met, many of these relative homes experience extreme stress that disrupt many of the placements.

Other programs have been somewhat more formal. These programs arrange to place children with relatives through the commitment process but offer little in the way of supportive services thereafter. In these situations host families are subjected to many of the pressures experienced in the completely informal settings, often resulting in placement failure.

Some jurisdictions offer either traditional levels of support or specialized support to families who care for their relatives. In this book these programs are referred to as kinship foster care. These programs are perhaps even more varied than are relative caregiver programs. Some, for instance, require relatives to complete traditional foster parent training. Others do not. Some require caregivers to plan for adoption. Others allow for long-term care as an option. Some use traditional case management to supervise and support the home. Others use a mediation model. Some provide the same array of services offered to traditional homes. Others offer a different continuum of services believed to be more appropriate for kinship homes. Yet another difference exists in the identity of the agency providing the services. In some areas it is a state agency, in some areas a private agency; in some areas it may be both. Kinship programs have received a great deal of attention and support in recent years as child welfare agencies look for alternative ways of handling a growing influx of children.

Role of the Foster Parent

The role of foster parents in a kinship or relative home is very much like that of parents in a traditional home. They are responsible for providing a home for and overseeing the daily activities of children much in the way that a biological parent would. One likely difference is that other family members are likely to be more involved in the care and supervision of the children.

Role of the Case Manager

Obviously, the role of the case manager varies according to the level of support a home can expect to receive from the child welfare agency. Where relative care programs call for little involvement with the case manager, contact with a child welfare agency employee may be rare. Where kinship programs offer intensive services, the case manager may be very involved with the family, particularly in the early days of the placement.

Role of Outside Agencies

Participation by outside agencies also varies. When services are limited, the child welfare agency may provide few referrals, limiting the access of many families to outside resources. When the state is very involved, wraparound services may require frequent visits by other agencies. When a mediation model is used for a kinship home, the case manager may facilitate a series of family meetings in which concerned family members negotiate an effective arrangement among themselves, deciding what services a child may receive and which agencies will provide them.

A Typical Day in a Relative or Kinship Home

A typical day in a relative or kinship home is much like a day in a traditional home, and perhaps even more like a day in the source home. Placement with relatives tends to normalize the child's situation more so than do other forms of placement. Children are surrounded by familiar people who are likely to share similar worldviews and cultures. They are more likely to attend familiar schools, see familiar people, and participate in familiar environments. It is this familiarity that makes care by family members so attractive to so many practitioners.

MISCELLANEOUS HOMES: THE HODGEPODGE OF NECESSITY

This and the previous chapter have been organized and methodical, presenting the system of care for children in care as patterned, consistent, and clearly differentiated. In the real world the patterns are far less consistent and the separation between types of homes far less distinct. Many jurisdictions are sadly understaffed and underfunded. Recruitment and retention of foster homes are an ongoing problem for many. As a result, homes that are intended to be of one type are, in fact, a blend of types. It is common, for example, to find that homes housing the children of relatives also care for children who would fit the profile for both traditional and therapeutic homes. On the surface, it may appear that such a situation is inexcusable. In reality, child welfare workers may face incredible pressures to place children. When the hour is late and they are faced with several children yet to be placed, they may call on parents who are particularly compassionate. Those parents, knowing that their role does not include providing shelter for some children, may agree to receive them despite the circumstances. When they do, despite their excellent intentions, the home type is compromised, resulting in a blend that may or may not have the strengths it had when it kept only those children who could be identified as appropriate for that setting.

CHAPTER SUMMARY

This chapter provides an overview of specialized foster care settings and the strengths and challenges to successful placements. It is essential that specialized foster placements have appropriately trained and supported staff/foster parents with adequate resources to facilitate a successful placement for special needs children in their care.

 TEST YOURSELF

1. **Acceptance criteria for psychiatric placements may vary among jurisdictions or even within jurisdictions.** True or False?

2. **The pattern over the last several years has been to shift service provision away from state agencies, transferring direct service to private agencies.** True or False?

3. **Therapeutic homes serve children with significant developmental, behavioral, and psychological problems.** True or False?

4. Parents in therapeutic foster homes are taught to diagnose mental illnesses in the children in their care. True or False?

5. An array of services that is intended to be comprehensive (i.e., address every aspect of the a child's problem) is referred to as wraparound. True or False?

6. Criteria for referral to a psychiatric institution do not include

(a) Danger to self or others

(b) Severe levels of cognitive impairment that preclude successful living in a more traditional environment

(c) Whether children have committed both status and delinquent offenses

(d) Uncontrollable psychotic episodes

7. Many psychiatric institutions use token economies, in which

(a) Greater levels of freedom and responsibility may be earned through continuous appropriate behavior

(b) Children are provided with vocational training that will enable them to earn an income after they are released

(c) Children receive a token or special benefit for taking their medication on a regular basis

(d) The personal belongings of children who are admitted are kept in a locked room and may be redeemed by submitting a token.

8. Medical foster parents may engage in such supportive activities as

(a) Crisis counseling, medical diagnosis, and administering medication

(b) Managing medical equipment, conducting laboratory tests, and prescribing certain medications

(c) Administering medication, managing medical equipment, and changing dressings

(d) Assessment of psychiatric issues, administration of psychotropic medication, and behavioral intervention

9. Experts have noted that placement with relatives can

(a) Minimize the trauma of removal, accommodate cultural needs, and help ease the burden on the case manager

(b) Accommodate cultural needs, help ease the burden on the foster care system, and strengthen the relationship between caregiving agencies

(continued)

(c) Minimize the trauma of removal, accommodate cultural needs, and create strong boundaries between the source family and the caregivers

(d) Minimize the trauma of removal, accommodate cultural needs, and help ease the burden on the foster care system

10. Historically, many children have been placed in the homes of relatives

(a) Always with the approval of the court

(b) Always with support from child welfare agencies

(c) Sometimes with no support from child welfare agencies

(d) Only after extensive assessment and search for other alternatives

Answers. 1. True; 2. True; 3. True; 4. False; 5. True; 6. c; 7. a; 8. c; 9. d; 10. c.

Seven

ESSENTIALS OF REUNIFICATION

D espite recent movement in both policy and practice toward more long-term custody alternatives, reunification with the source family remains the primary goal for most jurisdictions. Given the prevalence and strength of American norms supporting the primacy of the family, reunification seems likely to remain the primary goal for a great many cases for many years to come. Because of this probability, it is vital to understand what conditions are likely to result in a successful return to the source home and what conditions suggest that a return may not be appropriate.

It is important to remember that children who have been removed from a source home have experienced significant trauma. They have been removed from a familiar environment and caretakers they may have loved, shifted through a series of bewildering and perhaps frightening environments, and placed in the hands of strangers. If the placement goes well and children become comfortable in a foster home, the trauma may be to some degree recreated when they return to their source homes. If the source home is not ready for the child's return and maltreatment recurs, the original trauma may be repeated. For children who already suffer from separation anxiety, attachment disorder, and related problems, the result can be devastating.

PREPARATION FOR REUNIFICATION

Careful preparation can minimize or eliminate the potential trauma of reunification. Several events may alert the case manager to the fact that reunification should be considered. The first signal is often a nearly completed case plan. When source families have shown diligent and persistent effort in working on the plan and completion seems imminent, case managers should consider proposing to the court that steps be taken to prepare both child and family to be reunified. At other times the recommendation may come from a mental health professional, from an attorney, or from the judge. When conditions appear to be right for reunification, the possibility should be discussed in a hearing, and the opinions of several experts should be sought. Experts may include the case manager, various professionals who have been involved in the case, attorneys for all parties, and the guardian ad litem. A guardian ad litem is a court appointed guardian whose responsibility is to advocate for the well being of the child. This individual may or may not be an attorney, depending on individual state guidelines.

Case managers observe the progress of both children and parents to determine the degree to which case plan goals are being met. Professional counselors such as social workers or psychologists may offer their opinions or provide the results of psychological testing. Mental health practitioners may submit their opinions in writing, as may school personnel, medical providers, and other professionals. Several attorneys may express opinions, including the attorney for the child welfare agency, the attorney for the child, and the attorney for the source family. When guardians ad litem are not attorneys, their opinion may also be sought. Judges review the cases and hear the recommendations of the concerned parties. This may occur in a regularly scheduled status hearing or in a hearing requested specifically for this purpose.

If the judge determines that conditions are right to move toward reunification, the case manager should work with the other parties in the case to develop a plan. Several strategies are often incorporated into the process, including increased visitation with the source family and counseling and psychoeducation for children and families. When the process is done properly, children have several weeks to prepare themselves for the coming change. The case manager should thoroughly investigate the thoughts and feelings of the child, the source home, and the caretaking home regarding the possibility of a return. If the case manager has any doubts during these discussions, he or she would provide appropriate intervention to alleviate them. If the concerns were particularly severe, a new hearing might be requested to determine whether the reunification process should continue.

The reunification plan would likely include longer, more frequent visits between children and source families. For example, the child might visit for entire weekends when only days or afternoons had been permitted in the past. Case managers would carefully monitor both child and family before,

Putting It Into Practice

Reunification should be a process in which both child and family are carefully prepared. An example of a well-planned reunification might include the following steps:

1. Recognizing that conditions are right for reunification to occur
2. Obtaining the court's approval to proceed in a formal hearing
3. Consulting with involved professionals to determine what strategies to include in the preparatory process
4. Arranging longer, more frequent visits between children and source families
5. Careful monitoring of visits to support the process
6. Focusing interactions with the case manager on issues related to reunification
7. Focusing interactions with involved professionals on issues related to reunification
8. Working with the family to develop a family safety plan (FSP)
9. Ensuring that appropriate resources are in place
10. Obtaining final approval of the court for reunification to occur

after, and during the visits to ensure that interactions during the visits indicate that a return to the home is appropriate.

In addition to increased visitation between children and their source homes, the reunification plan might include increased interactions among children, families, and the case manager. During these visits the case manager would focus on issues related to reunification. Similarly, visits with mental health professionals might focus on psychological readiness. In addition to preparing the families, case managers and mental health professionals should attempt to determine whether the criteria for reunification are met on facilitating the development of a family safety plan (FSP). Both the criteria for reunification and the FSP are discussed in greater detail later in this chapter. In addition, case managers should ensure that children and families are aware of the personal and community resources that they may need and that they know how to access those resources.

The final step in reunification involves obtaining the approval of the court. This typically occurs at a hearing in which the case manager presents the results of the reunification plan along with reports from professionals who have been involved. If the judge is satisfied by the report and with the measures that have been put in place through the FSP, the child may be returned to the source family.

CRITERIA FOR REUNIFICATION

In some cases the factors surrounding reunification make it very clear that the time has come. Other cases may be much more difficult. Frequently, case managers and judges must consider multiple conditions in order to make a good decision.

Successful completion of the case plan is often a prerequisite for reunification. A well-designed case plan will have considered the problems that contributed to the original maltreatment and have addressed them. Children and source families are sometimes reunited before the completion of the plan if the parties have made sincere efforts to complete all its requirements and the judge is convinced that the unfinished requirements do not jeopardize the health of the child.

Other than successful case plan completion, the most obvious factor that must be considered is *the safety of the child*. The source family must have demonstrated sufficient change to make it reasonable to believe that the child will not be harmed if reunification occurs. This might mean, for example, that dangerous conditions within the home have been corrected, that a parental substance abuse problem has been addressed, that a perpetrator has been effectively excluded from the home, or that a parent has mastered anger management techniques and demonstrated a knowledge of acceptable disciplinary alternatives. Other protective factors would include the presence of a strong social support network, an awareness of and ability to utilize family strengths, and a clear, strong desire on the part of both parent and child to achieve reunification (Rycus & Hughes, 1998). If the probability that maltreatment will occur is high, the child should not be returned to the source family.

A third factor that may be considered is *the stability and competence of the source family*. Even though a family may have successfully completed the case plan and reduced immediate danger of maltreatment, ongoing or recurrent stressors may cause the probability of harm to increase again at some future point. If the family appears to be reasonably stable and competent to deal with a recurrence of stressors, reunification may be considered.

In an ideal world, concern for the *safety of a child in state custody* would not be an issue. In reality, however, children sometimes experience maltreatment at the hands of foster parents, child welfare workers, or other children. When resources are stretched and placement options are limited, judges may be forced to consider whether children may be at lesser risk if they are returned to their source homes.

The degree to which these conditions exist can be determined by answering a series of questions about each case. Satisfactory answers to these questions indicate a stronger probability that reunification will be successful. Unsatisfactory answers indicate a lesser probability of success. Questions should be asked across several dimensions of family functioning including the child, the perpetrator, the nonoffending caretaker, the family, and other social systems.

QUESTIONS RELATED TO THE CHILD

The first group of questions that should be asked when reunification is considered are those related to the children and their well-being. Of particular interest are issues related to the child's desire to return to the source family, the likely effects of reunification on the child, the likely effects of continued custody on the child, and the availability of services that may be needed should reunification occur. Rapid Reference 7.1 lists these questions, which are further explored in the following sections.

≡Rapid Reference 7.1

Questions Related to the Child

1. Does the child express a desire to return to the custody of the caretaker?
2. Has the child made sufficient recovery from any medical problems to permit reunification?
3. Has the child made sufficient recovery from any psychological problems to permit reunification?
4. Is reunification therapeutically indicated for the child?
5. Does the child (if age-appropriate) exhibit sufficient awareness of the nature of abusive behavior to permit reunification?
6. Have adequate supports, such as psychological services or educational programming, been put in place to allow the child to continue to progress and grow?

1. Does the Child Express a Desire to Return to the Custody of the Caretaker?

One of the primary child-related factors to consider is what the child wants. Children who are strongly opposed to returning to their source homes are unlikely to do well there. If a child does not want reunification, the worker should try to determine the reason for the resistance and whether the child's issue can be addressed. Some concerns may be alleviated through counseling, psychoeducation, or other interventions. Strong or persistent concerns should be investigated thoroughly to determine whether there is some history that has not yet been discovered. When a child's objections to reunification cannot be alleviated, workers may need to consider other alternatives.

Questions related to the desire of children to return to the source home can best be answered through questions asked directly of the children as well as observation of their behavior prior to and during visits with source caretakers. If professionals, such as a psychologist or a social worker, are involved in the case, they should be consulted and their opinions sought. Caseworkers and foster caregivers can also inquire regarding the child's readiness. It is also important that they observe the children's behavior prior to visiting with the parents and, whenever possible, during at least a portion of the visits. If children appear anxious, withdrawn, or fearful or display other unusual behavior, it may indicate that they are uncomfortable with the reunification or that they have additional issues that need to be addressed. When this is the case, it is important that the case manager, the foster caregiver, or a professional therapist further investigate these possibilities.

2. Has the Child Made Sufficient Recovery From Any Medical Problems to Permit Reunification?

Some medical problems may be best treated while a child is in custody. If, for example, the source family lives in a remote geographical area and has transportation difficulties, they may not be able to care adequately for a child whose illness requires frequent or intensive treatment. In such cases it would be important to ensure that the child's illness or injury was adequately treated before proceeding with reunification.

The issue of medical readiness for reunification can only be adequately answered by a medical professional. When medical services have been provided throughout the intervention period, the attending physician or practitioner should provide the opinion regarding readiness. If medical care has been terminated at some point, it may be appropriate to obtain the approval of the practitioner who provided the original care or of some other medical professional.

3. Has the Child Made Sufficient Recovery From Any Psychological Problems to Permit Reunification?

In some cases source families may make rapid progress toward their case plan goals, but maltreated children may not progress as rapidly in dealing with issues related to attachment, bonding, trust, depression, and other psychological problems. In order to optimize the probability of successful reunification, it is important that children have dealt with these problems sufficiently so as not to interfere with their successful functioning. The judgment of readiness is often best made by a psychologist, social worker, or psychiatrist who has the opportunity to assess both the child and the source family.

Judgment about a child's psychological readiness for reunification should be made by a qualified mental health professional. In some instances the case manager may be educationally and professionally qualified to make that judgment, but given that case management is typically an entry-level position in child welfare agencies, this is unlikely. Children who have been in the care of a mental health practitioner can be evaluated by that practitioner.

4. Is Reunification Therapeutically Indicated for the Child?

Closely related to psychological recovery is the issue of whether reunification is therapeutically indicated for the child. Children who experience depression or anxiety at the suggestion of returning to their homes may not be ready for reunification. Similarly, those who are making progress on attachment issues in a foster home may be best served by remaining in that setting.

As with psychological readiness, therapeutic indication should also be judged by a qualified professional. Ideally, any children being considered for reunification should receive an evaluation. In reality, budgetary constraints often make this impossible. In many jurisdictions, only those children who have been more severely maltreated or who have demonstrated significant behavioral problems are likely to receive evaluation or counseling. In these cases both readiness and therapeutic indication may need to be made by case managers or judges who lack the professional expertise for such decisions. If this is the case, it is important that case managers have extensive conversations with children and foster caregivers to determine whether attitudinal or behavioral problems need to be addressed before reunification can occur.

5. Does the Child (If Age-Appropriate) Exhibit Sufficient Awareness of the Nature of Abusive Behavior to Permit Reunification?

Although children must understand that they are not responsible for the maltreatment they have experienced, they can often be taught things about abuse and abusive behavior that will allow them to avoid being harmed in the future. For example, teaching children to notice indicators of escalating anger in a potential abuser may allow them to remove themselves from threatening situations before maltreatment occurs.

Thorough discussions of these issues between the case manager and children are usually adequate to help children reach an appropriate level of understanding. In some cases, such as instances of severe abuse or where children experience learning disabilities, it may be necessary to employ the services of a mental health or educational professional. Readiness can typically be assessed through interactions between the child and whoever has provided the training.

6. Have Adequate Supports, Such as Psychological Services or Educational Programming, Been Put in Place to Allow the Child to Continue to Progress and Grow?

Many children and families who are reunited are in need of ongoing resources and support. Before reunification is attempted, caseworkers should ensure that these services are in place and that all participants know how to access them.

Case managers and judges are often able to make a determination regarding readiness by reviewing the original assessment, the case plan, and the other documents in a child's record. Needs and strengths that were identified can be evaluated to determine the degree to which they have been met (needs) or optimized (strengths). Where unmet needs or unoptimized potentials exist, additional services should be put in place.

QUESTIONS RELATED TO THE PERPETRATOR

If the perpetrator will be involved in the child's life following reunification, it is critical that certain questions receive satisfactory answers. These questions focus on the well-being of the child, the perpetrator's desire and willingness to be reunified, and the perpetrator's perceived commitment to avoiding further maltreatment. Rapid Reference 7.2 lists the questions, which are elaborated in the following.

1. Does Reunification With the Perpetrator Appear to Be in the Child's Best Interest?

This question is answered in part by the answers to Questions 3, 4, and 5 in the previous section. It is possible, however, that even if children are psychologically prepared to return to the custody of a formerly abusive caretaker, it may not be in their best interest to do so.

If, for example, it seems doubtful that the former perpetrator will be able to maintain the improvements made during the implementation of the case plan, or if the nonperpetrating caretaker appears unable to protect the child from lapses by the perpetrator, it may be best not to return the child to the source home.

≡*Rapid Reference 7.2*

Questions Related to the Perpetrator

1. Does reunification with the perpetrator appear to be in the child's best interest?
2. Does the perpetrator express a desire for reunification?
3. Does the perpetrator express a desire for reunification in appropriate terms?
4. Has the perpetrator completed all components of the case plan successfully?
5. Has the perpetrator taken responsibility for the past abuse and for refraining from abusive behavior in the future?
6. Has a relapse prevention plan been put in place for the perpetrator, and does he or she display a willingness to comply with it?

Assessment of the readiness of the perpetrator is best performed by a mental health professional. Case managers and foster caregivers may provide additional information through observation of children's behavior prior to caregiver visits and interactions between caregiver and child. A positive assessment is also supported by the presence of a successfully completed case plan. Although mental health evaluations are desirable in near every case, they are often precluded by budgetary problems for less severe cases. In such cases, case managers and judges must rely on case plan outcome as a measure of readiness.

2. Does the Perpetrator Express a Desire for Reunification?

In some instances the former perpetrator may lack the desire for reunification. If this is the case, the child's presence is likely to be seen as burdensome and may be the occasion for further maltreatment. This situation may arise when one caretaker from the source home strongly desires the child's return while the other does not. In either case the likelihood of repeated harm to the child is increased.

The degree to which the perpetrator desires reunification is best assessed by a mental health professional. When a professional opinion is not available, case managers may have in-depth conversations to try to assess perpetrator readiness. Similarly, they should observe interactions between perpetrator and child to determine whether their actions are consistent with their words.

3. Does the Perpetrator Express a Desire for Reunification in Appropriate Terms?

In cases where the sincerity of the perpetrator is in doubt, case managers should carefully monitor the type of response that is given to questions about desire for the child's return. Where financial considerations or the approval of authority figures (e.g., the grandparents) may be an issue, the way in which the perpetrator discusses children and their return may be particularly important. The desire to be with the children should be sincere, as demonstrated by regular visitation with the child, sustained contact with both the child and the case manager, devoted effort on the case plan, and appropriate language used in the expression of desire for the child's return.

Appropriate expression of desire can be assessed by a mental health practitioner or by the case manager. In either instances, the same processes as were described in the previous two questions can be used.

4. Has the Perpetrator Completed All Components of the Case Plan Successfully?

Unless there are extraordinary extenuating circumstances, perpetrators should have successfully completed every component of the case plan before reunification should be considered. Case managers should also be satisfied with the consistency and sincerity of the perpetrator's effort.

To ensure that case plans have been completed, the case manager should thoroughly review the case records. Perpetrators should have completed all requirements, and, ideally, their weaknesses and strengths should have been addressed. Successful completion of a demanding case plan is often powerful evidence of a perpetrator's sincere desire for reunification.

5. Has the Perpetrator Taken Responsibility for the Past Abuse and for Refraining From Abusive Behavior in the Future?

It is critical that perpetrators take full responsibility for their actions, not engaging in excuses or blaming their history of maltreatment on the child or other people. Although the initial response to allegations by many parents is denial, those who are successful in changing their behavior accept the responsibility for what they have done and acknowledge that they are responsible for behaving differently in the future.

Acceptance of responsibility is often assessed by mental health practitioners or by the case manager. It is typically evaluated by asking questions about past incidents of abuse and determining where the perpetrator places the blame. If perpetrators fix blame outside themselves (e.g., on the child or on circumstances), they have likely not fully accepted responsibility for their behavior.

6. Has a FSP Including a Relapse Prevention Component Been Put in Place, and Does the Perpetrator Display a Willingness to Comply With It?

Good case planning requires help in developing strategies that will minimize the probability of maltreatment after reunification. These strategies should include support systems, referrals to resources, contingency plans, and follow-up meetings. Such plans (discussed in greater depth earlier) are often most successful when the perpetrator participates in their development. An unwillingness to participate or disinterest in participating often signals a lack of commitment.

Case mangers should work with all family members to develop the FSP and should obtain the agreement of each to comply with its contents. Involving family members helps to improve the acceptance of the plan and enhance motivation. It also means that family members understand their roles and those of others so that they can support one another in carrying out the plan.

QUESTIONS RELATED TO A NONOFFENDING CARETAKER

Certain questions must also be answered about the nonoffending caretaker. These focus on the well-being of the child, the desire for reunification, and the competence of the caretaker to prevent further maltreatment. Rapid Reference 7.3 summarizes the questions discussed in the following sections.

≡ Rapid Reference 7.3

Questions Related to the Nonoffending Caretaker

1. Does reunification with the nonoffending caretaker appear to be in the child's best interests?
2. Does the nonoffending caretaker express a desire for reunification?
3. Does the nonoffending caretaker understand his or her responsibility in the past abuse and in preventing future abuse?
4. Has the nonoffending caretaker completed all the components of the case plan successfully?
5. Can the nonoffending caretaker understand and verbalize the FSP that has been put in place to avoid further abuse?
6. Has the nonoffending caretaker dealt with his or her own issues related to the abuse?

1. Does Reunification With the Nonoffending Caretaker Appear to Be in the Child's Best Interests?

Under certain circumstances it may not be in the best interests of children to be returned to nonoffending caretakers. If, for instance, the nonoffending caretaker is not competent to provide adequate care or support, reunification may not be desirable. In another example, if the nonoffending caretaker seems unwilling or unable to protect the child against further harm from the perpetrator, reunification may not be appropriate.

This question is best answered by a mental health professional who has had ongoing contact with everyone who will reside in the home after reunification. If the perpetrator is also to be in the home, the professional should, at a minimum, have several interviews with that person. When a professional cannot be involved, case managers should also talk with all those who will reside in the home and should attempt to ascertain what is in the best interests of the child given the likely effect of living with all persons involved.

2. Does the Nonoffending Caretaker Express a Desire for Reunification?

It is important that the nonoffending caretaker express a strong and convincing desire for reunification. Situations in which an offending caretaker is doubtful about a return should be viewed cautiously to determine whether this lack of motivation makes the caretaker less disposed to protect the child from the perpetrator.

The nonoffending caretaker's desire can best be assessed by (a) reviewing case plan compliance, (b) talking with the caretaker, and (c) observing interactions between the caretaker and the child. When the nonoffending caretaker has fully complied with a well-prepared case plan, appropriately expresses the desire to be reunified, and demonstrates that desire in interactions with the child, then there is strong evidence of genuine desire for reunification. When mental health practitioners are involved in the case, their opinions should be sought as well.

3. Does the Nonoffending Caretaker Understand His or Her Responsibility in the Past Abuse and in Preventing Future Abuse?

Nonoffending caretakers must recognize and acknowledge issues related to failure to protect the child from past maltreatment. They must also accept their responsibility to protect the child from future harm. This would require that the caretakers be willing to admit their failures in the past, commit to provide protection in the future, and be able to describe specific actions that might be taken to avert future instances of maltreatment.

This question is best answered by a mental health professional. When this is not an option, the case manager should have a discussion with the caretaker, focusing on perceptions of why the original abuse occurred, what caused the abuse to occur, and what might contribute to abusive situations in the future. Case managers should also ensure that any plans for dealing with circumstances that might lead to maltreatment are well known by the caretaker.

4. Has the Nonoffending Caretaker Completed All the Components of the Case Plan Successfully?

Just as the perpetrator must successfully complete the entire case plan, so must the nonoffending caretaker. Clearly, the two will have had some shared tasks and some individual tasks. The case manager must supervise these processes carefully to ensure that each does the appropriate amount of work on each task. This will help to ensure the appropriate level of commitment and desire on the part of both parties.

This is a critical component of assessing readiness. Whether the person making the recommendation is a mental health practitioner, the case manager, or both, the entire record should be reviewed to determine the degree to which the plan's specifications have been met. If any component has not been met, case managers should at least consider delaying the reunification.

5. Can the Nonoffending Caretaker Understand and Verbalize the FSP That Has Been Put in Place to Avoid Further Abuse?

The caretaker must understand the conditions that may lead to new instances of maltreatment and must be willing to take steps to address those conditions. Verbalizing the plan helps ensure that the caretaker is familiar with it. Listening to the manner in which it is recited may give the case manager some idea of the caretaker's sincerity regarding its implementation.

The caretaker's ability to understand and verbalize the FSP can be assessed by the case manager by simply asking the caretaker to repeat and explain it. Judges sometimes seek answers to this question themselves by asking the caretaker to describe the plan in court.

6. Has the Nonoffending Caretaker Dealt With His or Her Own Issues Related to the Abuse?

Caretakers who have not been perpetrators may face a variety of issues related to the maltreatment. Guilt is often one of these, as caretakers feel shame at not having intervened in the past. Similarly, they may feel powerless against the perpetrator or may blame the victim. These and other issues must be successfully addressed before reunification can be considered.

This question should be answered by a mental health professional. Case managers are unlikely to have the training or experience to deal with these issues, and they are additionally unlikely to be able to devote the time necessary to do so successfully given their other responsibilities.

QUESTIONS RELATED TO THE FAMILY

Additional questions must be asked about other members of the family and about the family as a whole. These questions relate to family issues, resources, and willingness to support the reunification (see Rapid Reference 7.4).

≡Rapid Reference 7.4

Questions Related to the Family

1. Are there issues remaining within the family that need to be dealt with before reunification can occur?
2. Have other family members complied sufficiently with the terms of the case plan?
3. Do all members of the family understand their role in the FSP, and can they express it in an age-appropriate fashion?
4. Are other members of the family sufficiently protected from the potential for abuse?
5. Have other members of the family dealt with their own issues regarding the abuse?

1. Are There Issues Remaining Within the Family That Need to Be Dealt With Before Reunification Can Occur?

Family issues may include scapegoating of the victim, guilt, fear, anger, and an assortment of other conditions. These problems should be dealt with before a child is returned to the source family. Scapegoating occurs when other members of the family single out one individual to be blamed for all the family problems. Often the person who is scapegoated is the one who is abused. The atmosphere of blame is a powerful force in supporting and perpetuating maltreatment. It must be eliminated before a healthy return to the family can be made. Other family members may also be paralyzed into inaction by guilt, fear of the abuser, anger, and other problems. Dealing with these issues will increase the probability of a successful return.

Family issues are often best assessed by a mental health professional, particularly one who is skilled in working with families. When a professional is not available, the case manager should attempt to make this determination through individual and collective discussion with family members.

2. Have Other Family Members Complied Sufficiently With the Terms of the Case Plan?

All members of the family should fulfill their obligations in the case plan. Although the most critical participants are usually the caretakers, failure to participate by siblings and extended family can jeopardize the plan's success. The unwillingness of one family member to participate may not in itself be sufficient to prevent reunification, but its effects should be considered. If, for example, an older sibling refuses to participate in family counseling, this deficiency might be overcome by providing parents with additional training on how to cope with this child.

Family participation can be assessed through a thorough review of the records in which all plan criteria are identified and the degree to which they have been reached is evaluated. The case manager is often able to make this determination.

3. Do All Members of the Family Understand Their Role in the FSP, and Can They Express It in an Age-Appropriate Fashion?

Ideally, every member of the family needs to understand the strategies that have been put in place to avoid the recurrence of maltreatment. If one individual is unable or unwilling to participate fully, the plan can be adapted so that others compensate for the deficiency. Having participants describe the plan and their role in it is an important way of ensuring that they understand the part they must play.

As with the other types of questions, issues regarding the FSP can often be assessed by the case manager through individual discussions with all family members. A collective discussion may also be useful to determine whether members understand how their parts in the plan interact.

4. Are Other Family Members Sufficiently Protected From the Potential for Abuse?

The reintroduction of a child into a home is a happy event, but it is also often a source of increased stress. Resources that are often limited are stretched. Family members are faced with temptation to fall into the old interactional and behavioral patterns that contributed to the original maltreatment. The new skills that family members have developed are sometimes strongly tested. The high stress levels and new challenges may endanger not only the child being returned, but other children as well. The case manager should ensure that resources and strategies are in place to protect other children in the home.

This question is best answered by the case manager and any involved mental health professional working together to assess the situation. Case managers bring expertise in the antecedents of maltreatment in general and of maltreatment within the family in question. Mental health professionals bring more general knowledge of the intrapsychic dynamics of the family with whom they have worked. Those who have provided family counseling may be particularly helpful because they can speak to both individual and family issues.

5. Have Other Members of the Family Dealt With Their Own Issues Regarding the Maltreatment?

Other children may have been traumatized by watching their sibling be harmed. They may experience depression, anxiety, or their own problems with attachment. The case plan should have included treatment for these children, and they should have reached an acceptable point in dealing with these issues before reunification can occur.

When mental health practitioners have been involved in a case, they can address this issue. Alternatively, a professional who has not previously been involved might be asked to assess readiness. When an outside professional is not an option, case managers must use individual and family meetings to develop their own opinions about the readiness of family members.

QUESTIONS RELATED TO OTHER SOCIAL SYSTEMS

The status of the family's social network is often critical to successful reunification. Personal relationships with extended family, friends, and other neighbors can provide important resources. Needed services can be accessed from social service providers, schools, and churches.

Physical needs can often be met through income maintenance programs, medical providers, and housing programs. These resources should be put in place prior to reunification to optimize the probability of success. This should be in the form of a list and narrative included within the FSP. Rapid Reference 7.5 highlights the questions that should be asked regarding other social systems.

1. Have Other Social Systems (Such as Extended Family, Neighbors, and Friends) Been Recruited to Support the Family in an Appropriate Manner?

Many families in which maltreatment occurs are closed systems, insulated from outside influences and therefore from the potential support that others might provide. Extended family, neighbors, and family friends can offer a variety of types of assistance including emotional support, babysitting, and help with housekeeping. During the intervention period, the family should have been taught to value and utilize those resources. The ways in which the family will use these resources should be understood and clearly documented in the FSP.

This question can be answered by formulating a list of all known members of the extended family, friends, and neighbors and by discussing what roles they might play with the family. Family members might then be asked to investigate and report on the willingness of these individuals to perform the identified tasks.

≡ *Rapid Reference 7.5*

Questions Related to Other Social Systems

1. Have other social systems (e.g., extended family, neighbors, and friends) been recruited to support the family in an appropriate manner?
2. Have other social systems (e.g., school, church, and social service providers) been accessed so that ongoing services for special needs will be available?
3. Have other social systems (e.g., income maintenance programs, medical providers, and housing programs) been accessed to ensure that the physical needs of the child and family will be met following reunification?

2. Have Other Social Systems (Such as School, Church, and Social Service Providers) Been Accessed so That Ongoing Services for Special Needs Will Be Available?

Although the conditions that contributed to the original maltreatment should have been addressed during the intervention period, it is likely that the family will require ongoing sources of social support, educational assistance, counseling and psychoeducation, and other services. Before reunification is attempted, family members should know where these resources are located and how they can access them.

To address this question, case managers might begin by developing a list of the family needs that will require ongoing support and the strengths that might best be utilized through ongoing contact with external resources. They could then identify the necessary resources, learn methods of contact, and include the results within the FSP.

3. Have Other Social Systems (Such as Income Maintenance Programs, Medical Providers, and Housing Programs) Been Accessed to Ensure That the Physical Needs of the Child and Family Will Be Met Following Reunification?

In cases where the physical needs of the family may have been a factor in the maltreatment, the case manager should ensure that services are in place to meet those needs. Stressors from finances, medical needs, housing difficulties, and similar conditions can greatly increase the probability that maltreatment will recur. The presence of appropriate services can help to alleviate those stressors.

The same procedure can be used to address this issue as was suggested for Question 2. Needs and strengths should be identified and detailed, resources identified, and contact methods described. The results should be included in the FSP.

DEVELOPMENT OF A FAMILY SAFETY PLAN

The importance of the FSP has surfaced several times in this chapter. The FSP is essentially an organized strategy for family activities that will help to ensure that the gains made by completing the case plan are sustained and that the probability of future maltreatment is minimized. The components of an effective FSP are listed in Rapid Reference 7.6.

It is important to note that the contents and appearance of FSPs may vary between jurisdictions. Some may not include all the components discussed here. Some may include additional components. The structure of each component may also vary. For example, a title other than "antecedent" may be used to describe the situations mentioned in Section 1, or the section may be written as a narrative rather than in numbered sentences.

⁼Rapid Reference 7.6

Components of an Effective Family Safety Plan

1. A description of conditions that may have contributed to maltreatment in the past
2. A series of strategies to use should those conditions recur
3. A list of personal and community resources that the family can access to continue to address its needs and maximize its strengths

Section 1: A Description of Conditions That May Have Contributed to Maltreatment in the Past

Conditions and situations that cause or contribute to maltreatment are often referred to as antecedents. Antecedents may include elevated stress levels, substance abuse, arguments, accidents, and specific types of behaviors or interactions. These should be noted in detail. For example, a plan in which a biological father had been abusive when stressed about finances or when drinking might include the following:

- *Antecedent 1:* Dad sits down to pay the bills and becomes increasingly anxious.
- *Antecedent 2:* Dad shows the physical characteristics (tense manner, short temper, reddened face) of escalating anger.
- *Antecedent 3:* Dad displays both Antecedent 1 and Antecedent 2.
- *Antecedent 4:* Dad displays either Antecedent 1 or Antecedent 2 and is drinking.

As in this example, the presence of multiple antecedents often heightens the risk of abuse. When multiple antecedents are present, more rapid and drastic steps may be necessary.

Section 2: A Series of Strategies to Use Should Those Conditions Recur

For each antecedent, specific strategies should be developed to help avert the recurrence of maltreatment. The descriptions of the strategies should include information about what family members should take what actions and what additional steps should be taken if the initial strategies fail. For example, strategies for dealing with each antecedent may be listed beneath it.

- *Antecedent 1:* Dad sits down to pay the bills and becomes increasingly anxious.
  - *Alternative A:* Mom will remind Dad of his anger and will encourage him to use stress management techniques taught by a mental health professional.
  - *Alternative B:* Older brother will ask Dad to take a break from the bills and join him for a walk or watch a television show with him.
  - *Alternative C:* Grandmother will take the child who has been abused in the past to play in the park while Dad finishes the bills.

- *Antecedent 4:* Dad displays either Antecedent 1 or Antecedent 2 and is drinking.
  - *Alternative A:* Entire family will confront Dad on his behavior and drinking.
  - *Alternative B:* Entire family will leave the house to allow situation to deescalate.

Section 3: A List of Personal and Community Resources

The FSP should contain a list of the needs and strengths of the family along with the resources that can be accessed to help meet the needs or to develop the strengths. In the case of the family mentioned in the previous two sections, the FSP might include the following resources.

- *Antecedent 1:* Dad sits down to pay the bills and becomes increasingly anxious.
  - *Resource A:* Source of financial assistance: County Government Human Services Agency, 777-888-9999
  - *Resource B:* Stress management training: Human Development Agency, 777-111-2222
- *Antecedent 4:* Dad displays either Antecedent 1 or Antecedent 2 and is drinking.
  - *Resource A:* Substance abuse treatment: Addiction Recovery Center, 777-333-4444
  - *Resource B:* Stress management training: Human Development Agency, 777-111-2222

CHAPTER SUMMARY

Reunification is a critical event representing the culmination of the case planning and intervention processes for many children. In order to increase the probability that reunification will be successful, it is important to plan the reunification process carefully, to develop strategies that maximize the probability of success, to develop an effective FSP, and to ensure that the appropriate reunification criteria are met.

TEST YOURSELF

1. **Children who have been removed from abusive homes are always grateful to escape that environment.** True or False?

2. **Often, the first sign that the time to consider reunification is near is a nearly completed case plan.** True or False?

3. **In a reunification plan it is often wise to increase visitation with all family members.** True or False?

4. **Children should be considered safe as long as they are in state custody.** True or False?

5. **The desires of the child regarding reunification are of little importance.** True or False?

6. **Judgment about a child's psychological readiness for treatment can best be made by**

    (a) The case manager

    (b) A mental health practitioner

    (c) A physician

    (d) A judge

7. **Children may be taught to notice indicators of escalating anger in a potential abuser so that they can**

    (a) Telephone the case manager to have their case reopened

    (b) Remove themselves from threatening situations before maltreatment occurs

    (c) Ask a neighbor to observe the interactions with the potential abuser

    (d) Use behavioral interventions to redirect the potential abuser's attention

8. **The sincerity of a former perpetrator's desire to be reunited the child can be assessed by examining**

    (a) Records of psychological treatment, records of medical treatment, records of attendance at 12-step meetings, and the degree to which the FSP concurs with the recommendations of the case manager and the court

    (b) Effectiveness in the use of anger management techniques in therapy, adequate knowledge of nutritional requirements, clear understanding of the accessibility of social service resources, and a clear knowledge of the rules of home safety

(continued)

(c) Interactions with the child, interactions with other family members, interactions with the court, and interactions with other professionals who are involved in the case

(d) A history of visitation with the child, regularity of contact with the child and case manager, degree and consistency of effort on the case plan, and the use of appropriate language in expressing the desire for the child's return

9. Scapegoating occurs when

(a) Perpetrators are excluded from their family because of the maltreatment

(b) The nonoffending perpetrator is blamed for the abuse by the child welfare system

(c) Other members of the family single out one child to be blamed for all of the family's problems

(d) The family grows resentful toward the caseworkers and blames them for family problems

10. The family's personal social network is

(a) Not very important to the success of the reunification

(b) Very important to the success of the reunification

(c) Important only for cases of physical abuse

(d) Important only for cases of neglect

Answers. 1. False; 2. True; 3. True; 4. False; 5. False; 6. b; 7. b; 8. d; 9. c; 10. b.

Eight

ESSENTIALS OF ADOPTION

W hen efforts to reunify children with their source families are not successful, child welfare workers may move for the termination of parental rights (TPR). When parent's rights are terminated, the parents legally cease to be parents, and all their rights and responsibilities as parents are transferred to the state. At this point children have three options, as described in Rapid Reference 8.1. Foster care was discussed in an earlier chapter. Independent living is the subject of the next chapter. The process of adoption is here.

THE TERMINATION OF PARENTAL RIGHTS

As with all the primary processes in child welfare, TPR requires the approval of the court. The decision to proceed with TPR is usually initiated by the recognition of one or more of five conditions: (a) when it is recognized that the source family does not want custody of the child, (b) when it is recognized that the source family is incapable of caring for the child, (c) when the source family cannot be located for an extended period of time, (d) when the source family is deceased, or (e) when no suitable kinship arrangement can be made in which custody can be arranged without TPR. When one or more of these conditions is believed to exist, the case manager, the attorney for the child, or the guardian ad litem may request a hearing to propose TPR and to explain the rationale for their proposal.

A motion to terminate the rights of the parents does not guarantee that the termination will occur. In a TPR hearing members of the source family or their attorney may object to the motion or may offer evidence to counter the claims of those who filed the motion. In some cases they may introduce family

Rapid Reference 8.1

Primary Options for Children Whose Parents Have Had Their Rights Terminated

1. Adoption
2. Long-term foster care
3. Independent living program

members or friends who are willing to take responsibility for the child so that their rights are not terminated.

Although some source families oppose TPR, some do little to prevent it and may even request it. When source families have already had several children removed, they may offer little resistance. In other cases, substance-addicted mothers who have become impregnated while earning money to support their habit may relinquish their rights from the maternity ward.

Judges may decide whether to terminate rights in a single hearing or may request that additional information be provided at a future hearing. Emphasizing the primacy of the family and judges, policy often requires that a high standard of evidence be met to show that TPR is in the child's best interests. The lack of sufficient evidence to warrant termination or a strong challenge from the source family may result in additional hearings.

If parental rights are terminated, case managers are asked to develop a long-term plan for the children involved. They may have come to the hearing with a plan in hand, in which case they might present it to the judge for approval. In other situations the judge might schedule an additional hearing to go over the plan. As mentioned earlier, plans typically have one of three general goals: adoption, long-term foster care, or independent living.

The ideal goal for many children whose parents' rights have been terminated is adoption. In fact, the adoption may already have been in the works if an extended family member or family friend has shown willingness to adopt. In other cases the children may have characteristics that make them easy to place for adoption. Generally, children who are infants, Caucasian, and who display no special needs are relatively easy to place. Older children, minorities, and children with medical problems, learning disabilities, behavioral disorders, and other special needs have historically been more difficult to place (Kapp, McDonald, & Diamond, 2001). In some jurisdictions, children who have reached a designated age (typically early to middle adolescence) may refuse to be adopted. When children are likely to be difficult to place, or when they refuse to be adopted, a goal of long-term foster care or independent living may be accepted. Many jurisdictions also have programs that are intended to facilitate the adoption of children with special needs. These programs are described later in this chapter.

THE ADOPTION PROCESS

Rapid Reference 8.2 presents an overview of the adoption process. Adoption begins with the matching of children and prospective adoptive parents. Parents are recruited to adoption programs through strategies that are similar to those used to recruit foster parents. In fact, many jurisdictions combine their recruitment efforts so that the same funding and outreach efforts are used for both. Indeed, adoptive parents are often found among applicants for foster parenting and among the current foster parents. Relatives, extended family, and friends of the children may also be recruited, as may others who have been close to the children, such as teachers, church members, or neighbors.

Potential adoptive parents may be introduced to children in a variety of ways. They may meet in individual meetings with an adoption worker present but acting as unobtrusively as possible. They may be introduced on a playground with a group of other children or in a meeting at a fast-food restaurant. If the first meeting goes well, additional meetings may be scheduled. As time passes, longer visits are arranged and may even include weekend visits or visits over a period of several days. Adoption workers monitor the progress of both children and prospective parents to determine how likely it is that an adoption might succeed. Mental health professionals might also be consulted regarding the degree to which the prospective family fits the child.

≡Rapid Reference 8.2

An Overview of the Adoption Process

1. Matching children with prospective parents
2. Evaluating compatibility through a series of visits
3. Seeking the approval of the court to proceed
4. Rechecking backgrounds and home environment
5. Getting the court's final approval for the adoption

When the adoption worker believes that the match is suitable and that all parties are ready to proceed, a hearing is scheduled in which the child welfare agency seeks the court's permission to proceed with the adoption. At the hearing, the judge would review the evidence presented and then might order further evaluation to ensure suitability. Even though the prospective adoptive parents would have been thoroughly screened at the time of their recruitment, the judge might order additional background checks, psychological evaluations, and home studies. Although it may seem that these additional studies would be unnecessary, they have sometimes uncovered serious problems in a potential parent's background that have prevented the adoption from proceeding.

The results of the evaluations would then be presented to the judge, who might decide to grant or deny the adoption. If the judge did not approve, contact between the child and the prospective parents would end. If approval were given, the paperwork would be completed to make the prospective parents the legal parents of the child.

It is important to remember that these procedures may vary between jurisdictions. Hearings and investigations may proceed in an order different from the one presented here. In some areas the court's permission may be required to initiate any visits between children and perspective parents. The overall process, however, is fairly consistent between jurisdictions and includes matching children with prospective parents, evaluating their compatibility through a series of visits, seeking the approval of the court to proceed, rechecking backgrounds and home environments, and getting the court's final approval for the adoption.

MATCHING CHILDREN AND FAMILIES

Rapid Reference 8.3 lists the steps to follow in matching children and families for adoption. One of the most important steps in facilitating an adoption is matching the needs of the child with the strengths of the prospective family. This can be conceptualized as a three-step process including (a) identifying the needs of the child, (b) identifying the family's strengths, and (c) assessing the fit between the child's needs and the family's strengths. It is also important to consider any significant weaknesses the family might have or any characteristics that might negatively impact the parent-child relationship.

≡Rapid Reference 8.3

Steps in Matching Children and Families for Adoption

1. Identify the needs of the child
2. Identify the strengths of the family
3. Assess the fit between the child's needs and the family's strengths
4. Consider any significant weaknesses the family might have
5. Consider any characteristics of the family that might negatively impact the parent-child relationship

Identifying the Needs of the Child

Children's needs should be made clear in their case records. Many children receive extensive evaluation during their journey through the child welfare system. Case records should contain a step-by-step recounting of evaluations, interventions, and outcomes. If the records are in order, the adoption worker should be able to compile a list with relative ease. Unfortunately, child welfare records are often abysmal with large gaps in chronologies and omissions of critical information. When case records are incomplete and adoption workers are unable to reconstruct them, adoption workers must conduct a new assessment. This is perhaps best accomplished by using the same tools used to assess children by the protective service workers and by referring them to outside professionals such as psychologists and physicians for in-depth evaluation. Based on the information obtained in the assessment, the adoption worker can prepare a list of the needs experienced by the child that will need to be addressed in the adoptive home.

Identifying the Strengths of the Family

Family strengths can be assessed in a variety of ways. The instruments described in Chapter 3 for assessing the source family can be used by the adoption worker as part of a series of interviews and discussions with family members. Where funds are available, mental health professionals may also be accessed to evaluate families. All the family's strengths should be listed during the assessment process, not simply those that are clearly related to the needs that the child is known to have at the time of the assessment.

Additional needs may be discovered during the adoption process that some of the family strengths may address. In addition, the importance of strengths not seen as relevant early in the assessment process may become clear at some later point.

Family strengths should be listed and thoroughly described. Assessors should be careful to include information about the family as a whole and about its individual members. Sometimes, assets that are not clearly visible in family interactions are more readily recognized in individual members.

Assessing the Fit Between Strengths and Needs

After lists of the child's needs and the family's strengths have been prepared, they should be compared to determine how well they fit. In a good fit, most or all of the child's needs will be clearly addressed by one or more of the family strengths. In other cases, unaddressed needs can be met by providing resources to the family or by ensuring that ongoing services are in place for the child. The fit between a child and an adoptive family can rarely be considered perfect, so the real issue is whether a sufficient degree of fit exists to allow the adoption to be successful and in the best interests of the child. Rapid Reference 8.4 details the questions to raise when considering the fit between family strengths and a child's needs.

The process of determining whether strengths match needs is relatively simple. The list of family strengths is compared to the list of the child's needs. In comparing the lists, the adoption worker must consider not only whether individual needs are met but also the degree to which they are met. For

≡Rapid Reference 8.4

Questions to Answer When Determining the Fit Between Strengths and Needs

1. Do family strengths match the child's needs?
2. Can unmet needs be met by identifying resources to bolster family strengths?
3. Can unmet needs be met by accessing outside resources?
4. Is the degree of fit acceptable when resources are in place?

example, a child who has substantial educational needs might be a good match for a home in which one parent was an elementary school teacher. On the other hand, the degree to which that match would be good might be affected by the amount of time the parent had available to spend with the child. After the lists have been compared, workers can consider whether additional resources might be accessed either to bolster the strengths of the family or to compensate for deficiencies. In the previous situation, for instance, an extended family member might assume some of the teaching parent's other responsibilities to allow for more time with the child. Alternatively, a tutor might be located to help with the child's lessons. The final question about degree of fit is important because perfect matches are rare. Some of the child's needs may not be met by a potential adoptive family, and resources may not be present to address them. If this is the case, caseworkers should try to determine how important that need is and the likelihood that failure to address it will lead to problems after the adoption. Given the problems in many child welfare systems, the worker should also weigh the likelihood that the child may languish in foster care against the probability of problems in the adoptive home.

Considering Family Weaknesses

Potential adoptive families may have problems or weaknesses that are not sufficient to prevent selection as an adoptive family but that can or should be addressed as a part of the adoption process. Those who have weak social support networks, for instance, might be encouraged to develop more and stronger friendships. Those who have financial problems may be referred to income maintenance programs or agencies that provide employment training. Addressing family weaknesses can be critical to the success of the adoptive placement. The presence of a new child in the home can exacerbate stress levels and result in placement problems or even failure.

Considering Other Characteristics

It is also important to consider the unique characteristics of each family when arranging an adoption. In some cases, factors are present that are not weaknesses but still might jeopardize the adoption. An example is a single couple who lives a highly structured, orderly life and is considering adopting a child who has significant behavioral problems. In this case, the couple would need to have a full understanding of the consequences of bringing a child with these kinds of issues into their home. They might need to spend time with a therapist and have the child visit their home for several days at a time on several different occasions. If they seem flexible enough to deal with the change that would inevitably come, the adoption might proceed. If they do not deal well with the challenges presented by a child with behavioral problems, some other alternative might be considered.

PREPARING THE CHILD

In order to strengthen the probability that an adoption will succeed, children need to be prepared in very specific ways. Simply moving them from a foster home to an adoptive home can recreate the trauma experienced when they were taken into custody. By placing them suddenly in an unfamiliar environment, workers would significantly compound the possibility that the adoption might fail.

Dealing With the Child's Issues

One important factor in preparing children for adoption is helping them resolve as many issues related to their maltreatment and experiences in the child welfare system as possible. When the issues cannot be resolved (as is often the case), resources should be put in place to ensure that the issues receive ongoing professional attention. Many children will have difficulty bonding with their new families. Others will be very needy and require a great deal of support and attention. Proper intervention can make the process easier for both children and parents.

Increasing Exposure to the Adoptive Family

Children can also be prepared through increasing exposure to the adoptive family. Early meetings may last only an hour or two and may take place with an adoption worker or foster parent present. As time goes on and the time for the adoption hearing approaches, visits may lengthen to days or weekends without the worker being present. Workers should talk with both children and families following each visit to determine whether any issues or needs have arisen.

Communication Between the Child and All Involved Parties

Children who are old enough to do so often need to communicate about the process with all involved parties, including adoptive parents, adoption workers, foster parents, and, in some cases, the source family. Conversations with adoptive families may include feelings about the impending adoption, hopes for the future, and plans for dealing with issues. Communication with foster parents and adoption workers may include expressions of gratitude, verbalizations of concern, and discussions related to the coming change in their relationships. When source families have maintained contact with a child who is being adopted (e.g., when children are adopted by other family members), issues related to the process may need to be discussed.

Arranging Ongoing Contact With Significant Persons

In some cases it may be appropriate to arrange for children to have ongoing contact with the persons they have known during their time in state custody. They may, for example, want to have regular visits with foster parents, caseworkers, or members of their source families. In many cases these kinds of visits may be beneficial to children. If they are desirable, arrangements should be made with all parties before the adoption is made official. All parties should understand whether such visits will occur and the procedures that will be followed if they do.

PREPARING THE FAMILY

Preparation of an adoptive family can be viewed as a five-step process: recruitment, screening, assessment, training, and integration. The specifics of the process may vary between jurisdictions, but each of these elements should always be present.

Recruitment

Adoptive parents may be recruited along with foster parents or through separate processes. Recruitment is sometimes accomplished through broad processes targeting large groups of people. Examples include media advertising, speaker's bureaus, and visits to religious organizations. At other times recruitment may be very focused, such as when an extended family member or family friend is asked to consider adoption. An active recruitment program is essential to successful adoptions. Many families might be willing to consider adoption yet will not take the first step without some prompting. Many agencies have developed very creative ways of making potential parents aware. For example, many have used catchy billboard advertising, television spots, videotapes, and other media to enhance public awareness.

The down side of mass advertising is that people who are not desirable adoptive parents may apply. This necessitates an effective screening process that includes background checks, home visits, psychological testing, and intensive counseling by adoption workers during the training process. Persons who are recruited individually must go through the same processes.

Screening

Screening occurs in stages beginning with the initial interview and continuing up to the moment of adoption. In the initial conversations between recruiters and prospective parents, questions are asked about the recruit's legal history, motivation for adoption, parenting philosophies, and other relevant topics. The recruiter also shares information about the adoption as well as the challenges presented by adoptive parenting. Some applicants are eliminated from the process at that point, either because the screener recognizes something about them that would make them undesirable or because the applicants recognize that adoption is not for them. Those who pass the initial interview receive a background check in which police records and child welfare agency records are checked. Different jurisdictions have different criteria for excluding prospects. Most, perhaps all, exclude those who have a history as a perpetrator of abuse. Some exclude anyone who has committed a felony. Others allow felons to proceed as long as the felony was not violent and no effort was made to conceal the history of offense.

Applicants who pass the background check may receive psychological assessment. Although not all jurisdictions include psychological assessment, many have a system in which some sort of formal testing is done. For some it might be a simple pen-and-paper questionnaire that is scored by the recruiter. For others there might be interviews with a mental health professional. Those who pass the assessment are able to begin the training process.

Training procedures and curricula vary across jurisdictions. Most training programs, however, provide opportunities for self-screening by recruits who discover that the rigors of parenting are not for them and for the trainers to "counsel out" those who they believe are not well suited to adoptive parenting.

Screening also occurs in the matching process described earlier. The final screening occurs in the courtroom, where the judge must be convinced that it is appropriate to proceed. It is interesting to note that new information about the background of recruits sometimes comes to light during adoption hearings. More than one adoption has been halted in its late stages because someone uncovered a previously unknown problem.

Screening represents an attempt to identify characteristics of potential adoptive parents that might make them unsuitable for that responsibility. Rycus and Hughes (1998) identified twelve categories of problems that might exclude an applicant from becoming an adoptive parent. These categories can be found in Rapid Reference 8.5.

It is important to remember that falling into one of these categories may not automatically result in exclusion. For instance, a single incident of domestic violence many years ago may not be sufficient to cause an applicant to be screened out. Similarly, having experienced childhood maltreatment may not be a barrier as long as the applicant has received treatment and appears to have dealt with those issues so that they will not cause difficulties in the adoption.

Assessment

Applicants who pass through screening often progress to an assessment stage. As mentioned earlier, this may be as simple as the completion of a questionnaire or an interview with an experienced adoption worker. In other cases it may involve interviews with and evaluation by a mental health professional. Assessment is a point at which the significant strengths and weaknesses begin

≡Rapid Reference 8.5

Characteristics Indicating Potential Screen-Out for Prospective Parents

1. Either having been the perpetrator of sexual abuse or having some significant sexual disorder such as pedophilia or voyeurism
2. Being an active substance abuser
3. Suffering from a current, untreated severe mental illness such as schizophrenia, bipolar disorder, or paranoia
4. Having been the perpetrator of some form of maltreatment of a child in the past
5. Having a history of arrest and conviction, particularly for felonies
6. Having a history of domestic violence as perpetrator, particularly repeated incidents
7. Having a history of substance abuse with a short-term recovery period
8. Having unresolved issues related to one's own experience of maltreatment in childhood
9. Having unrealistic expectations for the behavior of children
10. Having had significant problems raising one's own children
11. Having a history of recurrent problems with a mental illness or psychological disorder
12. Having significant family problems or problems within the social support network

to be noted, providing information that can be used later in the matching process. Assessment also helps workers identify family needs that can be addressed through referral to resources and serves as yet another opportunity for screening. Many mental health problems, for example, are uncovered during the assessment stage. There are also cases in which recruits may be referred for specialized assessment. One example would be a prospective parent who reports a history of substance abuse. If adoption workers suspected that the abuse was ongoing, such an individual might be referred to a substance abuse specialist for evaluation.

During assessment, workers and professionals look for the presence of or the opportunity to develop certain characteristics. Rycus and Hughes (1998) provided a list of 10 such characteristics, which are outlined in Rapid Reference 8.6.

≡ *Rapid Reference 8.6*

Desirable Characteristics for an Adoptive Family (Rycus & Hughes, 1998)

1. Appropriate expectations and motivation for adopting a child
2. Sufficient personal maturity to deal with the stressors presented by adoption
3. Stability and strength in relationships within the family and the family's social support network
4. Effective characteristics, skills, and strategies for dealing with stressors
5. Strong family links with the world outside the family such as friends and community groups
6. Adequate parenting skills and attitudes toward parenting
7. Strong social skills, particularly empathy, and perspective-taking
8. A strong belief in their rights as parents to act in their child's best interests
9. An active, hands-on parenting style
10. A genuine, long-term commitment to effectively parenting the child

It is important to remember that the assessment is intended to determine whether these characteristics or the capacity to develop them exists within a recruited family. In some cases these characteristics may be developed or strengthened by the child welfare agency's training program. In other cases a referral to some outside resource may be enough to help the recruited family make the necessary changes.

Training

The next step in the preparation of adoptive parents is training. Another possible point for screening out those who may not do well as adoptive parents, the training period is also intended to (a) provide families with critical information about child welfare, the consequences children experience from maltreatment, and the ways in which those consequences may affect an adoptive family; (b) provide them with basic information and skills to deal with the challenges of adoption; (c) allow trainees to begin to develop relationships with trainers and adoption workers; and (d) facilitate the development of relationships with other parents who are experiencing the same process.

Training programs generally contain material from several areas. Minimally, they should cover the following topics:

1. An overview of the child welfare system focusing on what children experience after they are taken into custody.
2. A discussion of the adoption process, including a summary of the legal process, a description of the function of the child welfare agency, and an outline of the role and responsibility of the adoptive parents.
3. Self-assessment and training on how to use community resources to maximize strengths and address weaknesses.
4. Information on problems related to attachment disorders, mental health problems, and separation issues along with strategies for dealing with them.
5. The short- and long-term effects of maltreatment on child development.
6. Parenting techniques for children who have experienced various types of maltreatment (sexual, physical, neglect, abandonment).
7. Parenting techniques for managing behavioral problems.
8. Parenting techniques for normal behavioral management.
9. Understanding and supporting the participation of others who may need to remain in contact with the child (caseworker, foster parent, source family).
10. Communicating with a child about adoption and the issues related to it.

Matching

Those who complete training await the matching process discussed earlier. In some jurisdictions, in fact, matching begins during training or before. Many child welfare systems are overburdened and underfunded, needing more adoptive parents than they can recruit. In these settings there is often pressure to identfy suitable parents as early as possible. In fact, when relatives or friends of a child's family are being considered, the matching process actually begins in the earliest stages of the process.

Integration

The word *integration* is used here to refer to the process of gradually integrating the child into the family through the strategies discussed earlier in the chapter, such as counseling, psychoeducation, and visitation. This is the final step in the process of preparing the family. After a suitable period of integration, the hearing to determine whether adoption will occur is scheduled. The integration period is discussed in greater detail in a subsequent section.

PREPLACEMENT SERVICES

The term *preplacement services* is used in various ways across jurisdictions. In this section it is used to indicate services delivered during the integration period. Preplacement services are designed and delivered with very specific goals in mind. Those goals may be conceptualized as goals related to the adjustment of the child, to the preparation of the adoptive family, to the relationship between child and adoptive family, and to the soon-to-be integrated family and its social systems.

Goals Related to the Adjustment of the Child

The preplacement goals for the child include minimizing the stress associated with a move to the adoptive home, helping the child develop a feeling of involvement and participation in the process, laying the groundwork for the development of positive new relationships, and providing an environment in which future issues can be effectively addressed. The services provided during this period should be directed toward those goals.

The move to a new home is likely to be stressful for children, even when the move is a natural part of the adoption process and is very much desired. Children have been through the process of removal from their source home and resettlement in at least one other home. Many have moved through a series of homes before they are matched with prospective adoptive parents. Each of these moves will have generated some degree of stress as the children have adjusted to strange new environments, new sets of norms and values, and different interactive styles within the home.

It is also important that children feel that they have been involved in the process of preplacement planning. Many of the children in state custody have felt that they have little control over their lives from the day of their birth. Their experiences in child welfare are unlikely to have improved their perceptions. They may have been removed from their source homes against their will, shuttled through a series of temporary homes that they did not choose, and finally matched with an adoptive family that they did not select. Participating in the planning of the integration process may provide them with some sense of participation in and control over their own lives.

A third goal is laying the groundwork for the development of positive new relationships. Some children will have enhanced their ability to form attachments during their time in the child welfare system. Many others will have remained unchanged or will have had their ability to bond with others, particularly adults, even further weakened. The integration period is a time in which attachments can be encouraged and the beginnings of positive relationships can be promoted.

Preplacement services should also provide an environment in which future issues can be effectively addressed. Adoption is often a challenging process even for families that have been well-prepared. Problems and issues inevitably arise, many of which may have been unanticipated. Although it may be impossible to anticipate every challenge, it is possible to equip the family with resources to deal with many of those problems.

Goals Related to the Preparation of the Adoptive Family

The adoptive family must be prepared with information about the child, about the child's social systems, and about dealing with specific problems the child may experience. While the training period included general information about adoption and adoptive children, the integration phase focuses on information and skills specific to the child selected for adoption.

Adoptive families must receive extensive information about the children being integrated with them. They must know about psychological and behavioral issues, medical problems, educational status, religious preferences, and cultural characteristics. In addition, they should become familiar with the child's likes, dislikes, habits, fears, hopes, and other personal factors. Knowing what to expect and how to deal with it is a significant help to the adoptive family.

Parents will also need information about children's social systems. It may be in the best interests of some children to maintain contact with source families, foster families, case managers, guardians ad litem, and others with whom they have become close. They may also have friends from before or during their time in state custody with whom ongoing contact may be important. Parents should also be made aware of schools they have attended, programs in which they have participated, and other places from which they may have made friends or derived social support.

Adoptive families should also be prepared to deal with specific problems children may have or experience. They should receive thorough education about any psychological, medical, behavioral, educational, and social issues children may have and be taught specific techniques for dealing with those issues.

Goals Related to the Relationship Between Child and Adoptive Family

The integration period should also be a time in which relationships between adoptive families and children are developed and strengthened. This is usually accomplished through a series of visits between families and children that are closely monitored by adoption workers. The visits are often followed by debriefing sessions in which case managers or mental health professionals discuss thoughts and feelings about the visits with both children and families.

Goals Related to the Soon-to-Be Integrated Family and Its Social Systems

It is important to ensure that adequate resources are in place to make the adoption as positive as possible. This includes both the personal support network and the social service network. Adoption workers should implement strategies to ensure that the following conditions are met.

In the personal support network, workers should attempt to ensure that extended family members and friends are aware of and supportive of the adoption. Those who are particularly close to the family may need some personal information about the child and some understanding of the issues that may be involved in the early part of the adoption. Those who will be involved in child care or family activities may need more detailed information.

≡*Rapid Reference 8.7*

Strategies for Successful Integration

- *Communication:* There should be regular meetings between all parties.
- *Planning:* The visitation plan should include date, times, lengths, and locations of the visits between families and children.
- *Visitation:* The visitation process should gradually intensify.
- *Additional service provision:* These should be utilized when necessary.

The social service support network is also critical. The process of putting resources in place was discussed as a part of the family safety plan. The plan is often developed during the integration phase.

Strategies for Successful Integration

The goals for the integration period are met through the use of specific strategies that are summarized in Rapid Reference 8.7.

Communication is critical for and between all parties. Workers should arrange to have regular meetings with everyone involved to explore thoughts and feelings and to facilitate interaction. If misunderstandings arise, they should be addressed as soon as possible.

Planning is also vital. A visitation plan should be worked out that specifies dates, times, lengths, and locations of the visits between families and children. Both adoptive parents and children should be included in the planning process, as should others (e.g., source or foster parents) who may be involved.

The *visitation* process should gradually intensify. The initial visit should be in a place that is very safe and comfortable to the child and should be of a relatively short duration (probably no more than an hour or two). Later visits may move to a neutral location such as a park or restaurant and should last for longer times. Still later visits should move into the adoptive home and should be extended first to overnight and then to several days.

When problems arise during the integration process, workers should determine whether additional *service provision* is necessary. When problems are sufficient to require additional intervention, workers should immediately arrange referrals. All parties should then discuss whether the situation requires a revision of the integration plan.

Special Situations

Special situations may allow or require modification of these processes. When foster parents adopt children already living in their home, for example, a visitation plan is clearly unnecessary. Similarly, when relatives adopt a child, it is unlikely that they will need as much background information as adoptive parents who did not previously know the child. It is vital, however, that workers not neglect critical processes in these kinds of situations. Familiarity between parents and children does not mean, for example, that additional services may not be necessary to support the adoption process.

POSTPLACEMENT SERVICES

Postplacement services refers to a set of services provided to the child and adoptive family after the child has been placed in the home and after the adoption process has been completed. The primary objectives of these services are much like those for preplacement. They are essentially directed toward meeting the needs of the child and family as described earlier and, in addition, toward enhancing the relationships within the newly reconstituted family.

Although the goals for postplacement are similar to those for preplacement, the emphasis shifts to maintenance rather than preparation. For example, issues identified during preplacement may not have been fully addressed prior to the actual move-in date. Intervention during postplacement would focus on maintaining and furthering gains made during preplacement. Similarly, as new issues arise in family relationships as the family spends increasing amounts of time together, workers would focus on strengthening the bonds developed during preplacement.

One important aspect of postplacement services that typically does not receive much attention in preplacement is crisis intervention. Introducing a new child into a family system brings with it many changes. These changes may produce reactions from any or all members of the family. When these reactions are intense, crises often result. If managed improperly, these crises can result in instability or disruption of the placement. Postplacement service workers monitor homes to detect escalating problems and provide intervention where necessary.

When problems are detected, postplacement workers begin with a thorough assessment. The assessment is directed toward determining what factors may have created or contributed to the problem. They develop an intervention, often working with family members to plan it, and then participate in carrying it out. Once the situation is stabilized, workers focus on helping the family develop strategies to avoid the recurrence of the conditions that produced the crisis.

Postplacement services should also include a plan in which ongoing services are identified and listed to facilitate the process of reaching the goals. The plan should be sufficiently specific that all participants understand their roles, yet sufficiently flexible to adapt to evolving circumstances and crisis events. As with the preplacement plan, the postplacement plan should be developed in a collaborative process between workers and family.

DISRUPTIONS

Researchers have clearly identified the processes experienced by adoptive families. For some families these processes result in successful outcomes in which the adopted child and the new family remain happily together. For others the process breaks down, and children are removed from the home forever. Understanding these processes is vital to the success of the family and of postplacement planning. The stages on which the following sections are based, were identified by Partridge (1991), were described by Rycus and Hughes (1998), (see Rapid Reference 8.8 for a summary).

≡Rapid Reference 8.8

Typical States in a Failed Adoption

- The honeymoon
- Diminishing pleasures
- Blaming the child for the problem
- Looking outside for support
- The critical moment
- The ultimatum
- The last straw
- The decision
- The aftermath

The Honeymoon

The honeymoon period is the period immediately after the adoption's finalization. The family members are excited and enthusiastic. All are on their best behavior and are hoping for the best. Behaviors and attitudes that may be resented later are accepted or even appreciated during this stage.

Intervention does not seem necessary at this point, yet the effective postplacement worker will be aware of signs of impending problems. Questions such as, "How do you think you will feel about that if it happens in 6 months?" and "How are you going to handle that situation if it continues?" may help parents prepare for future events. Similarly, for children who are old enough to understand, workers and mental health professionals can work with children and parents to modify behavioral problems before they reach crisis proportions.

Diminishing Pleasures

The second stage in the escalation of problems in an adoptive family has been referred to as diminishing pleasures. In this stage the initial euphoria and excitement have worn off, and the family members are confronted by the reality of learning to live together. The parents are increasingly intolerant of the adopted child's attitudes and behaviors. The child may become increasingly resistant or may begin to act out in more extreme ways. Family relationships become increasingly strained.

The period of diminishing pleasures is critical for sustaining the adoptive family. Intervention at this stage has a very good chance of preventing further deterioration and is often more effective than is intervention in later stages. Interventions may include counseling for parents and the application of behavior modification techniques with children. Parents may need to develop more realistic expectations for the children's behavior, learn new parenting and behavioral modification techniques, and learn new anger management techniques.

The Adopted Child Is Seen as the Problem

During this blaming period, the parents develop a negative, accusatory attitude toward the child. Tension rises, and parents become increasingly intolerant. Children may respond in a variety of ways, including open hostility, passive aggression, depression, withdrawal, or similar behaviors. Their reactions provoke further reaction and blaming from the parent so that the problems in the family enter a period of cyclic escalation.

Intervention during the blaming period may be more difficult than in the earlier periods because ideas about and attitudes toward other members of the adoptive family may have developed. Counseling is likely to be necessary for all parties to counter the assumptions that underlie the blame and behavioral problems. Parents may need the same type of parenting and behavioral management training offered in the second stage, but perhaps more intensively. They may also need more active encouragement from the worker to use those techniques, particularly if they appear to have failed. Children may need counseling and, depending on their age, may respond well to anger management or other social skills training.

Going Public

After blaming, but keeping most of the trouble private, the family may take their woes to friends, relatives, neighbors, and others. Sometimes the decision is not made by the family but is forced by children's behavior at school, a recreational program, or a religious function. At other times, particularly if the behavioral problems are focused in the home, parents may begin to discuss the problems with those with whom they are close. The advice parents receive from outside sources—surprisingly enough, even from schools and religious sources—is often very biased and reinforces their inaccurate perceptions of the problem. Children are likely to sense extraordinary hostility and may return it openly. They are also very likely to fear that maltreatment will occur or that they will be taken into custody again.

Intervention at this stage is difficult, in part because the problem has progressed so far and in part because parents may now be receiving biased advice and support from outside sources. Parents are likely to need counseling, lessons in child management and behavior modification, and instruction regarding the advice of inexperienced outsiders. Visits with other adoptive parents who have reached this stage and have worked out issues with their adopted children may be helpful. Families may also benefit from a respite arrangement in which the child stays with another family for brief periods of time. Children will need counseling, emotional support, and behavioral guidance. Often, they can benefit from spending time with adults with whom they have had a positive relationship in the past.

The Turning Point

At the turning point, the events that have led to the growing alienation between parents and children come to a head. Some major event, such as a theft, a disruptive temper tantrum, an act of violence, or sexually inappropriate behavior, causes parents to decide that they have had enough. They begin to consider ways to terminate the adoption.

Intervention at this stage is very difficult and often impossible. After parents have reached the point that they are willing to give up on the child, a tremendous psychological barrier stands in the way of successful intervention. Children, too, are likely to be emotionally wounded and exceptionally unhappy with their living arrangements and their lives. Only with extraordinary intervention, perhaps with the child on respite from the home, can there be any real hope of success. Workers would do well to consider at this point whether the probability of failure and its concurrent damage outweighs the probability of success.

The Deadline or Ultimatum

Parents who have passed the turning point often establish an imaginary line at some point in the future beyond which they are not willing to go with the child. They may establish some goal (often unrealistic) that the child must reach. For example, they might tell children with anger management problems that they must go for one month without losing their temper. If they lose their temper only once, they will have to leave.

Once again, intervention at this point is difficult if not impossible. Strong emotions will be present on both sides. Many parents at this stage may have already decided that they want children out of their homes but are looking for something to provide justification for their actions. They see the failure to make the deadline as justification to themselves and others that they have made every effort to keep the child. Children may be no more amenable to intervention at this point than parents. It is likely that the trauma they experienced in their source home, their removal, and perhaps in their journey through a series of foster homes has been recreated to the point that they do not want to be in the home.

The Final Crisis

The final crisis may preclude the ultimatum. Frequently, families in which relationships have deteriorated to this point find that some incident occurs that, whether big or small, is sufficient in the minds of the parents to warrant disruption. The final crisis generates substantial trauma and instability. Intervention is unlikely to be successful after this point.

The Decision to Disrupt

Following the child's failure to meet the ultimatum or some final crisis, the family is likely to request the child's removal. When workers have been in touch with the family, this should have been anticipated or perhaps precluded by an earlier removal. Requests for removal may also come from a child or some involved professional. Children should be moved to a safe alternative home as quickly as possible.

The Aftermath

Both child and family are likely to have experienced significant emotional trauma and injury as a result of their experiences. Although there may be a tendency to try to gloss over the experience and move on, the child should have conversations with the caseworker and receive supportive professional services. If the family is willing, they should also receive professional help.

Adoption disruption can be devastating, but it can also be avoided in many cases. One of the keys to effective postplacement services is a strong and consistent relationship between the worker and all members of the adoptive family. The postplacement plan should cover all known contingencies, and regular visits with both child and family should alert the worker to the need for intervention.

CHAPTER SUMMARY

Adoption is a wonderful alternative for some children who cannot return to their source families and who are willing to allow an adoption to proceed (Triseliotis, 2002). The process has a number of steps, each of which should be carefully followed. Careful attention to the processes known to be effective can strongly increase the probability of an adoption's success.

 TEST YOURSELF

1. **When efforts to reunify children with their source families are not successful, child welfare workers may move for the termination of parental rights (TPR).** True or False?

2. **Policy emphasizes the primacy of the family, and judges often require that a high standard of evidence be met to show that TPR is in the best interests of the child.** True or False?

3. **Parents are recruited to adoption programs through strategies that are similar to those used to recruit foster parents.** True or False?

4. **The procedures used by child welfare agencies and juvenile courts do not vary between jurisdictions.** True or False?

5. **Children's case records should contain a step-by-step recounting of evaluations, interventions, and outcomes that children have experienced while in the child welfare system.** True or False?

6. **After lists of the child's needs and the family's strengths have been prepared, they should be compared to**

   (a) Determine whether the child's needs are too extraordinary for adoption

   (b) Determine whether a family is suitable to adopt

   (c) Determine the degree of case manager involvement needed

   (d) Determine how well they fit

7. **Potential adoptive parents who have weak social support networks might be encouraged to**

   (a) Develop more and stronger friendships

   (b) Seek counseling for their antisocial ways

   (c) Seek mental health counseling

   (d) Move to a new community

(continued)

8. Early meetings between children and prospective adoptive parents should take place

(a) In a place where the child feels secure

(b) In the prospective parent's home

(c) In a child welfare case manager's office

(d) In the office of a mental health professional

9. Preparation of an adoptive family can be viewed as a five-step process

(a) Recognition, recruitment, involvement, review, and assignment

(b) Identification, screening, assessment, integration, and evaluation

(c) Recruitment, screening, assessment, training, and integration

(d) Identification, recruitment, assessment, training, and integration

10. Among other things, the training period for potential adoptive parents is intended to

(a) Expose them to the children with whom they have been matched

(b) Provide them with an opportunity to self-select out of the program

(c) Get to know the upper-level administration in the child welfare system

(d) Interest them in switching to the foster parent program

Answers. 1. True; 2. True; 3. True; 4. False; 5. False; 6. d; 7. a; 8. a; 9. c; 10. b.

Nine

ESSENTIALS OF INDEPENDENT LIVING

The last several years have brought increasing concern about the problems experienced by children who spend years in the child welfare system and then "age out" into a world for which they are virtually unprepared (Collins, 2001). Recently, a number of policy initiatives at both federal and state levels have created an assortment of programs for these children (Stoner, 1999). The programs are designed to support the transition from foster care to self-sufficient living for children who (a) are currently in foster care and recognized as unlikely to leave that program before their 18th birthday, (b) have recently left foster care because they have reached the age of emancipation but have not yet reached 21 years of age, and (c) have been in foster care in the past but are currently homeless or on runaway status from foster care and have not yet reached the age of 21. Programs for the first two categories of children are referred to as *independent living*. Programs for the homeless and those on runaway status are referred to as *transitional living*.

The structure of the independent living program is very different from the other components of the child welfare system such as protective services, foster care, or adoptions. In the other programs federal guidelines are very specific, leading to some consistency in the structure of these programs across jurisdictions. The federal law creating independent living is much more general, however, naming broad categories of services to be provided and leaving the decision to state and local child welfare agencies to decide what the structure of the program will be. To understand how these programs operate in different jurisdictions, it is important to know some basics of the laws that have created them.

FEDERAL POLICY

Independent living as it is today was created by the Foster Care Independence Act (FCIA) of 1999, often referred to as the Chafee Act in honor of one of its primary sponsors, Senator John H. Chafee. Replacing and improving upon an older independent living program, the FCIA designated federal dollars for states that developed programs, defined goals that the programs should be designed to meet, gave general guidelines for eligibility, and identified categories of service that children should receive. The states were given a great deal of latitude in how to accomplish these goals. The result has been very different kinds of programs between states and jurisdictions, all directed toward the goals required by the Chafee Act (FCIA, 1999).

The *goals* identified in the act are listed in its discussion of its purpose:

(a) Purpose—The purpose of this section is to provide States with flexible funding that will enable programs to be designed and conducted

(1) to identify children who are likely to remain in foster care until 18 years of age and to help these children make the transition to self-sufficiency by providing services such as assistance in obtaining a high school diploma, career exploration, vocational training, job placement and retention, training in daily living skills, training in budgeting and financial management skills, substance abuse prevention, and preventive health activities (including smoking avoidance, nutrition education, and pregnancy prevention);

(2) to help children who are likely to remain in foster care until 18 years of age receive the education, training, and services necessary to obtain employment;

(3) to help children who are likely to remain in foster care until 18 years of age prepare for and enter postsecondary training and education institutions;

(4) to provide personal and emotional support to children aging out of foster care, through mentors and the promotion of interactions with dedicated adults; and

(5) to provide financial, housing, counseling, employment, education, and other appropriate support and services to former foster care recipients between 18 and 21 years of age to complement their own efforts to achieve self-sufficiency and to assure that program participants recognize and accept their personal responsibility for preparing for and then making the transition from adolescence to adulthood. (FCIA, 1999)

General *eligibility* guidelines were set by the FCIA. Much discretion was also left to the states, however. For example, the act uses the phrase "children who are likely to remain in foster care" as a standard for receiving services. It offers no assistance, however, in determining how states might decide which children are likely to remain in state custody until the age of 18. The result has been a broad range of approaches between jurisdictions.

The categories of service provided by the act were also identified in the statement of purpose just presented. Extracted from the rest of that text, the categories of service included for children in foster care and those children between the ages of 18 and 21 who have been in foster care can be found in Rapid Reference 9.1. The Act also provided opportunities for health care by allowing states to offer Medicaid coverage to both categories of children.

The FCIA also provided funding for the proposed services along with guidelines that states could follow in applying for the money and instructions for the development of a five-year plan for the implementation of funded programs. Within these broad guidelines, states have been free to develop their own sets of programs and approaches.

STATE POLICY

The approaches of the different states to the implementation of the FCIA have varied widely (see Rapid Reference 9.2 for two examples). For instance, one state might respond to the requirement that independent living programs provide assistance to children to ensure that they complete their high school education by developing school-based tutoring programs in partnership with the school system. Another state might provide assistance to foster parents that would help them provide educational support for the children. In response to the requirement that 18- to 21-year-olds be given assistance with housing, one state might issue a room-and-board payment to the program recipient, while another might pay the money directly to the landlord.

≡ *Rapid Reference 9.1*

Services Available for Children in Foster Care

1. Assistance in obtaining a high school diploma
2. Career exploration
3. Vocational training
4. Job placement and retention
5. Training in daily living skills
6. Training in budgeting and financial management skills
7. Substance abuse prevention
8. Preventive health activities
9. Education, training, and services necessary to obtain employment
10. Help to prepare for and enter postsecondary education
11. Personal and emotional support

Services Available for Children Between 18 and 21 Who Have Been in Foster Care

1. Financial assistance
2. Housing
3. Counseling
4. Employment
5. Education
6. Other appropriate support

One plan calls for the use of classes and training sessions using resources that are already available. The other proposes similar activities but intends to use partnerships with external resources to accomplish the same goal. Clearly, as suggested by Rapid Reference 9.2, independent living workers in Tennessee would be likely to engage in very different activities than would the workers in Georgia.

Many states use some system of case management by an employee of the child welfare agency or an agency with which it contracts. In some states case managers supply many of the direct services. In other states they engage only in assessment, referral, and advocacy activities.

SAMPLE CASES

Just as activities may vary between jurisdictions, they may also vary by the category of youth served. Children who have not yet reached the age of

≣*Rapid Reference 9.2*

A Comparison of State Responses to One Goal of the Foster Care Indpendence Act

GOAL: "to help youths receive education, training, and services necessary to obtain employment"

Tennessee

1. "Provide independent living classes".
2. "Encourage, support, and advocate for youths to obtain job training in the community".
3. "Assist youths in completing applications, resumes, mock interviews, and identifying references" (University of Tennessee, 2002).

Georgia

1. "Utilize the Interest Determination, Exploration, and Assessment System (IDEAS) to formally assess vocational aptitude and to assist youth in career goal setting."
2. "Through workshops, conferences, and mentoring programs young adults will be exposed to professionals representing a variety of employment fields."
3. "Through collaboration with the Department of Labor and Workforce Development, youth are provided summer and long-term employment opportunities." (Houston, 2001).

emancipation may receive services built around the foster home or institution in which they live. Those who are aging out of foster care may transition into university housing or an apartment. Those who have been homeless or on runaway status may need immediate services to help them find the basics such as shelter, food, and clothing.

In the Foster Home

Children who are residing in foster homes and have been recognized as unlikely to leave foster care before their 18th birthdays are likely to receive services that are built, at least to some extent, around the home or institution in which they reside. Because housing is not an issue for them, room-and-board payments are not an issue. Rather, services and program dollars can focus on education, training, mentoring, and the other components of the FCIA.

DON'T FORGET

Just as activities may vary between jurisdictions, they may also vary by the category of youth served.

Many independent living programs use case managers who engage in the familiar process of assessment, case planning, intervention, and evaluation. Although much of the information they need for the assessment may be available in the case file, the assessment for readiness for independent living is likely to require different kinds of information than are found in standard foster care assessments. The services identified in the FCIA address the areas that need to be considered and are summarized in Rapid Reference 9.3.

One of the areas where assessment is critical is *education*. This is implicit within the FCIA's requirements for assistance in obtaining a high school diploma, career exploration, and vocational training. Effective assessment includes determining both children's current grade and their actual level of functioning. It also requires an understanding of their career interests and goals, their interests and hobbies, and their natural strengths and capacities. Educational assessment is perhaps best done through referral to those trained in professional educational testing. Where this is not possible, some computerized programs or pen-and paper instruments can be administered by the case manager. One example is the Interest Determination, Exploration, and Assessment System (IDEAS) included in the Georgia plan.

Another critical area for assessment is *career planning*. Career planning is closely related to education for several reasons. First, children's educational plans must be considered. If they want to attend college, they will need to be

⩵Rapid Reference 9.3

Critical Areas for Independent Living Assessment

- Education
- Career planning
- Daily living skills
- Financial management
- Personal care and prevention
- Housing plans
- Personal emotional preparation

prepared accordingly. If not, vocational training may be a possibility. If children do not want additional schooling, the assessment should focus on identifying the types of jobs they might want and might do well in and on strengths and weaknesses related to getting those jobs.

The third critical area for assessment is *daily living skills*. These include such activities as housekeeping, cooking, doing laundry, driving, accessing public transportation, and shopping. In order to live independently, foster children will need to be able to do these things successfully.

Financial management capabilities should also be assessed. Youths who live on their own will need to be able to budget, plan, maintain checking and savings accounts, and use ATM and credit cards. Those who lack knowledge and skills in any of these areas will need assistance in developing those capacities.

Personal care and prevention is used here to refer to the FCIA's requirements concerning substance abuse prevention and preventive health activities. In fact, the entire area of hygiene, nutrition, healthy behavior, access to medical and dental resources, and medical insurance is vitally important. Case managers determine what children need in each of these areas.

It is also important to know what children who will be leaving foster care will be doing for housing. For some (e.g., those who will be attending college), the decision may be as simple as an apartment or dormitory. Others will need to consider how to obtain suitable housing, whether to live with roommates, and how to screen prospective roommates. Case managers need to know the degree to which housing is an issue and what skills and knowledge youths need in order to be able to acquire it.

Personal emotional preparation is another important issue for children who will be leaving foster care. This issue may be best answered by consultation with a mental health professional. If the professional recognizes that work is needed to prepare the child, services could then be delivered.

Based on the assessment of these areas, the case manager would work in collaboration with children, foster families, and other significant persons to develop a case plan. The case plan would then become the basis for the intervention. Case planning was discussed in great depth in an earlier chapter. Here it should suffice to say that the same method for developing the plan that was described there can be used for this plan. It is even more important at this stage that children be included in the planning. This will improve their level of acceptance and give them a greater feeling of control over their future. It also models an effective planning process for them.

Putting It Into Practice

Problem Statement

Sherry is a 16-year-old African American girl who has declined to be considered for adoption. She currently resides with a foster family (the Greens) and has resided with them for the past four years. She has resided in three other foster homes since being removed from her mother's home at the age of 8 due to neglect. Sherry is happy with her living arrangements, as are the Greens. She has declined to be considered for adoption. Sherry has clear plans for her future. She wants to attend a local university to become a teacher. She recently received an assessment for independent living. The assessor reached the following conclusions regarding the areas required for independent living:

1. *Assistance in obtaining a high school diploma.* Sherry does not appear to need any support in this area. She is doing well in school, and barring unforeseen circumstances, her graduation seems certain.

2. *Assistance with career exploration.* Sherry has chosen a career that seems fitting and attainable for her. Her choice has remained stable over a period of at least two years.

3. *Referral to vocational training.* Because Sherry has chosen a career that is fitting and attainable, there is no need for vocational training.

4. *Job placement and retention.* Sherry will probably receive assistance from college financial aid programs. In addition, she will need some money for her daily expenses because her aunt and uncle have financial limitations that will prevent them from providing expense money. The case manager will help Sherry develop a resume, identify jobs, complete application processes, prepare for interviews, and negotiate positions.

5. *Training in daily living skills.* Sherry has good skills except in the area of financial management. The caseworker will follow the procedures listed in Number 6.

6. *Training in budgeting and financial management skills.* Sherry will need to understand budgeting and financial management. She will be referred to the XYZ Financial Services Agency for her training.

7. *Substance abuse prevention.* Sherry has not received substance abuse prevention training. She will be referred to the ABC Recovery Agency for training.

8. *Preventative health.* Sherry does not have problems in this area. No referral is necessary.

9. *Education, training, and services necessary to obtain employment.* The activities Sherry will need have already been listed.

10. *Help to prepare for and enter postsecondary education.* The activities Sherry will need have already been listed.

11. *Personal and emotional support.* Sherry has substantial emotional support from her family and her friends. She does not appear to need additional support.

Case Plan

1. Within 30 days the case manager will help Sherry develop a resume, identify jobs, complete application processes, prepare for interviews, and negotiate positions. The intent will be to help her earn money for her daily expenses because her aunt and uncle have financial limitations that will prevent them from providing expense money.
2. Within seven days the case manager will refer Sherry to the XYZ Financial Services Agency for her training in budgeting and financial management.
3. Within 30 days the case manager will refer Sherry to the ABC Recovery Agency for substance abuse prevention training.

Intervention follows the development of the case plan. During the intervention phase, the steps identified in the case plan are completed and new components of the plan added if needed. The case manager is involved in overseeing the plan and in encouraging the youth. Ideally, the plan has included some way of measuring improvement so that adjustments can be made if necessary.

For Those Who Have Aged Out

Services for those who have aged out of foster care are often accessed when a youth has been out of foster homes for some time and then returns to a child welfare office to request services available under the FCIA. One of the earliest priorities for many of these youths is arranging stable housing. Because they are beyond the age for which they would qualify for foster care, the FCIA's room-and-board funds may be accessed. When stable housing has been obtained, youths can be assessed for needs related to the independent living program. The FCIA provides several categories of service, including financial assistance, housing, counseling, employment, education, and "other appropriate support." Some states have also taken advantage of the dollars that make Medicaid available to meet the youth's medical insurance needs.

Putting It Into Practice

Problem Statement

Billy is an 18-year-old Caucasian male who left the foster care system seven months ago when he attained the age of 18. Since leaving foster care, he has moved through a series of temporary residences, mostly with friends and extended family members. He also reports having spent a few nights "on the streets." He reports that he has been unable to continue schooling (he has completed the 11th grade), find employment, or obtain medical care because of his transience. He also reports having been smoking marijuana "as often as I can get it." He also reports that he has been asked to leave virtually every home he has lived in because of problems with anger. He has presented at one of the field offices of the child welfare agency asking for assistance.

Case Plan

1. *Financial assistance.* Billy is in need of room-and-board payments at a minimum. The case manager will immediately help Billy secure an apartment and will facilitate the application and financial processes involved. The case manager will also ensure that utilities are arranged and that Billy has suitable food and supplies.
2. *Housing.* The apartment should provide suitable long-term housing for Billy.
3. *Counseling.* Billy appears to need counseling in at least two areas. First, he needs to deal with the issues that cause him to become so angry that he has been asked to leave the homes where he has stayed. Within one week the case manager will refer Billy to the Community Mental Health Center with a request for assessment, counseling, and anger management training. Billy also may have issues with substance abuse. Within one week the case manager will refer Billy to the Substance Abuse Prevention and Treatment Center for an evaluation and counseling or training if it is needed. The case manager will work with the financial officers at those institutions to negotiate services until a determination can be made about Medicaid eligibility.
4. *Employment.* Billy needs assistance in understanding and negotiating the processes of job application and interviewing. He also needs a thorough assessment with regard to his interests, skills, and knowledge to begin the process of career planning. Within one week the case manager will have arranged an appointment with the Career Selection and Advancement Center for an assessment and services. Within two weeks the case manager will have helped Billy prepare a resume and job applications and will have role-played telephone calls to prospective employers with him. When Billy does obtain an interview, the case manager will prepare him with discussions of appropriate dress and demeanor and will role-play interviews with him.

5. *Education.* Billy is a bright young man who should at least complete his high school education or obtain a GED. He is motivated to do so. Within two weeks the case manager will help Billy apply for admission to the Help Young Adults Finish High School (HYAFHS) program. The case manager will also see that Billy has the supplies and transportation he needs to participate in the program. Billy may also wish to consider either college or vocational training. The case manager will ensure that he receives appropriate testing and educational counseling through HYAFHS.

6. *Other appropriate services.* Billy will also need several additional services. Within one month the case manager will arrange adult education classes in budgeting and preventative health. Within one week the case manager will arrange for Homemakers Services to visit Billy's apartment and train him in the basic techniques of housekeeping. Within one week the case manager will have helped Billy enroll in activities at the County Recreation Facility near his new apartment.

Intervention would, of course, consist of following the case plan and then evaluating it for success and adjusting it as necessary. During the intervention period the case manager should maintain a posture of close observation and facilitative mentoring with regard to the youth's activities. It might be easy to assume that an 18-year-old, for example, should be able to complete the application process at any agency alone. In fact, those who have grown up in unstable foster homes and have had difficulties maintaining a stable home thereafter may lack some of the basic social skills needed to complete the application process successfully. Where these skills are lacking, the case manager should both help the youth develop them and assist in the processes when the youth's skills or knowledge are lacking.

For the Runaway or Homeless

The third category of juveniles eligible for services under the independent living program are those who have run away from foster care or who have become homeless. Often, these children have lived difficult, desperate lives surviving on the streets. They may have been victimized and may have victimized others. Their need for assistance is often critical. Runaway and homeless children may come to the attention of the independent living program in several ways. One possibility is that they simply hear of the program and show up at a child welfare office or a foster home at which the have resided in the past. At other times another child or foster parent may notify the independent living program of a child's whereabouts. Some come to the attention of the program because they have been arrested or detained by law enforcement.

The critical nature of the problems often experienced by these children makes quick, effective intervention vital. Housing and food are typically immediate issues, as may be medical care. The case plan may be developed after at least some arrangement has been made to address these critical issues. A case plan for a youth who has been a runaway or homeless might contain the following:

Putting It Into Practice

Problem Statement

Nichole is an 18-year-old female who identifies as being of mixed race. She resided in a foster home until the age of 15, at which point she reports running away to escape ongoing sexual abuse by one of the foster parents. She has lived in a variety of settings since that time, including the homes of friends, the homes of men she met, and on the street. She reports having survived by shoplifting, selling drugs, and prostitution. She has completed the 8th grade and reports that she was tested for a learning disability during her last year of school. She states that she can remember neither the results of the test nor the disorder for which she was tested. Agency records provide no information on the test or the disorder. Nichole also has a history of moodiness with bouts of depression and periods of great activity and angry outbursts. She has no specific career ambitions but states that she would like to do something to help kids have better lives. Nichole displays excellent financial management skills, something she says she learned from a man she met while on runaway status from foster care.

Case Plan

1. *Case management.* Nicole will be assigned a case manager who will help her locate immediate temporary housing and develop strategies for arranging permanent housing. The case manager will facilitate immediate housing by checking with the two local runaway centers to see whether beds are available for older adolescents. If no beds are available, the case manager will access flex funding to obtain housing for up to three nights. To obtain permanent housing, the case manager will check the list of recently established housing for others from independent living to see whether any are in need of a roommate. If there are such persons on the list, the case manager will arrange meetings between the potential roommates to let them determine compatibility.

   The case manager will ensure that Nicole has adequate food by furnishing grocery vouchers from flex funds. The case manager will accompany Nicole for the first three trips to the grocery to ensure that she has an understanding of the use of the vouchers and of the process of shopping.

Nicole is in need of a physical examination and testing. The case manager will refer her to the County Medical Clinic for examination and evaluation.

2. *Education and training.* Nicole has indicated a desire to pursue a GED. The case manager will refer her to the County Human Development Agency to enroll in one of its classes.

3. *Employment.* Within one week of Nichole's entering the program, the case manager will help her apply for at least five jobs and will help her prepare for interviews. They will purchase clothing appropriate for the interviews using flex funds. Within two weeks of entering the program, Nicole will be referred to the Job Support Training Program to enter its assessment and training process.

4. *Financial management.* Nicole does not appear to need assistance with financial management.

5. *Mentoring.* The case manager will refer Nicole to the Community Faith-Based Mentoring Program to be paired with one of its available mentors.

The sample case plans presented in this section vary widely in content and structure. This is, in fact, consistent with the potential appearance of case plans in different jurisdictions. Independent living programs may offer very different resources between jurisdictions. Some may be able to address areas of need not considered by the FCIA by accessing local funding sources and programs. Some may use FCIA requirements as an outline for assessment and case planning. Others may use a different system entirely. What is important to gain from the model case plan is a sense of the types of needs that youths who receive independent living services have and the types of plans that are developed to help them.

CHAPTER SUMMARY

The FCIA provides opportunities for children who either will be or have already aged out of foster care to access a range of services to help them live successfully on their own. The broad requirements of the act provide a general guideline from which each jurisdiction has developed its own program based on the needs of the children and the types of resources available in its area. Assessments and case plans are developed using both the federal guidelines and the programming opportunities developed at state and local levels.

TEST YOURSELF

1. Among other groups, the independent living program is designed to support children who are currently in foster care and recognized as unlikely to leave that program before their 18th birthday. True or False?

2. The Foster Care Independence Act (FCIA) of 1999 offers extensive guidelines that states must use in order to determine which children are likely to remain in state custody until the age of 18. True or False?

3. The FCIA provides opportunities for health care by allowing states to offer Medicaid coverage to youths who receive services under the plan. True or False?

4. Children who are residing in foster homes and have been recognized as unlikely to leave foster care before their 18th birthdays are likely to receive services that are built, at least to some extent, around the home or institution in which they reside. True or False?

5. Daily living skills include such activities as housekeeping, cooking, doing laundry, driving, accessing public transportation, and shopping. True or False?

6. Personal emotional preparation may be best assessed by

   (a) Administering a pen-and-paper questionnaire

   (b) Consulting case records for prior evaluations

   (c) Consulting with a mental health professional

   (d) Conversing with the youth and the foster parents

7. The most immediate need for children who present for independent living services and have been homeless or on runaway status is often

   (a) Medical care

   (b) Housing

   (c) Mental health counseling

   (d) Job training

8. **Which of the following statements is most accurate regarding the FCIA and its provisions for medical insurance?**

   (a) It makes no provision for medical insurance.

   (b) It provides funds allowing youths to purchase private coverage.

   (c) It utilizes partnerships with local health departments.

   (d) It allows states to offer Medicaid to covered children.

9. **The federal law creating independent living can best be described as**

   (a) Naming broad categories of services, leaving decisions regarding program structure to the state

   (b) Requiring a very strict and consistent program structure across jurisdictions so that programs vary little

   (c) Mandating state action but offering little in the way of financial support to accomplish its goals

   (d) Being shortsighted with little or no real services offered or provided to children aging out of care

10. **Under the FCIA, services to children who have aged out of foster care include**

    (a) Financial assistance, housing, counseling, employment, education, and other appropriate support

    (b) Case management, career counseling, private medical insurance, GED education, and mental health counseling

    (c) Career counseling, mental health counseling, microenterprise loans, and assistance in purchasing homes

    (d) Financial assistance, housing, counseling, private medical insurance, and microenterprise loans

Answers. 1. True; 2. False; 3. True; 4. True; 5. True; 6. c; 7. b; 8. d; 9. a; 10. a.

Ten

ESSENTIALS OF CULTURAL COMPETENCE IN CHILD WELFARE PRACTICE

The population of the United States is changing. An ongoing influx of immigrants, coupled with a robust birth rate among those who have immigrated here previously, has produced a burgeoning population of persons whose primary culture is other than that of mainstream America (Lum, 2000). In fact, the U.S. Bureau of the Census (1992) has projected that by 2050, non-Hispanic Whites, historically the dominant group, will barely constitute a majority of the population. The changing mix in the population means that the people receiving social services are likely to change. Researchers have already noted increases in minorities in child welfare, juvenile justice, and children's mental health (Ellis, Klepper, & Sowers, 2000).

Researchers and clinicians have also noted that culture, including language, interaction patterns, and fundamental ways of thinking, affects people's willingness to seek services, willingness to receive services, and willingness to consider change (Atkinson, Morton, & Sue, 1998). Those whose cultural perspectives are ignored by a practitioner or an intervention often respond poorly, resulting in a failure to make positive change. When practitioners are aware of and sensitive to fundamental characteristics of a culture during their interactions with persons of that culture, the probability of success is enhanced (Devore & Schlesinger, 1996). This makes cultural sensitivity, awareness, and, where it can be developed, competence of critical importance to those who work within the child welfare system (O'Hagan, 1999).

The ability to work effectively with persons of other cultures cannot be taught in a single chapter. It is possible, however, to introduce the reader to the foundational concepts of cultural competence and cross-cultural effectiveness. It is also possible to provide examples of some of the characteristics that often vary among individuals and families across cultures. An accepting, willing attitude toward others and behavior that demonstrates awareness of the importance of some aspects of a family's culture often go a long way toward eliminating the barriers that cultural differences may present. These, then, represent the goals of this chapter: (a) to help the reader begin to understand what culture is and why it is so important to effective practice and (b) to provide specific examples of the characteristics of some individuals and families of various cultures that may be relevant to effective practice.

CULTURE AND ITS RELEVANCE TO PRACTICE

Culture is a very important yet elusive concept. It has been defined in various ways. One very useful definition, provided by Barker (1995, p. 87), characterizes culture as "the customs, habits, skills, technology, arts, values, ideology, science, and religious and political behavior" of a group of people. Although this statement accurately explains what culture is, it does not describe the degree to which people are affected by their participation in it. Culture permeates the lives of people to the point that they act and think in ways of which they are unaware based on things that they have learned from their culture. Culture affects the way people see themselves, their families, the world, the government, spirituality, and many other areas. Culture is sufficiently important that it can totally disrupt an intervention without the child welfare worker or the intervention's recipient ever understanding why. It is crucial in determining the ways in which persons from one culture behave and think, yet it may be nearly invisible to members of other cultures.

Practitioners who are working with persons from their own cultures face many barriers to success. Factors such as mental health problems, anger, stubbornness, and substance abuse issues hinder effective practice. A lack of understanding of the other culture presents another potential barrier. If, for example, the practitioner unknowingly says or does something that is offensive to persons from the client's culture, the

> **DON'T FORGET**
>
> Culture is the customs, habits, skills, technology, arts, values, ideology, science, and religious and political behavior of a group of people (Barker, 1995).

CAUTION

Culture permeates the lives of people to the point that they act and think in ways of which they are unaware based on things they have learned from their culture. Culture affects the way people see themselves, their families, the world, the government, spirituality, and many other areas. Culture is sufficiently important that it can totally disrupt an intervention without the child welfare worker or the intervention's recipient ever understanding why.

rapport between the two may be seriously damaged. If the practitioner is unaware and the client is from a culture in which mentioning the offense would be inappropriate, the incident may pass unnoticed by the practitioner but be resented by the client. This scenario might well result in the failure of the intervention.

Not every intervention between persons of different cultures is doomed, but many may be negatively affected if steps are not taken to minimize the misunderstandings that might arise because of cultural differences. These steps include efforts on the part of individual practitioners and the agencies for which they work to develop greater levels of understanding of and ability to interact successfully with members of other cultures. As the ability to interact successfully with another culture or group of cultures increases, practitioners move through stages that might be referred to as cultural sensitivity, cultural awareness, and cultural competence.

Stages of Cultural Effectiveness

The stages of cultural sensitivity, cultural relevance, and cultural competence are not clearly defined. There is as yet no definitive way to assess who is culturally sensitive, who has become culturally aware, and who has progressed into cultural competence. There is, in fact, some disagreement about how these terms are used. Stages of cultural effectiveness, summarized in Rapid Reference 10.1 and described in this section, should help readers identify where they are and prompt them to take steps to become more culturally effective.

═Rapid Reference 10.1

Stages of Cultural Effectiveness

- Cultural insensitivity
- Cultural indifference
- Cultural sensitivity
- Cultural awareness
- Cultural competence

The least evolved stage of cultural effectiveness is *cultural insensitivity*. The culturally insensitive person is characterized by attitudes and behaviors that are prejudicial and discriminatory. These attitudes and behaviors might be anywhere on a continuum between open hostility and a quiet insistence that others should adapt to the culture of the practitioner. Culturally insensitive people are so far from being able to relate to persons of other cultures that it is unlikely that they can be effective in working with them in child welfare settings.

The next stage of cultural effectiveness is *cultural indifference*. Culturally indifferent people have no animosity toward people from other cultures but are indifferent to their presence and unaware of the importance of culture to effective interaction. A child welfare worker who is culturally indifferent, for example, might conduct a protective investigation of a Hispanic family's home and see statues or other religious icons that are a part of the family's practice of an Afro-Caribbean religion. Not being aware of or understanding the family's culture, that practitioner might believe the icons to be evidence that the family engages in strange activities that endanger the child. In extreme cases, particularly if the worker has not advanced far beyond cultural insensitivity, this misunderstanding might result in the removal of children from their homes.

Cultural sensitivity is a term often used to indicate the third stage of cultural effectiveness. Those who have developed cultural sensitivity have the capacity to relate to those of another culture in a manner that makes them comfortable, and insensitive behaviors may be forgiven because the client recognizes the good intentions and attempts at accommodating cultural differences. Although those who are culturally sensitive might lack the knowledge and skills to conduct an assessment or do in-depth counseling, they might be able to do case management, transportation, and other direct service. For example, a worker who is culturally sensitive might be able to work as the case manager for a family of Southeast Asian descent, referring them to resources, advocating on their behalf, and brokering services, but might refer them to an agency with more qualified personnel for assessment and counseling services (Ellis, Klepper, & Sowers, 2001b).

P. Sandau-Beckler (personal communication, August 13, 2001) identified a stage that falls between cultural sensitivity and cultural competence. She refers to this stage as *cultural relevance.* Those who are at the level of cultural relevance are able to interact with members of other cultures comfortably and understand enough of the nuance of the group to perform many, but perhaps not all, of the services required. For example, a practitioner might be comfortable interacting with a family and might understand the nuances of its culture well enough to interact successfully and even to conduct an assessment, yet might lack the language skills necessary to implement the intervention.

Cultural competence is achieved when the practitioner is able to function in such a way that culture is not a barrier to successful intervention. This requires a deep acceptance of the people from that culture, strong knowledge of the culture, the ability to interact well with members of that culture, and, in some cases, fluency in the language of that culture. A culturally competent worker, for example, might be able to participate in every aspect of a family's intervention in their native language.

Practitioners who wish to progress through the stages to cultural competence must often make many changes. They may need to change the way they view themselves, persons from their own cultures, and persons from other cultures. They may need to learn about the important characteristics of other cultures that must be respected in interactions with clients. They may need to learn to control some of their own tendencies in personal interactions, such as to minimize interruptions or to use appropriate amounts of eye contact. They may often find it important to know and use at least a few words in the native languages of the people with whom they will work.

Other Factors

Several additional factors may influence or interact with culture to affect intervention, particularly among families who have recently immigrated to this country. These factors include oppression, socioeconomic status, acculturation, racial-ethnic identity, national origin, education, immigration status, age, and gender (Ellis, Klepper, & Sowers, 2001a). Outlined in Rapid

Reference 10.2, these factors must also be considered when interacting with families and developing interventions.

One factor that must be considered in interactions with families is the degree of *oppression* that they have experienced. Immigrants may have fled from countries where they experienced blocked economic opportunities, ethnic hostility, or open violence. Those who have lived in this country for generations may have experienced prejudice and discrimination here. Oppression can produce negative self-esteem, anxiety, anger, and a lack of trust in other groups and in authority. Those who have been oppressed may have an inherent distrust of government employees such as child welfare workers. This distrust may be compounded if the worker is of a different ethnic background or functions awkwardly within the client's culture.

Socioeconomic status also has a major effect on the way in which families of various ethnic origins function. A poor family that immigrates into a ghetto with hopes of finding economic opportunities is likely to be very different from a family of entrepreneurs who moves to this country to expand its business. The former, for example, is likely to have few resources and may be very dependent on the social service system. The latter may be able to hire attorneys, pay for professional counseling assistance, hire homemakers, and access other resources. Poor families are much more likely to have their children taken into custody and are much more likely to experience difficulty in getting them returned.

A family's *level of acculturation* is also important. Acculturation refers to the family's ability to function within the dominant culture. Signs of acculturation include the ability to speak English, the ability to complete successfully necessary daily activities such as shopping, to find

Rapid Reference 10.2

Factors in Addition to Culture that May Affect Intervention

- Degree of oppression experienced
- Socioeconomic status
- Level of acculturation
- Racial-ethnic identity
- National origin
- Level of education
- Immigration status
- Age
- Gender

and retain employment, and to interact successfully with members of the dominant culture. A family that is highly acculturated is likely to have much better understanding of the court system and the processes that can be used to access social resources. A family that has not become acculturated may be bewildered by any experience with the child welfare system. These situations require much patient interaction to help the families understand what has happened and what they must do. The situation is further complicated by the differential levels of acculturation that often exist within families. Children of immigrant families, for example, often become acculturated much more quickly than do parents and grandparents. Children who can function better in society than can their parents may become highly manipulative and may actually use their understanding to control the family's behavior. This complicates many of a family's interactions with the child welfare system.

The *racial or ethnic identity* of a family may also be a factor in how it interacts with child welfare workers. Many new immigrants face being in the minority for the first time. Others may be forced to deal with being perceived differently than they have been in the past. For example, a person of Hispanic descent who has a dark complexion may have been seen simply as Hispanic in their native country but may be seen as Black by many Americans. These conditions may result in a challenge to the family's self-esteem. Their ethnic identity, once a source of pride to them, may become a source of dissonance or even shame.

National origin also creates differences among persons of minority cultures. Persons of African descent, for example, may be from many countries, including such diverse areas as the United States, Jamaica, Central America, and Africa itself. Families from those countries may be from very different cultures, and these differences may be reflected in areas such as language, family structure, communication patterns, and worldview. A worker who has developed competence in working with persons of African descent whose family is from Ohio, for example, is unlikely to have the same level of competence in working with a family from Kenya.

Level of education is another important factor. Parents with higher levels of education are likely to have more resources and to be better able to solve or participate in solving the problems that contribute to child maltreatment.

For example, a more educated person is often able to find better paying employment, alleviating the financial pressures that may contribute to abuse and neglect.

Immigration status produces important differences in family behavior and interaction (Ely, Dulmus, & Wodarski, in press). One clear example is a family in which some members are in this country illegally. Such a family is likely to react to the visit of a child welfare worker very uncertainly, frightened that in addition to the removal of a child they will also experience the loss of a family member if the immigration status is exposed. The situation is further complicated when the hidden family member is a key participant in the decision-making process. In such a case, for example, the worker may be confronted with apparently inexplicable decisions or demands that are funneled through other family members by the one who is not a legal immigrant. This family situation may be in clear contrast to that of a family in which everyone is a legal immigrant. Such a family is likely to have the fear and resentment that are common when children are removed but unlikely to display the unusual behaviors often present among families of illegal immigrants.

An additional important factor that creates differences among persons of the same culture is *age*. Just as generational differences are present among members of the dominant American culture, they are also present among other groups. Workers cannot assume, for example, that the views of a young Vietnamese couple will be the same as those of their grandparents. Although the communication and interaction patterns of the two couples may be similar and the Southeast Asian value of family solidarity may make differences difficult to detect, the younger couple is likely to be more open to and cooperative with Western ideas.

Gender is yet another characteristic that may produce differences among members of various cultures. Women play very different roles in various cultures. In many cultures, their role is also transitional, and women move through a process from a secondary role in a patriarchal society. In other cultures, particularly those of some African countries, families are matriarchal, and a mother or grandmother serves as the primary decision maker. In some cultures women may have the responsibility of arranging a family's social life. In others they may be reclusive, rarely leaving the home or interacting with others. It is vital to understand the norms within a culture regarding the behavior of women and how those may affect intervention planning (Ely, Dulmus, & Wodarski, in press).

DEVELOPING CULTURAL EFFECTIVENESS

It is clear that culture in combination with a number of other factors can cause one group of people to think, feel, and act differently than do people in another group, and even than other members of their own group behave. It is also clear that these differences can be very important to child welfare workers. Nonetheless, the ability to work effectively with persons of other cultures is an elusive goal. Many who are concerned about becoming culturally competent ask themselves questions such as, "How can I become competent? I can't speak their language. I don't know how they think." The good news is that there are many things practitioners can do to become more effective in working with persons from other cultures.

Obtaining Cultural Sensitivity

For some workers the first step in developing cultural effectiveness is developing cultural sensitivity. This is very often true for workers who have grown up in predominantly majority neighborhoods or have been raised in families that were not open to other groups. Those who are attempting to develop cultural sensitivity need to develop an attitude toward themselves, their own culture, and other cultures that will allow them to be comfortable with persons from other cultures and interact with those persons in ways that allow them to be comfortable. Although they may understand little about the customs of the cultural group with which they are working, they endeavor to let their clients know that they accept them and their customs. Several steps can contribute to developing the necessary attitudes and competencies.

Workers who develop a strong relationship with clients may also find opportunities to inquire about or participate in their cultures. Asking questions about a family's customs may provide strong rapport-building opportunities. Using a few words of a family's native language (even when spoken poorly) can also be very helpful in strengthening the relationship between family and worker.

Practitioners can enhance their sensitivity to other cultures by making friends of persons from those cultures. Friends are more likely than clients to feel free to educate them about how persons of their culture act and think. Understanding more of the culture and being acquainted with persons from it can greatly enhance cultural sensitivity.

Putting It Into Practice

Some practitioners have found it helpful to begin their relationships with clients of other cultures by openly describing their lack of knowledge of their culture and apologizing in advance for anything they may inadvertently say or do that might be offensive. For example, an adoption worker might approach a Cuban family by saying, "I really looking forward to working with you. I'm excited about the chance to introduce a child to a family that has as much to offer as yours does. I do have one concern, however, and my concern is much more about me than it is about you. You see, I've never had the opportunity to work with persons from another country before. I know a little bit about Cuba, but not very much. I understand that many of your customs are different from those of this country. I'm concerned that I may unintentionally do something that offends you or makes you angry. I want to let you know that my intentions are good, and that I will not deliberately do anything to offend you. If I accidentally do something that you find offensive, I hope that you will accept my apology in advance. If you're comfortable doing so, I hope that you will also tell me what I have done. I expect to be working with other families from your country in the future, and anything you can tell me about your customs will be very helpful."

Another good way of developing sensitivity is to attend events that honor the traditions and arts of another culture. Churches, recreational programs, universities, and other organizations often sponsor such events. Cultural fairs are excellent places to become acquainted with other cultures and to meet people from those cultures. Workers may be able to locate these events by watching newspaper advertisements from metropolitan areas in which large numbers of persons from other cultures reside.

Exposing oneself to and enjoying the literature, art, and music of other cultures can also promote sensitivity. The arts of many countries and cultures can be accessed through Internet searches. Literature can be ordered through interlibrary loan. Music from many cultures is available in record stores and on the Internet.

Those who wish to improve their cultural sensitivity may also participate in seminars and in-service training sessions that may be available through their own or other agencies. Local experts may be invited to attend staff meetings and talk about effective interaction with persons from specific cultures. Sociologists or anthropologists from local colleges or universities may be able to offer instruction.

Obtaining Cultural Awareness

Workers can also do many things to enhance their cultural awareness. Remember that cultural awareness refers to the capacity to interact with members of other cultures comfortably enough to provide many of the services required. This requires moving beyond sensitivity in that the worker must be sufficiently knowledgeable about and comfortable working within the behaviors and attitudes of members of another culture in order to be effective with them.

One important step in developing cultural awareness is reading the scientific literature about the characteristics shared by many members of other cultures. Many of these characteristics have also been identified as critical to consider within the counseling process. A few of those areas are discussed in greater detail in a later section of this chapter.

It is often possible to learn more about other cultures by asking persons from those cultures. It is occasionally possible to discuss some of these issues with clients, but the ability to do so depends on the nature of the question to be asked and the basic orientation of members of that culture toward being asked about their inner worlds. For example, it may be possible to ask clients about their culture's predominant religion, but it is likely to be inappropriate to ask questions about their sexual attitudes and customs. Similarly, persons from a Hispanic country may talk freely and proudly about their culture, whereas the value placed on commonality by persons of Southeast Asian descent may preclude them from talking freely about their customs. Although these factors may make discussion of a culture with clients difficult, it may be much easier with friends and acquaintances. When this is not possible, leaders from ethnic communities may be willing to provide insight.

Seminars and in-service training may be available to facilitate the process of developing cultural awareness. Local colleges and universities may offer helpful courses. If these courses are in departments such as social work, psychology, or counseling, they are likely to be very applicable to child welfare work. If courses are not available from those departments, sociology or anthropology courses may provide some of the basic information.

Practitioners can use role-playing and similar activities. Those who are familiar with other cultures can pretend to be clients and can interact with the trainee as members of those cultures might. The experience can be enhanced when an actual member of that culture is able to participate.

Aspiring to Cultural Competence

Cultural competence, the ability to perform all aspects of the intervention process, may be an elusive goal. In some areas of child welfare, such as adoption, it may be less elusive. In other areas, such as protective investigation or foster care, it may be a very elusive goal indeed. Protective investigators may walk into a home in which no member of the family speaks English well enough to understand what is happening. They may need to communicate with people who do not understand them and do not understand their right to be there. Foster care workers may be challenged by behavioral problems from children who do not understand or know how to deal with the cultural differences to which they are exposed.

Those who aspire to cultural competence must make a substantial commitment to its pursuit. They must develop a deep acceptance of and appreciation of the culture in which they will work and must have a balanced perspective with regard to their own culture. They must communicate well with members of the culture they serve and must become fluent in the language of that culture. They must understand and relate to the perspectives of their clients and must respond immediately and appropriately to issues that arise due to cultural differences.

Developing cultural competence requires spending substantial amounts of time with persons of that culture. Some agencies actually send workers to other countries to learn to work within the culture more effectively. Workers must engage in an ongoing program of reading, exposure to the culture in which they work, thoughtful observation of the habits of persons from that

DON'T FORGET

Those who aspire to cultural competence must make a substantial commitment to its pursuit. They must develop a deep acceptance of and appreciation for the culture in which they will work, and they must have a balanced perspective with regard to their own culture. They must communicate well with members of the culture they serve and must become fluent in the language of that culture. They must understand and relate to the perspectives of their clients and must respond immediately and appropriately to issues that arise due to cultural differences.

culture, and thoughtful evaluation of their own behavior when in contact with those persons. They may be required to learn a new language or to refine their knowledge of a language to accommodate regional differences. In many ways their own thoughts and behaviors must be modified so that they are able to function biculturally, that is, comfortably and effectively in two cultures.

EXAMPLES OF RELEVANT CHARACTERISTICS WITHIN SOME CULTURES

A central component of cultural competence is the awareness of important areas in which members of the culture receiving services are likely to differ from the dominant American culture. Whether practitioners are in the earliest stages of cultural sensitivity or have acquired a good measure of cultural competence, there are things to learn about persons from the culture they serve. This section includes a brief sampling of differences that are likely to be present in some cultures. These differences are also summarized in Rapid Reference 10.3. The cultures used in these examples include persons of African, Hispanic, and Southeast Asian descent.

Family Characteristics

The structure, composition, and patterns of interaction of families often vary from culture to culture. Families of African descent, for example, are often very different from those who are a part of or have adapted to the dominant American culture. Similarly, families of African descent that have resided within the United States for several generations are likely to be very different from those who have recently arrived from some other country. Further, families of African descent are likely to differ in important ways from families of Hispanic or Southeast Asian descent.

One way in which families often vary between cultures is their *structure*. In this context structure refers to their patterns of authority and decision making. Hispanic families, for example, often have patriarchal (male-dominated) patterns of authority and decision making. In these families the primary decision maker is frequently the father or a grandfather. Although workers cannot assume this to be the case in every family, they should be aware of the possibility when working with families of Hispanic descent.

≡*Rapid Reference 10.3*

Examples of Differences that Often Exist Between Cultures

- Family characteristics
  - Structure
  - Composition
  - Patterns of internal interaction
  - Patterns of external interaction
- Gender roles
  - Interactions with the community at large
  - Different levels of respect
- Interactive styles
  - Eye contact
  - Directness of speech
  - Frequency of touch
  - Personal demonstrativeness
- Religion
  - Honor the family's choice of faith
  - Regard the family's faith as an asset to intervention
- Language
  - Learn a few words or expressions
  - Speak as well as possible
  - Take lessons
  - Know you limitations

Families of African descent, on the other hand, may be structured matri-archally. Although some families may have altered traditional patterns through exposure to other cultures in other countries, many have maintained the female-dominated decision-making patterns present among some of the African cultures (Boykin & Toms, 1985). Workers must avoid the trap of assuming that a patriarchal or shared decision-making pattern is present when working with these families.

The presence of either a male- or female-dominated system of authority does not mean that the opinions of other family members should not be heard and considered. It is always important to show respect for every member of the family. There are also cases in which the appearance of traditional structure may be maintained while, in fact, some other member of the family controls decision making.

Families also may vary in *composition*. The traditional American family has often been conceived as two parents and their children. In recent decades this has changed to include single-parent families and families in which divorced parents may have new partners. Many families from other cultures include additional members in an arrangement sometimes referred to as the *extended family*. Extended families may include other relatives such as grandparents, aunts, uncles, and cousins or may include long-term family friends. Some cultures even have formal procedures by which adult nonrelatives are adopted into the family. When families contain extended members, it is often critical that they be included in family discussions and planning. They can also serve as important resources for an overstressed family.

Patterns of internal interaction differ among cultures. In some cultures the role of women is greatly diminished, and the needs and opinions of girls are given much less consideration than they are within the dominant American culture. In many Hispanic families, for example, girls have a very defined place. They are expected to fulfill specific domestic and social roles that are often very inconsistent with those in many American families. Workers must be careful not to interpret cultural patterns as abusive and must avoid unwanted meddling in family interactions that are culturally appropriate.

There are also differences in patterns of external interaction, that is, the way in which families interact with the outside world. Southeast Asian families, for example, tend to internalize problems and rely on their own resources to solve them. They may be respectfully resistant to outside help. Families of African descent that have retained the values of their ancestors may rely on their friends and neighbor far more readily. Workers must be aware of difference in these areas.

Gender Roles

Gender roles may vary within the family, but they may also differ in interactions with the community at large. In some homes, as with many Hispanic families, the husband is the visible leader, but the wife may be responsible for developing social interactions and relationships for the family and may handle many of its interactions with outsiders. In Southeast Asian families, women are often more reserved and may even be unlikely to speak with persons outside the family.

Women are treated with different levels of respect in various cultures. Although child welfare workers may be offended by conditions within the family that they believe to be oppressive toward women, they must be careful not to allow their personal feelings to interfere with their role in that home, caring for children who have experienced maltreatment. They may be activists for women's rights outside the home, but they must be careful not to interact with the family in ways that will undermine the intervention.

Interactive Styles

Persons from different cultures may have very different interactive styles. Failure to be sensitive to those styles may be perceived as an insult and may negatively impact the relationship between the worker and the family. Examples of important characteristics in interactive styles include eye contact, directness of speech, frequency of touch, and personal demonstrativeness.

Persons from some cultures, such as Southeast Asian or American Indian cultures, often use limited *eye contact* during conversation. They may even feel that looking into the eyes of another person for an extended period is offensive. Many within the traditional American culture place a great deal of importance on eye contact. They may see averted eyes as a sign of anger, disrespect, or dishonesty. Child welfare workers should be aware of the customs of the families they serve regarding eye contact and should attempt to adapt their interactions to be as inoffensive as possible.

Another area in which members of various cultures often differ is *directness of speech*. Western culture tends to place great value on directness and individuality. Some other cultures, such as those of Southeast Asia and the American Indians, use more nuance and inference. Many American Indians and persons of African descent may honor the ancient customs of storytelling to communicate important information and lessons. A worker's effectiveness can be enhanced by interacting in a manner with which the family is comfortable.

Frequency of touch may also be an issue among members of different cultures. Hispanic families may greet workers with hugs and hearty handshakes. Southeast Asians are much less likely to initiate or be receptive to physical contact, particularly in the early stages of a relationship. Workers should be receptive to appropriate gestures on the part of family members but should be careful not to initiate any sort of physical contact where it may be unwelcome.

Some cultures are characterized by higher levels of *personal demonstrativeness* than are others. Some value calm, quiet interactions. Others may be characterized by joking, loud laughter, and hearty interaction. Workers should not regard either of these behaviors with skepticism when they are characteristic of the members of the family's group.

Religion

Religion plays a very important role in the lives of people of many cultures. It both forms and is formed by the culture and thus is an integral part of life for many. It is also important to realize that there are many religions within the broad cultures discussed in this section. Among the Hispanics there are Catholicism, Protestantism, Afro-Caribbean faiths, and others. Persons of African descent may have embraced Christianity, a religion of the countries through which their families have passed, or some other faith. Southeast Asians may have retained one of the many traditional faiths of the region from which they come or may have adopted a faith in the new land. American Indians are likely to practice traditional religion, have converted to Christianity, or have become a part of the Native American church. Regardless of the faith that any individual or family may have adopted, it is likely to be very important to them. Child welfare workers must honor the choice of faith that families have made and should regard that faith as an asset to the intervention process.

It is critical that workers avoid viewing the faith of the families with which they work with skepticism. The faith of each individual is very important and very real to them. Some religions may seem strange to workers who were raised in the dominant American culture. It is important to remember that the worker's own faith may seem equally strange to the family. Viewing the family's faith with negativity or skepticism is likely to damage seriously the relationship between the worker and the family. Those who work with families from the Caribbean islands may encounter religions that have been treated as evil or dangerous in the press and popular literature. Workers should not fear these faiths or attempt to convert the families. Rather, they should encourage the families to draw upon their faith as a resource to help them deal with the problems they are facing.

Language

Child welfare workers can often enhance their effectiveness with persons from cultures other than their own by familiarizing themselves with and using some of the language and expressions of the family's native land. Families are often anxious to share a few words of their language. The use of some basic words such as "hello," "please," and "thank you" can enhance rapport. Workers may feel self-conscious about their accent when they try to speak another language, but families are likely to appreciate the effort. Workers should be aware that some languages, particularly some from Southeast Asia, rely heavily on inflection (the way in which a word is spoken) to determine meaning. The same word can mean two very different things in these languages depending on how it is spoken. When working with families whose native language relies on inflection, practitioners should be careful to use only those words that they can pronounce correctly.

Workers who wish to become proficient in a language may be able to find courses at local universities or language schools. Those who have developed friendships with persons from other cultures can practice the language with them. Becoming fluent in the language of families from other countries may be necessary for those who wish to attain cultural competency.

CHAPTER SUMMARY

As the population of the United States becomes more diverse, child welfare workers will need to develop greater skills in communicating with persons of other cultures. As they develop these skills, they will move through levels of effectiveness sometimes known as cultural sensitivity, cultural relevance, and cultural competence. Understanding the many aspects of the cultures with which they work can help practitioners move through the process.

TEST YOURSELF

1. **Researchers and clinicians have noted that culture, including language, interaction patterns, and fundamental ways of thinking, affects people's willingness to seek services, to receive services, and to consider change.** True or False?

2. **Culture has been defined as "the customs, habits, skills, technology, arts, values, ideology, science, and religious and political behavior" of a group of people.** True or False?

3. **Not every intervention between persons of different cultures is doomed, but many may be negatively affected if steps are not taken to minimize the misunderstandings that might arise because of cultural differences.** True or False?

4. **Cultural competence refers to the capacity to relate to those of another culture in a manner that makes them comfortable and in which insensitive behaviors may be forgiven because the client recognizes the good intentions and attempts at accommodating cultural differences.** True or False?

5. **Socioeconomic status has little to do with generating differences among persons from a given culture.** True or False?

6. **Those who have fled their native countries to escape oppression by the government are likely to**

    (a) Be open to and trusting of authority

    (b) Be afraid of and resistant to authority

    (c) Seek a green card in this country immediately

    (d) Learn English quickly

7. **Families that include illegal immigrants are likely to**

    (a) Be very open to the presence of a child welfare worker

    (b) Be resistant and evasive to a child welfare worker

    (c) Trust that the worker will not turn the illegal immigrant in

    (d) Seek help from their neighbors

(continued)

8. **When meeting a family from a culture with which the worker is not familiar,**

   (a) It is never proper to discuss the worker's cultural limitations

   (b) It is always proper to discuss the worker's cultural limitations

   (c) It may be proper to discuss the worker's cultural limitations

   (d) It is meaningless to consider the worker's cultural limitations

9. **Families of Hispanic origin are likely to**

   (a) Have a matriarchal structure

   (b) Have a structure in which authority is shared equally by the mother and father

   (c) Be reluctant to discuss the various aspects of their culture

   (d) Have a patriarchal structure

10. **Persons from Southeast Asian countries are likely to**

   (a) Be very demonstrative and open to touch

   (b) Be openly resistant to the worker

   (c) Be uncomfortable with open displays of affection

   (d) Engage in frequent and prolonged eye contact

Answers. 1. True; 2. True; 3. True; 4. False; 5. False; 6. b; 7. b; 8. c; 9. d; 10. c.

References

Achenbach, T. M. (1991). *Manual for Child Behavior Checklist 14-18, 1991 Profile.* Burlington: University of Vermont Department of Psychiatry.

American Psychiatric Association. (2000). *Diagnostic and statistical manual of mental disorders* (5th ed., Text Revision). Washington, DC: Author.

Atkinson, D. R., Morton, G., & Sue, D. W. (1998). *Counseling American minorities.* New York: McGraw-Hill.

Ballou, M., Barry, J., Billingham, K., Boorstein, B., Butler, C., Gershberg, R., Heim, J., Lirianio, D., McGovern, S., Nicastro, S., Romaniello, J., Vazquea-Nuttal, K., & White, C. (2001). Psychosocial model for judicial decision making in emergency or temporary child placement. *American Journal of Orthopsychiatry, 71*(4), 416–425.

Barker, R. L. (1995). *The social work dictionary* (3rd ed.). Washington, DC: NASW Press.

Boykin, A. W., & Toms, F. D. (1985). Black child socialization: A conceptual framework. In H. P. McAdoo & J. L. McAdoo (Eds.), *Black children: Social, educational, and parental environments* (pp. 33–51). Beverly Hills, CA: Sage.

Bradley, R. H., & Caldwell, B. M. (1977). Home observation for measurement of the environment: A validated study of screening efficiency. *American Journal of Mental Deficiency, 81*(5), 417–420.

Child Welfare League of America. (1991). *Core training for child welfare workers curriculum.* Washington, DC: Author.

Child Welfare League of America. (1994). *Kinship care: A natural bridge.* Washington, DC: Author.

Christmas, A., Wodarski, J. S., & Smokowski, P. (1996). Risk factors for physical child abuse: A practice theoretical paradigm. *Family Therapy, 23*(4), 233–248.

Christoffel, K. K., Scheidt, P. C., Agran, P. F., Kraus, P. F., McLoughlin, E., Paulsen, J. A. (1992). Standard definitions for childhood injury research: Excerpts of a conference report. *Pediatrics, 89,* 1027–1034.

Cline, F. W. (1992). *Understanding and treating the severely disturbed child.* Evergreen, CO: Evergreen Consultants.

Collins, M. E. (2001). Transition to adulthood for vulnerable youths: A review of research and implications for policy. *Social Service Review, 75*(2), 271–291.

Cowger, C., & Snively, C. (2002). Assessing client strengths. In A. R. Roberts & G. J. Greene (Eds.), *Social workers' desk reference* (pp. 221–225). New York: Oxford Press.

Cox, M. E., Buehler, C., & Orme, J. G. (2002). Recruitment and foster family service. *Journal of Sociology and Social Welfare, 29*(3), 151–177.

DePanfilis, D., & Zuravin, S. J. (2001). Assessing risk to determine need for services. *Children and Youth Services Review, 23*(1), 3–20.

Devore, W., & Schlesinger, E. (1996). *Ethnic-sensitive social work practice.* Boston: Allyn & Bacon.

Dulmus, C. N., & Wodarski, J. S. (1996). Assessment and effective treatments of childhood psychopathology: Responsibilities and implications for practice. *Journal of Child and Adolescent Group Therapy, 6*(2), 75–99.

Dulmus, C. N., & Wodarski, J. S. (2002). Parameters of social work treatment plans. In A. R. Roberts & G. J. Greene (Eds.), *Social workers' desk reference* (pp. 314–319). New York: Oxford Press.

Ehrle, J., & Geen, R. (2002). Kin and non-kin care: Findings from a national survey. *Children and Youth Services Review, 24*(1/2), 15–35.

Ellis, R. A., Ellis, G. D., & Galey, R. (2002). Evaluating kinship care alternatives: A comparison of a private initiative to traditional state services. *Advances in Social Work, 3*(1), 33–41.

Ellis, R. A., Klepper, T. D., & Sowers, K. M. (2000). Similarity, diversity, and cultural sensitivity: Considerations for intervention with juveniles of African descent. *Journal for Juvenile Justice and Detention Services, 15*(1), 29–41.

Ellis, R. A., Klepper, T. D., & Sowers, K. M. (2001a). Building a foundation for effective intervention: Understanding Hispanic juveniles and their families. *Journal for Juvenile Justice and Detention Services, 15*(3), 78–93.

Ellis, R. A., Klepper, T. D., & Sowers, K. M. (2001b). Toward culturally sensitive practice: Working with Asians in the juvenile justice system. *Journal for Juvenile Justice and Detention Services, 15*(2), 99–114.

Ellis, R. A., & Sowers, K. M. (2001). *Juvenile justice practice: An interdisciplinary approach to intervention.* Pacific Grove, CA: Brooks Cole/Wadsworth.

Ely, G., Dulmus, C. N., & Wodarski, J. S. (in press). Domestic violence: A literature review reflecting an international crisis. *Stress, Trauma, and Crisis: An International Journal.*

Ely, G., Dulmus, C. N., & Wodarski, J. S. (in press). Domestic violence and immigrant communities in the United States: A review of women's unique needs and recommendations for social work practice and research. *Stress, Trauma, and Crisis: An International Journal.*

Epstein, N. B., Baldwin, L. M., & Bishop, D. S. (1983). The MacMaster Family Assessment Device. *Journal of Marital and Family Therapy, 9*(2), 171–180.

Ewing, J. (1984). Detecting alcoholism: The CAGE questionnaire. *Journal of the American Medical Association, 252,* 1905–1907.

Faller, K. C. (1991). Criteria for judging the credibility of children's statements about their sexual abuse. *Child Welfare, 67*(5), 389–401.

Foster Care Independence Act of 1999. PL 106-199. (Dec. 17, 2002). Retrieved online from http://www.access.gpo.gov/nara/publaw/106publhtml

Gabor, P., Thomlison, B., & Hudson, W. (1994). *Family Assessment Screening Inventory.* Tempe, AZ: WALMYR.

Garvin, C. (2002). Developing goals. In A. R. Roberts & G. J. Greene (Eds.), *Social workers' desk reference* (pp. 309–313). New York: Oxford Press.

Geen, R., & Berrick, J. D. (2002). Kinship care: An evolving service delivery option. *Children and Youth Services Review, 24*(1/2), 1–14.

Holt, B. J. (2000). *The practice of generalist case management.* Needham Heights, MA: Allyn & Bacon.

Houston, M. (2001). *Georgia John H. Chafee Foster Care Independence Program 2001–2004 Application.* Atlanta, GA: Georgia Department of Human Services.

Hudson, W. (1982a). *Index of Family Relation.* Tempe, AZ: WALMYR.

Hudson, W. (1982b). *Index of Parental Attitudes.* Tempe, AZ: WALMYR.

Hudson, W. (1994a). *Children's Behavior Rating Scale.* Tempe, AZ: WALMYR.

Hudson, W. (1994b). *Index of Alcohol Involvement.* Tempe, AZ: WALMYR.

Hudson, W. (1994c). *Index of Drug Involvement.* Tempe, AZ: WALMYR.

Hudson, W. (1996). *Multidimensional Adolescent Assessment Scale.* Tempe, AZ: WALMYR.

Ingram, T. (1996). Kinship care: From last resort to first choice. *Child Welfare, 75*(5), 550–556.

Kapp, S. A., McDonald, T. P., & Diamond, K. L. (2001). The path to adoption of children of color. *Child Abuse and Neglect, 25*(2), 215–230.

Kluger, M. P., Alexander, G., & Curtis, P. A. (2001). *What works in child welfare.* Washington, DC: CWLA Press.

Kovacs, M. (1981). Rating scales to assess depression in school aged children. *Acta Paedopsychiatrica, 46*(5-6), 305–315.

Kubler-Ross, E. (1969). *On death and dying.* New York: Macmillan.

Leos, U., Bess, R., & Geen, R. (2002). The evolution of federal and state policies for assessing and supporting kinship caregivers. *Children and Youth Services Review, 24*(1/2), 37–52.

Levy, T. M., & Orlans, M. (1995). Intensive short-term therapy with attachment-disordered children. In L. VandeCreek, S. Knapp, & T. L. Jackson (Eds.), *Innovations in clinical practice: A source book* (Vol. 14, pp. 227–239). Sarasota, FL: Professional Resource Press.

Lindholm, K. J. (1986). Child sexual abuse within the family: CIBA foundation report. *Journal of Interpersonal Violence, 1*(2), 240–242.

Lowman, J. (1980). Measurement of family affective structure. *Journal of Personality Assessment, 44*(2), 130–141.

Lum, D. (2000). *Social work practice and people of color.* Pacific Grove, CA: Brooks Cole.

Lyons, P., Doueck, H., & Wodarski, J. S. (1996). CPS risk assessment: A review of empirical literature on instrument performance. *Social Work Research, 20*(3), 143–155.

Magura, S., & Mosas, B. S. (1986). Clinic as evaluation in child protective services. *Child Welfare, 63*(2), 99–112.

Mather, J. H., & Hull, G. H. (2002). Case management and child welfare. In A. R. Roberts & G. J. Greene (Eds.), *Social workers' desk reference* (pp. 476–480). New York: Oxford Press.

Mather, J. H., & Lager, P. B. (2000). *Child welfare: A unifying model of practice.* Pacific Grove, CA: Brooks Cole/Wadsworth.

McCroskey, J., Nishimoto, R., & Subramanian, K. (1991). Assessment in family support programs: Initial reliability and validity testing of the Family Assessment Form. *Child Welfare, 70*(1), 19–33.

McGinty, K., McCammon, S. L., & Koeppen, V. P. (2001). The complexities of implementing a wraparound approach to service provision: A view from the field. *Journal of Family Social Work, 5*(3), 95–110.

Miller, G. (1988). *The Substance Abuse Subtle Screening Inventory Manual.* Spencer, IN: Spencer Evening World.

Milner, J. S., Gold, R. G., Ayoub, C., & Jacewitz, M. (1984). Predictive validity of Child Abuse Potential Inventory. *Journal of Consulting and Clinical Psychology, 52*(5), 879–884.

O'Hagan, K. (1999). Culture, cultural identity, and cultural sensitivity in child and family social work. *Child and Family Social Work, 4*(4), 269–281.

Partridge, P. C. (1991). The particular challenges to being adopted. *Smith College Studies in Social Work, 61*(2), 197–208.

Pecora, P. J., Whittaker, J. K., Barth, R. P., & Maluccio, A. N. (2000). *The child welfare challenge: Policy, practice, and research.* New York: de Gruyter.

Polansky, N. A., Chalmers, M. A., Buttenwieser, E., & Williams, D. (1978). Assessing adequacy of child care: An urban scale. *Child Welfare, 57*(7), 439–449.

Reynolds, C. F. (1992). Treatment of depression in special populations. *Journal of Clinical Psychiatry, 53*(9), 45–53.

Rhoades, K. W., Orme, J. G., & Buehler, C. (2001). A comparison of family foster parents who quit, consider quitting, and plan to continuing fostering. *Social Service Review, 75*(1), 84–114.

Roberts, D. (2001). *Shattered bonds: The color of child welfare.* New York: Basic Books.

Rycus, J. S., & Hughes, R. C. (1998). *Field guide to child welfare: Foundations of child protective services.* Washington, DC: Child Welfare League of America Press.

Scannapieco, M., & Heger, R. L. (2002). Kinship care providers: Designing an array of supportive services. *Child and Adolescent Social Work Journal, 19*(4), 315–327.

Schmidt, B. D. (1979). *Child abuse/neglect: The visual diagnosis of nonaccidental trauma and failure to thrive.* Elk Grove, IL: American Academy of Pediatrics.

Stoner, M. R. (1999). Life after foster care: Services and policies for former foster youth. *Journal of Sociology and Social Welfare, 26*(4), 159–175.

Straus, M. A. (1979). The Conflicts Tactic Scales. *Journal of Marriage and the Family, 41,* 75–88.

Suarez, K., Smokowski, P., & Wodarski, J. S. (1996). The process of intervention with multiproblem families: Theoretical and practice guidelines. *Family Therapy, 23*(2), 117–134.

Terling, W. (2001). Permanency in kinship care: An exploration of disruption rates and factors associated with placement disruption. *Children and Youth Services Review, 23*(23), 111–126.

Testa, M. F., & Slack, K. S. (2002). The gift of kinship foster care. *Children and Youth Family Services Review, 23*(1/2), 79–108.

Triseliotis, J. (2002). Long-term foster care or adoption? The evidence examined. *Child and Family Social Work, 7*(1), 23–33.

University of Tennessee. (2002). *John H. Chafee Foster Care Independence Program.* Knoxville, TN: Social Work Office of Research and Public Service.

U.S. Bureau of the Census. (1992). Populations projections of the United States, by age, sex, race, and Hispanic origin: 1992 to 2050. *Current Populations Reports, P25-1092,* Washington, DC: U.S. Government Printing Office.

Walton, E. (2002). Family-centered services in child welfare. In A. R. Roberts & G. J. Greene (Eds.), *Social workers' desk reference* (pp. 285–289). New York: Oxford Press.

Wodarski, J. S., Rapp-Paglicci, L. A., Dulmus, C. N., & Jongsma, A. (2001). *The social work and human services treatment planner.* New York: Wiley.

Annotated Bibliography

Kluger, M. P., Alexander, G., & Curtis, P. A. (2001). *What works in child welfare*. Washington, DC: CWLA Press.

> *This is a systematic, comprehensive discussion of effective practices at every stage of the child welfare system. This book offers thorough discussions of best practices based on the research and practice of the greatest experts in the field.*

Mather, J. H., & Lager, P. B. (2000). *Child welfare: A unifying model of practice*. Pacific Grove, CA: Brooks Cole/Wadsworth.

> *This book emphasizes an integrated use of policy initiatives and practice methodologies. It uses a multisystemic approach in its discussions of practice, focusing on preventing child maltreatment and on successful alternatives to removal from the home, as well as foster care, adoption, and child sexual abuse.*

Pecora, P. J., Whittaker, J. K., Barth, R. P., & Maluccio, A. N. (2000). *The child welfare challenge: Policy, practice, and research*. New York: de Gruyter.

> *This comprehensive examination of policy, practice, and research in child welfare presents research findings and policy decisions that are tied to program design. The book covers a broad range of topics, including policy issues, child maltreatment, and income maintenance programs.*

Roberts, D. (2001). *Shattered bonds: The color of child welfare*. New York: Basic Books.

> *A thorough review and description of the discriminatory forces that operate to create and maintain an overrepresentation of minority children in state custody, this book looks at the critical decision points at which children are identified for inclusion or retention within the system as well as the consequences for the children who remain in custody.*

Rycus, J. S., & Hughes, R. C. (1998). *Field guide to child welfare: Foundations of child protective services*. Washington, DC: Child Welfare League of America Press.

> *A comprehensive source for practitioners, this book provides a wealth of information on best practices in child welfare, along with step-by-step guidelines for their use. The book covers the spectrum from identification of maltreatment through permanency planning and adoption.*

Index

About the Authors

Rodney A. Ellis is assistant professor at the College of Social Work at the University of Tennessee. He holds a master's of social work and a doctorate in social welfare from Florida International University. His primary areas of research interest include juvenile justice and child welfare issues, particularly in areas related to minority populations. Ellis has previously served as director of child welfare for the Florida Department of Children and Families, District X, and as the assistant director of the School of Social Work at Florida International University. He publishes in the areas of juvenile justice, child welfare, cultural competency, and social policy. His recent publications include "Harm by Her Own Hand: A Study of Internalized Violence Among Female Juveniles" (*Journal of Human Behavior and the Social Environment*), "Evaluating Kinship Care Alternatives: A Comparison of a Private Initiative to Traditional State Services" (*Advances in Social Work*), "Toward Culturally Sensitive Practice: Working With Asians in the Juvenile Justice System" (*Journal for Juvenile Justice and Detention Services*), and "Building a Foundation for Effective Intervention: Understanding Hispanic Juveniles and their Families" (*Journal for Juvenile Justice and Detention Services*). He has also authored a text entitled *Impacting Social Policy: A Practitioner's Guide to Analysis and Action* and coauthored a textbook, *Juvenile Justice Practice: A Practitioner's Guide to Analysis and Action*. He is currently working on a fourth text: *The Macro Practitioner's Workbook: A Step-by-Step Guide to Effectiveness With Organizations and Communities.*

Catherine N. Dulmus is assistant professor at the College of Social Work at the University of Tennessee. She received her master's and doctoral degrees in social work from the State University of New York at Buffalo. Dulmus's experience in social work practice includes both clinical and administrative positions in inpatient and outpatient mental health, as well as school social work. Her research focuses on the prevention of mental disorders in children,

…t work relates to violence and childhood trauma. Dul-
…e appeared in such journals as *American Journal of Orthopsy-*
…lies in Society, *Child and Adolescent Social Work*, and *Social Work*.
…on, she has coauthored two books: *Social Work and Human Services*
…ment Planner and *Adolescent Depression and Suicide: A Comprehensive*
…mpirical Intervention for Prevention and Treatment. She is coeditor of the
Journal of Evidence-Based Social Work: Advances in Practice, Programming,
Research, and Practice and associate editor of *Stress, Trauma, and Crisis: An*
International Journal. In 2002 she was awarded the Provost's Excellence in
Teaching Award at the University of Tennessee.

John S. Wodarski is director of research for the University of Tennessee's
College of Social Work. He received a master's in social work from the University of Tennessee and a doctorate in social work from Washington University in St. Louis. His main interests include child and adolescent health
behavior, including research on violence, substance abuse, depression, sexuality, and employment. Wodarski is the author of more than 35 texts and 310
journal publications and has presented his research at more that 235 professional meetings and conferences. He is coeditor of the *Journal of Human
Behavior in the Social Environment, Journal of Evidence-Based Social Work:
Advances in Practice, Programming, Research, and Policy*, and *Stress, Trauma,
and Crisis: An International Journal*. Over the course of his career Wodarski
has been the recipient of 56 individual awards from federal, state, and private
foundations and 21 institutional awards.